Mary Patterson

Walk in My Shoes

Also by Judianne Densen-Gerber, J.D., M.D.

WE MAINLINE DREAMS: The Odyssey House Story
DRUGS, SEX, PARENTS AND YOU (with her daughter,
Trissa Austin Baden)

Walk in My Shoes
An Odyssey into Womanlife

Judianne Densen-Gerber, J.D., M.D.

Saturday Review Press/E. P. Dutton & Co., Inc./New York

Standing Figure of Hatshepsut courtesy of The Metropolitan Museum of Art.

All the events depicted in this book are real, but certain names of people and places, as well as minor descriptive details, have been changed.

LIBRARY OF CONGRESS CATALOGING IN PUBLICATION DATA

Densen-Gerber, Judianne, 1934–
Walk in my shoes.

1. Densen-Gerber, Judianne, 1934– 2. Women—United States—Social conditions. 3. Women—Psychology. I. Title.
HQ1413.D4A36   301.41'2'0973   75–40326

Copyright © 1976 by Judianne Densen-Gerber, J.D., M.D.
All rights reserved. Printed in the U.S.A.
First Edition
10 9 8 7 6 5 4 3 2 1
No part of this publication may be reproduced or transmitted in any form or by any means, electronic or mechanical, including photocopy, recording, or any information storage and retrieval system now known or to be invented, without permission in writing from the publisher, except by a reviewer who wishes to quote brief passages in connection with a review written for inclusion in a magazine, newspaper or broadcast.

Published simultaneously in Canada by Clarke, Irwin & Company Limited, Toronto and Vancouver

ISBN: 0–8415–0435–0

A Dedication
To Womanlife—the affirmation of feminine being and
To Manlife—the realization of companionship

Contents

Preface xiii
Acknowledgments xxiii
   An Acknowledgment to Hatshepsut xxiii
   A Second Acknowledgment xxiv

Part I

Beginning Associations 3
   A Story 3
   Another Story, with Diversions 8
   A Final Story (and a New Journey) 20
   A Thank You to Nietzsche 28
   A Roadmap 28
   Background to an Evening in a Whorehouse 29
Selections from within a Whorehouse—I 38
   A Phone Call Later 62
   An Interlude during the Line-Up 69
Selections from within a Whorehouse—II 72
   it's all how you look at things 96
Bridges to Part II 99

Part II

Woman Faces Herself 115
   An Interlude 115
   A Speculation 116
   On Becoming Self-Actualized 121

An Intrusion into My Being   124
A Funny Story   127
Another Story   129
A Conclusion   131
A Dream   131
A Caveat   133
My Role Models in Reality   135
My Role Models in Fantasy   137

A Bridge to Woman Faces Her Mate   143
A Story   143
Two Closely Related Stories   143
A Final Story   149

Woman Faces Her Mate   153
A Recent Happening   153
The Game As Played by Men and Others   161
Defining and Enjoying the Orgasm   165
A Second Passing Aside   173
A Domestic Story   174
Of Clam Juice and Lambchops   175
A Story Where we Tickle Each Other   180
On Pain and Joy   182
Epilogue on Sex   185

Bridges to Woman Faces Her Child   188
First Bridge   188
Second Bridge   192
Last Bridge   202

Woman Faces Her Child   203
A First Story   203
An Aside   209
Another Animal Association   211
An Awakening   213
On the Need for Privacy   214
A Poem   220

A Bridge to Woman Faces Her Career   221
Woman Faces Her Career   227
A Male Speaks   239

A Bridge to Woman Faces Her Sisterhood   246
Two Proverbs (No, better yet, Two Inspirational Sayings) for the Sisterhood   251

A Manifesto for the Sisterhood   252
Woman Faces Her Sisterhood   256
   A Recalled Speech   258
   On Guiding Young Women   270
A Bridge to the Epilogue: Dialogue with My Editor   274
Epilogue   277
Appendix A   279
Appendix B   282
Curtain Call   288

Preface

Today begins for me with a daisy from the garden, brought broken and crushed in the small hands of my two-year-old, Sarah. She bounds into my bedroom with the words, "Here Mamma," followed by a kiss and then by the inevitable series of "No"s—first from her sixteen-year-old sister, Trissa, who is acting as a mother's helper this summer; second from her forty-year-old mother, who knows that today she must begin to write, and last from Sarah herself, to whom *no* says everything.

I awake to have my diet piece of toast, my cup of black coffee, my noncaloric squeeze and kiss from my husband, Michael, who still has a week or two before he must begin writing his first book, *Tales from the Morgue,* or interesting cases that often combine sex and death. Michael still has the breathing room to joke lightly about "the beginning."

As he gently kisses me, he teases that *he* has the first sentence for *his* book: "I have spent many fascinating, unforgettable moments in the morgue, not the least of which was making the acquaintance of my future wife and almost marrying her in the morgue chapel." Before I can comment, he meanders off to his writing desk, to one more day of the luxury of sifting papers and sorting materials. Yet today I must begin.

Begin what? It seemed so easy in 1972, when I had just completed my second book, *We Mainline Dreams,* to sign with Saturday Review Press to write a third book about myself—my being, my becoming. It had been a snap to write about my doing, my functioning, my career. Odyssey House was so much a part of my life that bits and pieces flowed onto tape and onto paper; memorabilia came out of scrapbooks, poetry out of letters, case histories out of charts, until we had almost 600 pages and still more to say. I should have realized that reporting was easy, story-telling a cinch, compared to the task of analyzing, feeling, suffering, laughing, cathecting—an odyssey into womanlife.

womanlife
WOMANLIFE
WOMANLIFE

What a strange word! Suggested to me by my editor, Ann La Farge, who has already become my friend, to mean the experience and essence of womanhood: described, delineated, defined, interviewed, known, touched, smelled, seen, perhaps even tasted, through that small part of womanlife that had been born *me.*

It seemed long ago, when I had promised Saturday Review Press a book on successful womanlife. The idea had begun during the spring of 1972, when I had served as the first woman visiting Fellow (their term; mine, more naturally and appropriately, is *Fallopian*) at the Exeter Academy, in New Hampshire. That year the school had reluctantly opened its doors to girls. I had been invited to join with them to show the students what women can accomplish and to influence the doubting-Thomas alumni and faculty that indeed it was not always a waste to educate females.

I played to mixed reviews. I said the word *shit* once. I challenged the faculty and student body to care about the world outside the secure grounds of the academy. I placed the demand that each Exonian give a tithe—10 percent—of his or her time to outer-directed causes, to give, not only to receive; to practice, not only to learn; to share, not only to grow.

I comforted the many faculty wives, intelligent and gifted, who served as unpaid dormitory housemothers but who had no other outlet for their manifold PhD'd talents because of Exeter's anti-nepotism rule and the lack of viable work alternatives for educated women within the reality of the cloistered New England town. This rule prevented husband and wife from working at the same place—but not father and son or two brothers. This construction fortuitously afforded the academy the work of two for the price of one.

But most of all, I reeled from one question after another, privately and repeatedly asked of me by a succession of Exeter girls: "Is it fair or possible for a woman to successfully marry, when she intends to have a full-time career?"

Changed was the expectation of my high school and college years—a time circumferenced by *The Feminine Mystique*—that marriage and children were givens and careers the failure alternative or at best occasional options. Today's acceptance is the career, fringed occasionally with the possibility of marriage but containing so frequently the rejection of child creation.

Female students questioned me about the how-to of combining successful marriage and motherhood with a career and the how-to of the simultaneous retention and perhaps even completion of my own personhood. Somehow, they perceived that I had not suffered a loss of self within my husband's formulation of his male being.

I was struck that it seemed so remarkable to these students that long ago my Mother had kept her own name (Mother was an early Lucy Stoner) and I had done likewise; and so remarkable that I had been able to remain *me* without fear or guilt and Michael to remain *him*self while we seemed to be doing some version of an *our* thing. Yet I was even more struck by the realization that it was inconceivable to almost all of these liberated young women that children were to be part of the journey. The idea was foreign to them first because they had bought the consciousness-raised new mystique of children being fetters to the development of true, complete self (i.e., dropout wife and mother) and second, because they carried the template of tradition that if the biological mother herself was not home for three-o'clock cookies and milk, irreparable damage to the young would be the inevitable result. The origin of this strange equation—no cookies and milk = juvenile delinquency + crippling neurosis—has always eluded me.

I thought of my own teen-age daughter and the someday grandchildren I so anticipated, and I reached out to these similar young girls with minds of such promise and bodies of such glory. Yet my story was not sufficient—they were all intelligent enough to realize an exception does not prove a rule.

I knew what to do. I would gather the stories of twelve successful women friends who had combined a marriage, a child or children, and a career, add mine, and write an inspirational masterpiece on this unique baker's dozen who had done it all. I would call it "Why Not Have Everything and a Little Bit More?"

And so I had said "Yes" to Saturday Review Press. I would write a book.

I chose the women carefully to prove my thesis—a YES YES to life and success, an affirmation of womanlife, that it could be done, that ours is not a world totally on male terms—for surely we had done it.

We:

Letitia Baldridge: head of her own public relations firm, former social secretary to Clare Boothe Luce and Jacqueline Kennedy; married, two children.

June Callwood Frayne: writer, lecturer, television personality, politician, well-known Canadian feminist, and worker in social causes; married, four children.

Joan Glynn: prominent Catholic laywoman, President of Marcella Borghese, a division of Revlon; former president of Simplicity Patterns, former vice-president of Bloomingdale's, and advertising agency executive; married, four children.

Lenore Hershey: creative and innovative editor-in-chief of the *Ladies' Home Journal;* married, one child.

Lucille Jarvis: prize-winning television producer for NBC—"The Kremlin," "The Louvre," "China," "A White Paper on Drugs"; married, two children.

Nancy Kelne: well-liked professor of secretarial sciences at Nassau Community College; married, one child.

Bernice Lavin: successful vice-president of Alberto-Culver (VO5), racehorse owner and breeder; married, two children.

Patricia Mink: feisty congressperson from Hawaii, leader in women's rights; married, one child.

Jacqueline Nokes: well-known television personality in the mountain states and pacesetter for Mormon womanhood in Utah; married, four children.

Jeanette Picard: first woman in space, having accompanied her famous balloonist husband on a flight in 1934. Consultant to NASA, and in her eightieth year one of eleven women ordained as priests in the Episcopal Church; widowed, two children.

Justine Wise Polier: daughter of rabbi and humanitarian Stephen Wise and Louise Wise, philanthropist who founded the adoption agency bearing her name; lawyer, family-court judge for over thirty years and now, in her seventies, guiding director of the Children's Defense Fund and the Field Foundation; married, three children.

Dorothy Speller, M.D.: black physician, leader in public health for the city of Philadelphia; married to the secretary of health for the state, three children.

And me.

I began the interviews and completed them in less than three months. They were easy, breezy, free-flowing, and filled with remarkable success. Surely, no young woman could fail to be impressed, inspired, convinced that it was possible. In fact, it was as easy as the new instant-pudding recipes. One whipped together the right ingredients, such as tremendous drive; encouraging, not sex-stereotyped parents; sufficient money; unbelievable self-esteem; and incredible opportunities, which often included a World War that sent the men overseas or a world-wide depression that forced acceptance of a second wage earner in the family.

The stories, on the surface so inspiring, were on reflection bland. Something was missing—hollow—empty. In a baker's dozen, you should see the doughnuts—here the focus was on the holes. Some days chicken, some days feathers. There was nothing. I wanted the young girls to believe because they wanted to believe, because they needed to believe—no, because we needed to believe—no, because *I* needed to believe.

And yet did I? As my days of interviewing ended, so did my days of being Aunt Agatha (the female counterpart of an Uncle Tom). By now it was the spring of 1973; my belly was swollen with the child that was Sarah. I was almost in my fortieth year, and at last I was ready to walk, to sit, and to talk with more than just the women at the top. A legal whorehouse in Nevada would soon afford me twelve additional reflections of womanlife. I vowed to interview those women with the same receptivity as I had the twelve women who had made it rather than always been made.

Indeed, I listened and learned, as a new world based on other values opened itself to me. I began to question my givens. I didn't have all the answers. Maybe I didn't even have the right questions. And something splendid happened to me.

I began to receive vibes from women all around me: good women, bad women; women of joy, women in pain; successful women, failureful women; women in repose, women in labor; women on pedestals, women in the gutter; rich women, poor women; imprisoned women in leg irons, perfumed women in gold chains; career women, housewife women; women married, women alone; educated women, illiterate women; women playing tennis, women on assembly lines; narcissistic women, martyred women; women just born, and women about to die.

Yet I knew that until I walked in all their shoes, looking back with understanding, ahead with courage, and around with awareness, I would never know myself, nor could I share with my daughters the specialness of the world and language of women, nor could I teach them to like being women and therefore themselves. And until they liked themselves, they could not like their fathers, their brothers, their lovers, their husbands, their sons. Sometime, someday, somewhere, women may know the possibility of male friends.

Forty years and the middle-age identity crisis surrounded the four years I have been walking—from 1972 to 1975. And then I arranged a meeting with my publishers to give back the advance, for I knew I could not write the book I had originally promised.

My editors asked why, and I shared. They walked a bit in my shoes. Stories poured out loosely, yet ultimately connected, and we experienced and learned. I told them of the becoming and the being. They listened, and I felt—albeit arrogantly and yet magnificently—that "it was one small step, yet one giant step for womankind." The language of women, so long spoken, like Yiddish, in the ghettoes, away from the world of power and influence, could now be written.

They said, "Write as you feel—no holds barred—let the reader organize, experience, accept, reject, agree, argue, but walk together."

Please—come walk with me.
    come walk in my shoes.

    Judianne Densen-Gerber, J.D., M.D.
    July 25, 1975

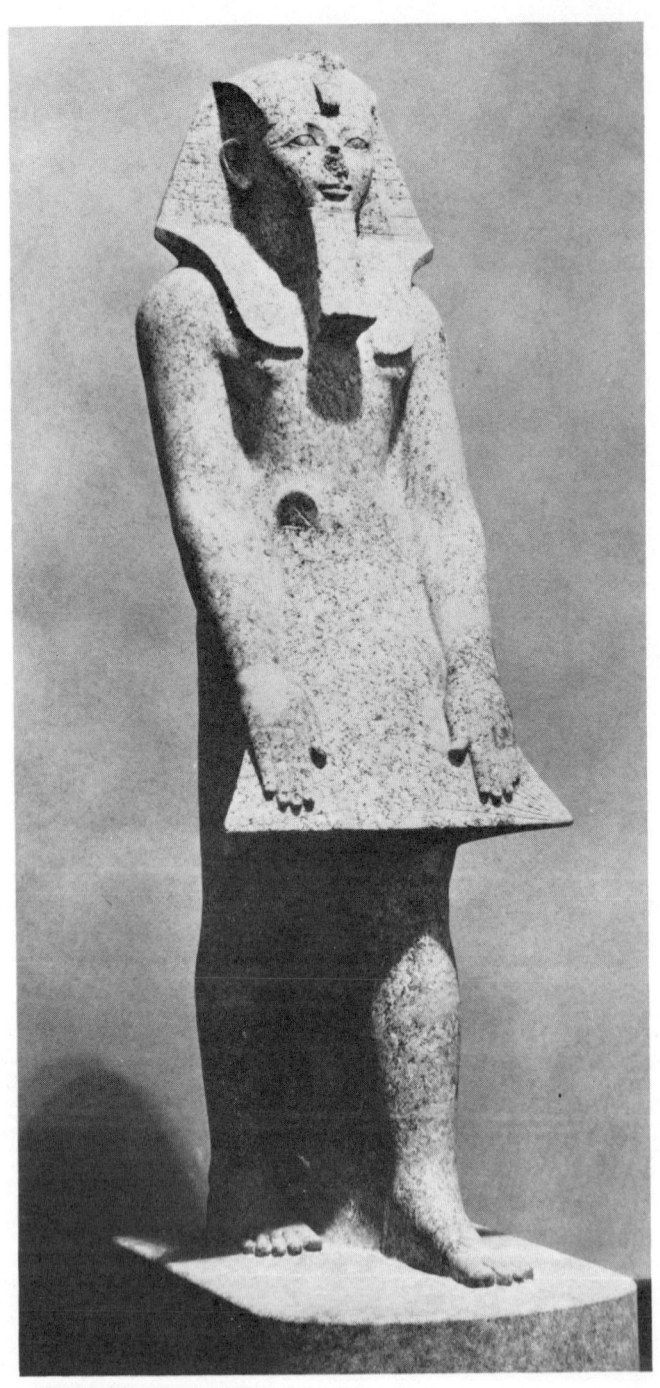

Acknowledgments

An Acknowlegment to Hatshepsut

To Queen Hatshepsut, one of the first of the daughters of Eve to walk forward for womanlife. Though her feet are bare, let us walk a moment in her steps.

Hatshepsut lived during the Eighteenth Dynasty at the height of Egyptian civilization, 1535–1480 B.C.

Hatshepsut was more brilliant and gifted than her two brothers and therefore favored by her parents. Because of her royal bloodlines and the Egyptian belief that she was of divine parentage, she was permitted an excellent education. She used the opportunity well and became a more capable ruler than either of her brothers. She is described as being strong-willed, feminine, religious (she was greatly influenced by Judaism, feeling a lifetime affinity with the Israelites), and a natural ruler of men.

Before her reign, and with the exception of her father's, for about 150 years Egypt had had a succession of weak rulers. She and her father loved each other greatly, and on the death of her mother, when Hatshepsut was a teen-ager, she became regent with him. This was her first coregency; the second was with her younger brother, Thutmose III. Coregency was imposed because Hatshepsut was a female; however, she was the deciding force in both regimes. In order to rule effectively, she had to wear a beard, as her picture shows.

Hatshepsut is honored not only because of her exceptional governing ability but also because of the role she played in the life of Moses and hence in Judeo-Christian heritage. King Thutmose I, her father, was the Pharaoh who ordered the killing of all male Hebrew babies in order to prevent a ruler from arising among them. When the babe Moses was placed in the river to escape death, it was Hatshepsut who found him, took him out of the bullrushes, and raised him as her son. It was her sense of values and guidance that shaped Moses and subsequently all of us (Exodus 1–2).

A Second Acknowlegment

To Landisi, a character from Pirandello.

Signora Cini says that she will only believe what she sees with her own eyes and feels with her own fingers.

Landisi admonishes her that she should show some respect for what other people see with their eyes and feel with their fingers.

Part I

Beginning Associations

A Story

Grandparents are essential to the successful rearing of children. The nuclear family—one man, one woman (i.e., a breeding couple), plus their offspring, living together and alone, facing life's responsibilities and privileges in the isolation and alienation of this highly mechanized technological world—is antithetical to the development and fulfillment of happy people. Even more destructive is the sadness of single parenting —often coupled with constantly changing partners—due to death, divorce, or never having been married.

It should be realized that the American Dream, romanticized togetherness model, is a new version of family life never known or tried before in the anywhere, anytime history of man and woman.

Before 1940 and our total surrender of self to the productivity and needs of American industry (needs which could have been met in many other less devastating ways if our business leaders had cared), families had roots, history, and heritage, which were passed on by grandparents, who had the leisure time and patience to relate to the young while parents toiled and worked, striving in their middle years to build self and maintain the family unit.

The task of the young is to grow, mature, and develop; the task of the parent is to secure, structure, and maintain; the task of the grandparent is to love, teach, and reminisce. The child is tomorrow, the future; the parent today, the now; the grandparent yesterday, the past. The child is amorphous, to be formed; the parent is delineated, sharp, value-bound; the grandparent is soft, accepting, forgiving.

The breeding couple, separated from the many hands and support of equally committed brothers, sisters, aunts, uncles, cousins, and grandparents, not only becomes isolated and alienated but weary and overwhelmed. These feelings lead to boredom, depression, anger, and many attempts at restitution, such as adultery, frequent job changes, alcoholism, and drug taking. The restlessness and frustration cause repetitive identity crises, with attendant struggles for control between husband and wife and between parents and children. That today's youth is lost, bewildered, frightened, destroyed, and destroying is explainable—indeed inevitable.

Many modern-day-family living problems are the result not of increased stress or demands but of a mistaken design in the nurturing model. Groups of people, loving and working together, can problem-solve horrendously difficult tasks; people all alone fall apart. How many people today live and work in the towns or houses that their parents or grandparents knew? How many families enter the birth of a new child in the family Bible or note anywhere the death of a loved one? The meaning of continuity over time, of the identity of the family and therein the worth of each of its members, has been lost and with it much value of the role of the womanlife, which formed the matrix (from the Latin *mater,* "mother") around which accretion occurred.

Most destructive is the phenomenon of relocation—so unnecessary even in military life, even less in business. True, people often must be transferred where the work is; but there is usually no reason why people cannot be moved in core groups of, say, ten families. I am sure that many women reading this book are remembering the experience of a new home, new friends, new church, or social groups. Who does not remember feeling icy cold when walking into a room of new faces and having to find self vis à vis other women in the pecking order?

Men have the common ground of their work, a slot where they fit when facing the new business situation. The vocabulary is familiar, the surroundings repetitive, the interpersonal relationships given. True, a woman has her husband's status to refer to within her new world, but still she must establish her place, and differing from the man who interacts with other men in relation to a set task, her definition is almost exclusively interpersonal. Many women have retreated to the world of fantasy and depression or withdrawn to alcohol and drugs when facing a new community and the possibility of rejection.

Each year my family rents a summer home in a different town. Michael thinks of the commute and will he be home in time to swim with the children. I desperately look for a friend (as happened this morning) to guide me to the market with the freshest fish. To negotiate the system and my role, I need other women. Indeed, I truly hate to walk into a room of unfamiliar faces.

I remember my Grandmother Sarah Densen with the greatest fondness. It is she who told me the stories of the family and comforted me when I was angered and hurt by my Mother. She taught me to cook and to keep a house. She told me of growing up in a time when only the sons were prized and taught to read and write. She shared with me her secret of how she made my Grandfather give her, not pearls or diamonds, as a wedding present but rather a tutor who would open the world of the written word to her.

Stories of a world before television, radio, telephones, cars, planes, delighted me as did the horsedrawn carriages, the babies born at home, and the bustles. Often I would ask, "But what did you do to pass the time or to communicate with each other?" And she would answer, "We would write letters, visit with each other, sew together, etcetera." Human contact was how she related. Even in her last years—and they lasted until she was in her nineties—she refused to go any reasonable distance both ways in her chauffeur-driven car. Whenever possible, she would take public transportation in one direction, with her car following behind. "How else," she would ask, "do you ever get to speak to new people and find out what is happening in the country?" She loved people, and they loved her.

Before each election she would call me on the phone to make sure I was going to vote and to remind me how hard she and others had fought to make the privilege a reality. Today, when I hear young women say they are not going to vote, as it is really meaningless, we have no real choices, and one vote doesn't count anyway, my mind sees my ninety-two-year-old Grandmother, white-haired, bent with arthritis, walking slowly with her cane to the voting booth because she had chained herself to the White House in the 1920s and had been forbidden by her father to read and write. As she pulled the lever, she affirmed that she was a person.

She also enriched my world with humor and earthiness. She did not have the uptightness of my Mother's generation, even though she had experienced a mother-in-law, my Great-Grandmother, who always covered the legs of her dining room table with bunting in order to prevent the men in the family from becoming sexually aroused and stimulated, particularly in the presence of young girls and women who were not their wives (a fairly common Victorian attitude). Her favorite loving story of my Grandfather was about a special realization she had on their wedding night. My Grandfather was known as Mike the Red, and he was very freckled. Grandma Sarah would say, "Judi, Grandpa was indeed freckled, and I knew I loved him when I realized he was freckled everywhere—even there."

Grandma was special to me, and she died in April 1973, shortly before her ninety-third birthday. My baby, Sarah, was born in July of the same year. I had wanted to name my first daughter, who is now sixteen, after my Grandmother; I called after the baby was born to ask permission. But Grandma said "No" because in the old Middle European countries of her grandparents, there is a superstition that with the passage of a name, travels the soul. Therefore, one is forbidden to name after the living, and to do so brings bad luck to all concerned. I was hurt but accepted the reason as part of her tradition.

Next came a daughter named Julianne Michael, born Mongoloid, who died in her first year of life, and two sons, Judson Michael, now twelve, and Lindsey Robert, now ten. After two and a half years of talking about having one more child, in 1972 Michael and I decided affirmatively on a self-made grandchild; we hoped it would be a girl. Since we knew it would be our last, we wanted to name her Sarah.

Because I had had a Mongoloid child and was close to forty when the instances of chromosomal abnormality are so much greater, Michael and I agreed on the obstetrician's advice to have me undergo a procedure called amniocentesis when I was sixteen weeks pregnant.

In February of 1973, I went to the amniocentesis specialist's office and lay down on a table under a machine that bounced sonar rays similar to radar off my abdomen. Outlined on the screen were the inches of my fat tissue, the baby's head, its spinal column, and mine. Carefully and painlessly, the doctor stuck a needle into my abdominal wall; watching the picture, he avoided the baby but entered the sac surrounding it and drew about fifteen cubic centimeters of fluid out into the attached syringe. The yellowish material contained cells made by my baby. A Band-Aid was applied, a Polaroid of the sonar picture was handed to Michael as the first entry in the baby book, and a fluid-filled test tube was given to me to deliver to the proper laboratory for cell growing and chromosome study. Finding the right lab was much more stressful and difficult than the procedure had been.

Six weeks later the doctor called to say we were expecting a normal, healthy girl. Her unique chromosome count—which also tells the sex of the baby—is matted and framed in pink and hangs on the nursery wall. At that moment in time, the baby moved from the impersonality of being an "it" to the warmth of being a "she." No longer did I have to wait the nine months, as I had with my two sons, suffering the anxiety of wondering and worrying if they would be abnormal, as their second sister had been. Michael and I experienced a special joy in the last four months of this pregnancy, due to the miraculous advances of medical science; anxiety gone, fear-free, knowing the special fact, the sex of the baby—it was a girl.

I wanted to share our joy and that fact with my Grandmother Sarah and to ask permission to name this baby girl after her, as I knew there would be no other children. My health and age mandated no more. On March 27, I called: "Grandma, it is going to be a baby girl. Michael and I want to call her Sarah. May I?"

Grandma responded, "Judi, it is wrong the way you doctors play God, putting needles in bellies and all. You new-fangled youngsters, what will you be up to next? Babies in bottles, I suppose. How can you be sure it will be a girl? I don't believe such things are possible. In my day . . ." I butted in: "Grandma, can I name her Sarah?" The answer came loud, clear, warm but unafraid: "Of course, dear, I intend to release my soul before she is born in July. My day is over, it is time for hers to begin. Pat Sarah welcome for me. Remember to tell her of me. Good-bye now."

That day in March she was in perfect health. One week later I walked to her funeral.

Sarah Handel Densen was born in New York in 1881 and died in 1973; Sarah Densen Baden was born in New York in 1973, and if she follows her Great-Grandmother, she will live to the year 2065, spanning three centuries and 184 years. There were those very special moments in time when the two lives existed together.

Continuity—the backbone of womanlife.

Another Story, with Diversions

How can we ever walk in anyone else's shoes? The projection of self into another's experience is the root problem of the existential dilemma. We are born alone, we feel pain alone, we die alone. Occasionally we have moments—fantasies that someone is with us, sharing, feeling, knowing—but most often it is an illusion. We, man and woman, seem to seek all through life the sensation of togetherness, a oneness with someone outside of ourselves.

Difficult as it is to know self, to know another is nigh onto impossible—and yet we grope, too often claiming understanding when we still are trapped within our own shadow and uniqueness. American Indian folklore expressed this very movingly: "You will never know my problems until you walk in my moccasins." This saying has been traced back to 1612.

Only when all women know and care about one another, from street whore to company president, from baby to grandmother, from bejeweled countess to welfare mother, from barren nun to Orthodox mother, can we appreciate womanlife; and only when we appreciate women, can we meaningfully share with men. Too long the sexes have lived separately, never speaking honestly across sex lines but only playing games. The time for batting our eyelashes has passed; now we must share experiences!

I believe that the world of women has its own language, which is seldom spoken to men. Witness the almost immediate rapport within the sisterhood. The women's movement has opened doors which not only encourage womanly communication but place a premium on respecting one another and on developing friendships.

Gone are the days of my college years when we had a clear understanding in our dormitory that when two girls made a dinner date together on a Friday night, the appointment was always subject to cancellation if a *man* called; first, because he was a male, and therefore superior company; second, his company meant we were selected; and third, because he would foot the bill, freeing our allowance for other things. I clearly remember that my allowance in part took into consideration a certain number of meals that would be paid for by my male escorts.

We have learned to respect other women as friends and important comrades. Gone, too, is the disrespect of considering the male merely a meal ticket (and on Friday night, which was fish night, any male would do). I remember one special year at college when the dietary department very cheaply bought a whole whale to serve on consecutive Fridays, since the Pope had declared whales were fish within the Friday abstinence rule. The whale made it a desperate year for Friday dates.

Just as a young man never fathomed why on a Friday a girl would accept a date ten minutes before the hour, in contrast to Saturday in which almost a week's notice was necessary (she feared he would think she was free at the last moment, a practice which mysteriously never extended to interfere with Friday feedings), he never fathomed whether it was he she was interested in or simply getting out. And she never quite knew what was expected of her in exchange for the dinner. The feelings of being exploited—she as a sex object, he as a meal ticket—were rationally felt on both sides.

Another commonly expressed attitude which totally denies the personhood of the male is embodied in the advice I am sure almost all the women reading this have been given by well-meaning women friends: "Honey, even if you don't like or care for him, you should go out with him; you can never tell who else you might meet."

Men, like women, need desperately to feel they are wanted, needed, liked for themselves. Both men and women should often pause to reflect on the many unthinking clichés in common parlance which express a lack of trust, profound distance, sexual exploitation, and mutual disrespect between the sexes. I cringe at snide remarks about men always being ready and willing, no matter what the woman is like, as well as at simple jokes about women drivers. An entire world of separation has been built and reinforced between men and women. Until we share openly and honestly, there will be only hostility and mistrust.

Recently, after I began to collect my thoughts concerning the language of women, I realized that even within my marriage I spoke to my husband on terms that he set. Obviously, with any two headstrong people such as Michael and myself there are times of conflict and differences of opinion. For the first fifteen years of our marriage I might cry, explode, or ventilate, but when it came down to problem-solving I had to logically answer each of his points as he tore away at my emotions with facts. I was almost forty before I realized that my feelings were *valid* facts that had to be considered in the resolution of any problem. He still is learning this and to express his own emotions, as well. I know now that Michael's blocking of his feelings is a sad result of the stereotyped mold that the male has been made to fit into. Always strong, always logical, the voice of reason versus the cry of hysteria (from the Greek *hyster*, "womb"). By my speaking to him in my language, he is slowly becoming free to be.

One night in October 1973 I was angry about something which I can no longer remember. I had just arrived home to join Michael in the kitchen. We were having a snack. I suddenly decided this one argument was going to be on my terms. It was the first time. I told Michael to be quiet and not push me to respond to his questions and formulations. For the next thirty minutes I ranted, raved, cajoled, cried, screamed, intellectualized, slammed doors, washed dishes, yelled, distorted, felt, argued, rationalized, ventilated, and resolved while he silently listened. At the end of the half-hour I stopped, feeling at peace with myself, with him and with the situation. It was the most satisfactory discussion I had ever had with Michael. I asked him at the end what he was thinking, and he replied, "I haven't understood a word you said." Our journey together since that time has been one of my being willing to share my ways with him and his being open to receive me as a valid person even if at first I appear hysterical and womanish. Michael tells me how much clearer so many things are to him now and how often I am proven right even though I have no factual basis which he can understand. If there is any "how-to" within these pages for a happy relationship, it is: begin to appreciate, not denigrate the self that is each other, and to travel on your terms, your partner's terms, and the together terms.

Though we learn through the exercise of intellectual functioning and conceptualization, most often the greatest insights are born in a flash of experience—an intuition of what it must be like to be in another's reality, to walk someone else's path.

So it was on the day I grasped the special pain of the black experience. It was a chance little occurrence, and yet the total was revealed. No matter how many times I had listened to stories of the suffering of blacks in their second citizenry, my perception had been limited to the intellectual formulations which, while they produce guilt, self-righteousness, and great changes in the legal and social systems, seldom produce empathy, caring, and sharing. It is only through gut-level awareness that new attitudes, in addition to behavioral modifications, are developed. Only when attitudes change can others feel safe and behavior be constant in design.

It was Christmastime of 1971, December 23, to be exact. I had gone shopping at Saks Fifth Avenue with one of Odyssey's directors, a young black man, I for presents for my family, he for his. He was a pleasant-looking man in his early twenties and well dressed always. Our task successfully accomplished, we emerged from the department store, both heavily burdened with our purchases, into the twilight of a snowfall at the height of that special holiday season symbolic to us all of the oneness of mankind—a time to love one another.

The twilight was cold and miserable, little more than twenty degrees; visibility was nil through the heavy snow, yet I was able to hail a cab. I sped home to the warmth of a holly-filled house, Christmas tree lighted and laden with ornaments collected through three generations, and happy expectant children who danced around me with greetings and merriment as the presents so obviously theirs were put aside for wrapping. I went upstairs to dress for pre–Christmas Eve dinner, only to remember I had forgotten to tell the young black man about an errand I urgently needed done first thing in the morning, before the stores closed for the holiday. I rang him up—no answer. I was surprised, knowing that the distance from Saks to his home on Gramercy Park, one of New York's better neighborhoods (he was earning about $15,000 a year), was less than to mine.

I rang him repeatedly over the next two and a half hours until he finally arrived home and answered.

"Rodney, where have you been?" I impatiently demanded. I was annoyed after calling and calling.

"I had to walk home," he replied, "and now I am having a hot rum, drying myself out, and attempting to do the same with most of the presents. I hope they are not ruined, but I definitely will need all new boxes."

Amazed I responded, "Why in God's name did you get it into your head to walk home on a wretched night like this? Are you crazy? You'll not only ruin everything you worked so hard to earn the money to buy but you will catch pneumonia."

He replied, "No cab would stop for *me*, Judi." He said it simply.

Suddenly I realized, as if I had been struck by lightning, why he sat for hours mesmerized by Nina Simone's record about the pain of being young, gifted, and black. Sure, the big things hurt and in the long run probably count more, but it is the little everyday things that equal the constant assault on your freedom to negotiate the system and that demoralize you until your self-esteem has been silently eroded.

It was a middle-aged, barely-educated Southern domestic, a black woman named Rosa Parks, who had such swollen feet and ankles at the end of a long day's work (a feeling familiar to many of us) that she simply sat down in the front of the bus. It was too far for her tired feet in old shoes to walk once again to the back of the bus as the sign and the driver demanded. It was this act that began the civil-disobedience demonstrations that so changed the face of this nation.

Great rhetoric in high places about important issues counts, but it is the little unprotested daily hurts that continue the ambiance of second citizenry all-pervasive in our society. Often the hurts are unconsciously inflicted. Only through flashes of insight and intuition do we escape the cages of our own realities to touch and feel the world of others. It is only through these experiences that we learn to appreciate, evaluate, or judge others within their own ways of living. This is why I ask you to walk with me in my shoes.

In April of 1971 I took a vow never to permit a slur or

discriminatory action against women or myself to pass uncommented upon. I promised myself never again to walk to the back of the bus. I hope other men and women reading this passage will similarly commit themselves. For men play an indispensable role in correcting the attitudes of other men. The taking of this vow may appear picayune, but to me it is essential. Let me illustrate why:

The happening that led me to take the vow occurred in Anchorage, Alaska. Michael and I had been sponsored by ITT to go there to lecture on the topic of heroin addiction. At that time the major route of entry for heroin was through the Northwest, the source our troops stationed in Southeast Asia. They brought drugs home with them. Alaskan officials were alarmed.

It is easy to trace the movement of heroin and how it is supplied. There are no secrets. Wherever its new ports of entry, some spills over to affect the young of the surrounding cities and an epidemic of addiction begins. In the sixties New York was the drug capital; in the late sixties and early seventies markets shifted to California; by 1971 Alaska, Montana, and other northwestern states were experiencing the problems. When stable markets had been developed and all the susceptible youths were afflicted leaving an insufficient number of new victims, the criminal cartels shifted their activity to the Midwest. Its young succumbed, too, and as I write now, it is Texas and the Southwest that are suffering. There is no mystery; simply, government does little if anything, and the toll is paid by American families. Furthermore, the profit incentive is phenomenal: a total production cost of $500 will easily yield $500,000 in the street markets. Ninety percent of the heroin in America today enters through the Mexican border; yet only this year the United States ended the border surveillance.

But rather than speculate, as we all can, about the reason for this official indifference, let us move on to the story from Alaska which illustrates another facet of what is wrong with our thinking. After Michael and I had completed our presentations, we were followed by a family-court judge of the district. Suddenly, during his speech, I sat at attention, unable to believe what I was hearing. The judge stated that addiction and juvenile delinquency had been readily predictable once men gave women the right to vote and permitted them to drive automobiles. The former made women believe they had the right to do anything they liked—even work rather than stay at home, where they belonged—and the latter gave them the freedom to travel. He was serious, and no one protested.

I stood up, blind with rage, brushed past Michael, and grabbed the microphone. I demanded an apology, that he be repudiated, disavowed, and removed from the platform. No one said a word. I felt everyone was more shocked by my unusual, unexpected behavior than by the content of his remarks. I turned to the one other woman speaker, a black woman. I confronted her, demanding she rise to the occasion. I challenged her to leave with me. She was paralyzed. She sat doing nothing.

I descended the steps from the stage amid much handclapping and some booing. The moderator began to explain with some liberal rhetoric about freedom of speech and how I should be more mature; Michael seized the microphone and started to defend me, saying it was an insult beyond what any rational person should be subjected to, and really an apology not a reprimand was in order and he would be the first to extend one.

I didn't need or want his apology. His commitment to me long ago had assured me of the safety of my personhood. Looking back now, I think perhaps I wanted him to punch the judge in the nose, but short of killing him, I needed nothing from Michael but to leave with me, for I needed to be held and comforted.

I yelled back, "Should Jews fight for Hitler's right of free speech or to build Dachau? Should Negroes preserve the right for the Ku Klux Klan to assemble? I vow to you all that you have noted only the first time I shall speak out. Never again, for any reason, will I stay silent in the face of denigration of me and femaleness, no matter how slight. I swear it, I swear it."

The pandemonium was too great, so the meeting was adjourned. I stood transfixed, waiting for Michael. People surrounded me, some supportive, others critical. Michael joined me; a black man had gone to him and told him I needed help. And strangely but fittingly I did.

It was the time of my menstruation. I was so excited I had not realized that I had bled until I was standing in a circle of blood.

Michael quietly said, "Judi, you need to go and clean yourself."

I looked down, and in my anger I said, "Get the judge—the floor needs mopping."

In the ladies room I cared for myself and cried until sufficiently purged to face the world of men.

In 1973, when I was appointed visiting law professor at the University of Utah Law School, a dinner was planned by the dean at one of Salt Lake's finest clubs, the Alta Club. I was delighted to accept, particularly because I had been there once before (prior to taking the vow) and had in quiet resentment accepted the fact that I was not permitted to walk through the front door. Ladies had to enter through the back entrance reserved for them. My aide—a former drug addict who, before his rehabilitation at Odyssey, had compiled a six-felony arrest record—in his maleness brazenly walked with our host through the front door. I—the lawyer and doctor, who had indeed successfully cured him—crept in my femaleness with my hostess up the back stairs next to the lavatories. The official reason given for this practice was that ladies entering through the front door would be girlishly chatting noisily, which along with their natural seductiveness, would distract the men from their important reading and other activities requiring concentration or repose. In 1970 I crawled, knowing my place; in 1973, knowing once again my place, I walked forward, back and forth through the front door. Dinner was delayed as several Utah ladies, one who was in her eighties, asked me (and of course I agreed) if I would walk them through the front door, as they had always wanted to but couldn't and now wouldn't do it alone. Another giant step for womankind! No back doors, no back seats.

In 1972 I journeyed to a famous California resort to lose weight, a perennial endeavor of mine, and to write this book about how to combine everything successfully—still blind, still believing, still an Aunt Agatha. Accompanying and helping me on the compilation of the material was a female aide. She rejoices in the glorious name of Freedom because she was born on November 11 after World War I had ended and her father still believed.

Freedom and I, after a day of spa reducing and book producing, sauntered into the dining room only to be seated at a table that would have been in the kitchen if the door had been hinged the other way. I asked to be moved to a window table, for I find that I enjoy a meal much more in pleasant surroundings with good views. The hostess informed me that the tables had been reserved for guests who had arrived previously but as soon as someone checked out, we would be moved. Daily meals proceeded amid the clang of pots and pans, bustling of waiters and waitresses, and the observation of new faces seated at window tables. I began to fantasize that sitting at a table in front of the rest room in a Chinese restaurant would be more delightful than this expensive resort.

After five days I confronted the maître d' (who naturally, in this instance, was a woman). She replied, "Oh, Dr. Densen-Gerber, you must realize by now that the window tables are reserved for couples. They do so appreciate and need the romantic atmosphere. We will be delighted to move you as soon as your husband arrives. We know you'll understand."

I explained firmly to her then and there that Freedom and I were a couple—we certainly weren't one person—we, too, had our digestion improved by a scenic atmosphere and were moving now—that very meal! Otherwise, the next morning, I would hold a press conference on the special considerations given women guests. They moved us. We finished the week and gratefully returned home, never to visit again.

Michael and I had a good friend in the early seventies in New York, a city commissioner and a doctor. He was a black man. He had a telephone in his car. It enabled him to call ahead for a reservation whenever he wanted dinner either for himself alone or with guests. He had found three or four restaurants in New York where he knew that the service would be polite and that a good table would be given him. He had to be very careful. It was important to him not to have to endure slights or be embarrassed before important visiting dignitaries or even good friends. He had learned how to insure himself against the hurts. After all, he was now earning over $60,000 a year and was responsible for the health of a large segment of New York's population. He had earned the right not to have to go through that any more.

Sometime in the last four years, I learned that I had the right not to have to go through that any more, either. Ladies, come walk with me through front doors to the best tables. We deserve it.

One last story especially for the men:

In 1974 I went to meet a newly appointed local commissioner who funded one of Odyssey's programs. I entered his office and extended my hand: a normal thing for a normal person in the normal business world to do. Observing protocol and etiquette—a woman extends her hand to a gentleman first—I extended my hand to shake his. The commissioner recoiled as if I were Eve's snake himself (herself?), saying, "Don't touch me; you may be unclean."

He is an Orthodox Jew; in his religion, menstruating women are considered unclean, and if he should touch one, he would have to be purified before he could pray again. Observing protocol and etiquette, he couldn't ask if I were menstruating.

I deeply respect freedom of individual religious choice, but if it means that all people cannot participate equally within the religion, I wonder—. Must women always sit behind curtains in the back? Would we permit customs which forced blacks or others to do so? I wonder ... I question, too, if tax exemptions should be permitted to groups which discriminate as part of their very definition against the personhood of their fellow Americans. I pay taxes *not* to aid them in defining me as second class.

Why women? Why do we wait and rationalize? Why is it always tomorrow for us?

I know this: people who choose life styles which discriminate against others may have the right to that private choice under our guarantees of individual freedom, but under my guarantee of equal opportunity, under the Fourteenth Amendment, they have *no* right, I repeat, *no* right to hold public offices and make decisions that influence my future. Could any man negotiate with any other man who considered him unclean to touch? How does one begin, tell me!

I wonder if any man can understand the feelings which are generated within a highly intelligent woman—educated as both a doctor and a lawyer and who every day makes decisions affecting over one thousand lives—by being considered unclean to city officials because of natural biological functions, by being unable to sit at a good table or to walk through a front door. Is this what success means in America if the person is housed in a female body?

On reading this, I realize that the militant tone will perhaps offend many people. Yet it is real and true and probably psychologically very healthy. It may seem strange to many that I remain devoutly religious, but I have no doubt that man and woman are equal before God. Mankind has made the distortion. I remain steadfastly American because I believe this is the system that allows for the greatest expression of personhood for both men and women, though I know that the struggle will be long and hard. I remain deeply happy, for in my home and in my work I have built a world of mutual respect for each participant, based on each one's personhood and not on his or her packaging. I thank my husband and sons, as well as my close male colleagues, for letting me believe and know, within a defined reality frame, that men and women can walk together side by side, holding hands. I tuck my daughters in at night with a special sense of safety.

A Final Story (and a New Journey)

In February of 1973, when I was five months pregnant and Michael and I were attending an American Academy of Forensic Sciences convention in Las Vegas, I decided the time had arrived for me to form a definitive opinion on whether or not prostitution should be legalized. Since I had treated so many prostitutes in my work, governmental officials as well as women's groups were asking me for my opinion. I needed to form one; yet my ambivalence was painfully present. I wanted the women protected and not exploited, but I couldn't relate to the concept of sex for sale. Xaviera Hollander's autobiographical best seller, *The Happy Hooker*, notwithstanding, I had never met a happy whore, and I had personally treated over four thousand women who had been or were prostitutes. Frequently, their teeth had been knocked out and so had all their underpinnings of self-esteem.

Indeed, women addicts are more difficult to treat because their self-esteem is more deeply eroded than that of their male counterparts. They usually present a triad of symptomatology: drug addiction, prostitution, and lesbianism. The latter sex pattern frequently arises out of their reactive contempt toward males. It is difficult to have had 3,076 male sex partners within a five-year run when you are walking the streets from eighteen to twenty-three years of age—as one young woman shared with me—and not view men within a most distorted and jaundiced framework.

Furthermore, for a man there is glamour in being a cat burglar, a cattle rustler (someone who steals meat from the local supermarket to sell cut-rate in lower income neighborhoods) or a car thief. For a woman there is no glamour in going in and out of a flea-bag hotel room to turn a twenty-dollar trick. Humiliation is added when you are really down and out and your "old man," your pimp, beats you if you don't make your evening's quota; then it's a two-dollar turn in a doorway or a five-dollar blow job in the back of a truck.

Prostitutes on drugs work rain or shine, day or night. It makes little difference whether or not they are sick, in withdrawal, pregnant, or menstruating. In fact, many are treated for chronic infections of the cervix caused by the jamming of cotton tightly into the opening of the cervix at those times of the month in order not to inconvenience the tricks. However, whenever possible on days of heavy flow, most of the girls perform either manual or oral services. "The show must go on" is the prime motto of this, our oldest profession.

The onset of labor is often the signal for a girl to go out to hustle one more trick for the road, thus ensuring sufficient funds for a last dose of heroin before she enters the hospital to face the pain of childbirth. Ironically, this last dose is euphemistically called the kiss-off. In addition, she is expected to leave a little extra money for her old man to tide him over the two or three days of her hospitalization, until she is strong enough to sign out against medical advice and begin once again to ply her trade.

When she signs out of the hospital to return to prostitution and drugs, her newborn baby usually accompanies her to share the life style she has chosen. The hospital staff conscientiously gives her a card noting the date that the new baby is to return to the well-baby clinic: this is the extent of society's responsibility to that helpless newborn human being unless he or she manages to survive until it is time to register for school. The little one belongs to his or her mother and will share the horror of her life. Occasionally abuse or neglect will become obvious to a neighbor or some other concerned citizen and some social agency may or may not intervene. Or the abuse will be so manifest that the child will be brought to the hospital or to the morgue (55 percent of child-abuse deaths in New York City are in homes in which addiction and/or prostitution are concurrent factors).

Society may justify its lack of concern or responsibility toward the prostitute or drug addict; it is much more difficult —or perhaps impossible—to rationalize its abandonment of her baby or children. The defense so often used—"Well, it's their free choice"—just doesn't fit.

Within the first year of my work with addicts I had an experience which vividly brought this home. Rocco, one of the ex-addict directors of Odyssey, came rushing into my room late one afternoon. He told me in a breathless voice that a former good friend of his, a schoolteacher from Connecticut he used to shoot drugs with, had just called to ask for help. The man's wife, a schoolteacher as well, had overdosed. She was unconscious and probably dying in a small walk-up apartment in Greenwich Village. Rocco pleaded with me to treat her, as his friend was afraid to seek other medical help because of the possibility of a police report and the subsequent loss of both their jobs within the school system.

Certainly, with a woman's life hanging in the balance, it was no time to stop to consider whether or not she was fit to teach or relate to young people or be an adequate role model. There was no time to debate the ultimate ethics. There would be time later. Now I had to be a doctor and go to the patient. Even today, ten years later, I remember my anxiety as we drove through the twilight streets from Sixth Street in the East Village to Christopher Street in the West Village. My doctor-self was filled with anxiety based in part on whether or not I would get there in time and if I did, would I be adequate to save her life? I was newly out in practice, and this was the first patient I had seen at home without the back-up facilities of a hospital and other colleagues with whom to confer. My lawyer-self was also busy working away. It was raising all kinds of questions such as, "Did I have a responsibility to inform the police?" "Should this couple be permitted to continue teaching?" And so forth. My personal self kept asking questions: "What was I walking into?" "What kind of people would I meet?" "Was I in any personal danger, as this was after all a criminal hangout —a shooting gallery."

I drove through the beautiful quaint Village streets, some with gaslights; past private townhouses, many of which cost well over a quarter of a million dollars; past churches that had served their communities for several centuries; past the Women's House of Detention, on Eighth Street, a mammoth fortress fortunately since closed but which on this day still had the women calling out the windows at their pimps, who angrily but patiently paced outside, waiting for the girls of their stables to be released now that bail had been posted or their sentences had been served; past sidewalk bistros and student cafes; past Village shops of craftsmen and artisans beginning to close for the night; and past average people hurrying home from a day's work to fix and eat dinner.

By the time we reached Christopher Street, Rocco was hanging out the car window, looking for the right house or for his friend, the husband of the dying girl. He had not been given the address of the building—since his friend knew it only by description. Rocco yelled, "Judi, stop here; that's it." I hastily parked the car much too close to a fire hydrant and hoped my MD plates would spare me a parking ticket. As always the streets were crowded, cars double-parked, and a girl . . . ?

We scrambled up the four flights to the top floor of the tenement. The door was ajar. I entered. A golden-haired girl in her late twenties was lying unconscious on the bed, a distraught but obviously very stoned man in his thirties was agitatedly pacing. Seven or eight children of all ages and sizes, representing every hue of the human race, were milling about, confused and frightened. The first words to break the silence were spoken by a tow-headed youngster of four or five, the same age as my older boy. He asked in a worried, high-pitched child's voice, "Is my mommy going to die this time?"

I leaned over, checked the respiration, heartbeat, and blood pressure of his young mother and was able to reassure him, "No, not this time." His mother moaned; she would live.

Later, my work finished, I asked about the other children. They were children of three different mothers, all drug-addict prostitutes, who by necessity shared child care, minimal as it was. The women counted on the odds that not all of them would be out tricking or copping or nodding or jailed at the same time. They gambled that one would always be available to mother. Unfortunately, this was not always the case, and on this evening the oldest child, a ten-year-old boy, was in charge. The Connecticut couple had been chance visitors and had been scheduled to leave before dinner. The youngest child, a girl, was not yet three and was still in diapers. The boy proudly opened the refrigerator in order to show me the four frozen meat patties and concentrated pink lemonade that he was planning to make for dinner. Except for the can and patties, the icebox was bare. The child was brown-skinned and barechested; he wore only cut-off jeans. I could not help noticing several burns in various stages of healing on his chest, arms, and hands. I asked him how he got them. He answered that fat splattered, and frying-pan handles got very hot, but he was learning.

I sent Rocco out for the basics and the trimmings for a good chicken dinner. He also laid in staples for breakfast and enough to cover the needs of the next two days. I changed diapers, washed dirty ones, hung them out to dry, treated diaper rash (it was a hot summer), cooked dinner, washed up, did some of the laundry, and found it was midnight. My patient was conscious and talking; it was time for me to go home. I tucked the children in; each kissed me and was kissed good night, and I slowly descended the four flights. I was a vastly changed person from the one who had ascended six hours previously.

The question *Will my mommy die this time?* haunts me to this day. What happens to a child who has to ask that question over and over again?

And what of the other children, alone, uncared for, without security during so many childhood days? They have no choice, and yet like all children, yours and mine, they are children who desperately need to grow in love, both received and given.

No, I did not call the authorities to come take these children. I was young. I didn't know whom to call, I had read the horrendous stories about our children's receiving centers. I wanted simply to go home to be comforted by holding my own children as quickly as possible. I didn't want to be further involved in general and involved in particular in the hours of filling out police and other bureaucratic forms. I was afraid of their mothers' anger if they returned home to find their children taken from them. I feared for my safety and my children's, since many of these women wielded knives. I withdrew; I was human.

Rocco checked on the children the next day. One mother

was home; she had just been released from jail on bond. Today Odyssey runs a major program to help these children and rehabilitate their mothers.

It was with these experiences and many others stored in my memory, that I rolled over in my bed in my hotel room with its mirrored ceiling in Las Vegas, to tap Michael, and say: "Today's the day I go to the whorehouse."

Michael teasingly reminded me that it isn't every husband who lets his wife go to the local whorehouse before he does. However, the terms of my agreement with the district attorney were that only I, accompanied by another woman, could go to interview the women. Indeed, it had taken three or four days to get clearance for us. The madam had not wanted a curiosity seeker and had first asked that I pay for the time of one of the women. That had not been acceptable, for obvious reasons. I had no intention of paying for a woman to turn a trick with me, and besides I wanted to interview more than one woman. After many calls and much persuasion, it was agreed that I and another woman, a psychiatric nurse from Las Vegas named Suzybelle, would make the visit on a Sunday evening. We would be able to visit one of the largest prostitution ranches in Nevada, the only state in the union where this activity is legal. Sunday was chosen, as it is usually the slowest business day. We were scheduled to leave in time to arrive by 9:00 P.M.

Due to my advanced state of pregnancy and the fact that I anticipated being up most of the night, I had had a quiet dinner with Michael in our suite—which was the one for honeymooners—and he had suggested we take a rest for about an hour. I awoke to look at myself in the mirror on the ceiling over the bed. I could not help chuckling at the picture: here I was, with swollen belly, in the lovers' suite in the International in Vegas, getting out of the bed to dress to visit one of the largest whorehouses in the United States. Only my husband would have been romantic enough to book the honeymoon suite at such a time, and as we looked at ourselves in the overhead mirror, it really was too much! I bent over, kissed him on the cheek, and gently said, "I'll be all right, honey. Don't worry. After all, we have made all kinds of contingency plans, just in case."

And indeed we had. I suppose you, like me, were warned as a child of the dangers of white slavery. I clearly remember the many times my mother cautioned me from the age of about six years on, not to walk too close to the side of the buildings after nightfall (she feared that I might be dragged into the alleyways and raped) or too close to the parked cars (she feared I might be pulled into a waiting car and sped off to a house of prostitution). I remembered the several years that I had walked home from friends' houses carefully measuring and keeping a midline position on the sidewalk and suffering heartbeat palpitations as I approached the corner, for there the cars were waiting.

And now somehow I was about to be driven far out into the desert—just myself and another woman—to voluntarily enter a whorehouse. The house was located in the middle of the desert because of the peculiarities of the Nevada law. In Nevada, whorehouses can be established only within counties with a population under 250,000, and they must be located sufficiently distant from schools, churches, and the main thoroughfare, so that innocent children and others are not adversely affected.

Michael and I had worked out a system whereby I would phone him every ninety minutes to reassure him I was safe. In my pocket, I had left only a five-dollar bill and the change necessary for the calls. I warned Michael not to gamble away my blackjack winnings, which I had banked with him because I was sorely afraid of being mugged or Mickey Finned and rolled—shades of pornographic novels, the *National Enquirer*, and *True Story*.

The phone rang in the suite. I was wearing my long-skirted tartan jumper; I looked proper and pregnant. I slung the strap of my tape recorder over my shoulder; it would give me legitimacy, purpose, and a modicum of additional safety. I answered and told Suzybelle I'd be right down. The elevator slowly descended twenty flights. I proceeded past the gaming tables in the lighted casino, partially filled with the strays who had not gone home after the gaiety of a fun-filled weekend and husbands impatiently waiting for their wives or women friends to descend, dressed for dinner. I greeted several other members of the Forensic Medicine Academy, but I didn't tell them of my anticipated caper. Waiting for me was a five-foot, two-inch, fiftyish uptight lady in blouse and skirt plus sensible shoes and steel-rimmed glasses, her gray hair piled up in a topknot. We exchanged "hellos" and started off for her car, a small Volvo; her "hello" had betrayed her origin as Alabama. A more unlikely pair to be going a-whoring, one cannot imagine.

Suzybelle and Judi. The drive through the desert was as isolated and other-worldly as it was beautiful. We chatted about small things, discussed our anxieties, joked about the strangeness of the situation, got to know each other as women, and returned again and again to discuss our expectations and the novelty of the situation. Curiosity and titillation drove away fear and concern.

And then, suddenly, in the middle of the desert was a myriad of neon lights, flashing on and off: "Margie's Place Michelob beer on draft." Multicolored lights were strung along an enormously long driveway which ended in a rambling bungalow-type building which had about thirty rooms. On one side were corrals for the horses, plus stables and riding rings. In the center was a small swimming pool. On the other side were the runways for the airplanes; this particular house had its own airport in order that junkets, business charters, and other groups could land here before, during, or after their main functions. Since that time I have always wondered if one of the reasons there are so few women executives is the inconvenience their presence would create on these special refueling stops. I did not see a tennis court, but then, it was before the current craze.

I turned to Suzybelle and said, "I guess this is it. I'm a bit scared. How about you? Are you . . . ?" and then I started to laugh—all was right within this world of ours, for the Master Charge card was in the window.

A Thank You to Nietzsche

Thank you, Nietzsche, for writing: "God created woman. In the act he brought boredom to an end—and also many other things. Woman was the second mistake of God."

And to you, Conrad, for writing: "Being a woman is a terribly difficult trade, since it consists principally of dealings with men."

And last, to you, Swift, for: "It is said of the horses in the vision, that their power was in their mouths and in their tails. What is said of horses in the vision, in reality may be said of women."

A Roadmap

I travel through the following sections on prostitution, bewildered and amazed, as if in a Fellini movie. The whorehouse does not seem to fit with my construct of men and women mutually moving forward in companionship and love; yet it fits perfectly because it is the jarring nonintegrable experience that makes me evaluate reality versus a tightly held, organized fantasy.

The whorehouse is a hyperbole of sexual distortion which caricatures all else I have to say. It is a caricature which brutally focuses on the necessity to find, to create, and to share something more between men and women. It shows us what we normally cannot see happening between the sexes because of the "togetherness coating" of the average American home. One reality of male and female relationships cannot be denied in the put and call of the whorehouse.

In the words of the French moralist Joseph Joubert, "A woman ought to have modesty, not only for herself, but for all her sex; that is to say, she should be jealous for every woman to keep the laws of her sex, for what harms the modesty of one harms the modesty of all. She who reveals her nakedness to the eyes of men in some degree dissolves all decent women; in showing herself unveiled, she exposes the others as well."

Background to an Evening in a Whorehouse

As the screen door slammed shut behind us, our eyes, constricting with the change in light, took in the typical barroom scene—a dart game, a billiard table off to a side, and two pinball machines with lights flashing and bells ringing. The shirtsleeved bartender was polishing the highball glasses as he listened to a customer pour out his suffering story. Not a woman was in sight. It seemed like McSorley's before the integration. (McSorley's: the famous men-only New York bar which sustained feminist demonstrations in the early seventies and was forced to become coed even to its lavatories.)

A bouncer-type man who had been standing at the screen door approached from behind to startle me by asking in a deep booming voice, "Are you Dr. Gerber?"

"Yes, I'm Dr. Densen-Gerber," I countered. "I have a—"

"Then follow me. Margie is waiting in the back, in the kitchen, for you," he interrupted in a tone that clearly indicated his annoyance at this female disruption of his routine.

We followed him through another doorway, heavily hung with curtains of glass beads. "Aha," I thought, "at least this fits into the picture of the dens of iniquity that Terry and the Pirates and grade-B movies about Sadie Thompson have given me."

To my delight, the first whore I saw was *fat.* She was Mexican and was wearing a purple Danskin leotard with a small scarf knotted around her neck. She was watching television and chewing gum. Her right hand held an open can of 7-Up. It was reassuring to note that obesity was not an occupational deterrent, and I chuckled to myself. All my life I have fought weight, and I am forever beginning, in the middle of, or cheating on a current diet. One's free associations and comforts are amazing. Certainly, I have never wanted the option of being a "lady of the evening," a *fille de joie*—terms which seemed so much more compatible to thinking in reference to myself than the word whore. Yet I felt strangely good that the first one I saw was fat.

She barely looked up to greet me. I later learned that the room she was sitting in is called the parlor. The parlor is the room to which a male customer or customers are brought. A bell rings throughout the girls' bedrooms, summoning all who are not busy servicing customers to assemble in the parlor for the "line-up." Indeed, the girls call this procedure "working on the line." Later I was to learn that they all prefer to work for a madam who has been on the line herself, as she can empathize and understand. Margie had been upwardly mobile, having worked the line in another place until she had enough money to buy land and build this one. She was now married, and her husband lived there, too. She was heavily invested in real estate, was chairperson of the local Chamber of Commerce and a member of the Governors' Campaign finance committee. Indeed, she was one of the town's business leaders, probably its largest taxpayer, and a recognized person in the community; but as the girls were to tell me repeatedly, if business was really brisk, she got right down and helped them out.

The mechanics of engagement are clear-cut and simple. The bell rings; the girls who are free line up in the parlor, wearing various outfits of their own choice but all more or less revealing: leotards, bikinis, baby-doll nightgowns, depending on what each one prefers. One girl, for instance, always keeps her breasts covered even in the most intimate of moments. That's her right and prerogative. All the outfits reveal the girls' entire legs, and all the girls wear excruciatingly high heels. This made me wonder about sadomasochistic activities and bondage and discipline performances, about which I later had the opportunity to ask. I learned that "leather work" of all types is permitted for a price but only with the man as the victim. Furthermore, as added protection when this is the "party" (the euphemism for sexual activity) contracted for, the man has to agree to leave the door of the bedroom ajar, and a security guard is posted outside within easy hearing distance. This ensures that the customer can not turn mean on the girl. I was amazed and pleased to find that the girls are always physically protected and safe—a far cry from the real-life situation of the forty thousand whores who work the streets of New York, many of whom are as young as thirteen or fourteen years old.

During the minutes that the girls are lined up and the man is making up his mind not a word passes between them. Once he chooses, she leads him back to her room and the negotiations begin. The basic party, which is "single-time straight-sticking in the missionary position," starts at $10. All else is additional, and it is up to the girl to sell. She will keep 50 percent of the fees charged, and the majority of the girls net between $120,000 and $200,000 a year. This house has thirteen girls; so it grosses roughly between $1.6 million and $2 million a year. The madam told me that after she subtracts overhead, taxes, and so forth (and there are no police payoffs or other bribes because all the activities are legal), she nets approximately $500,000.

Most of the girls save over $100,000 a year. Many set an amount they wish to accumulate before retiring from this business, investing in another career, and settling down comfortably with a husband and children. It usually takes them between five and ten years to reach their individual goal. Most retire by thirty-five, though one woman still working was forty-five.

After negotiations are completed and "parties" to be performed, agreed upon—and these parties can be quite extensive and expensive, sometimes involving several girls—the girl asks the man if he wants the relationship to take place there, in her bedroom, or in the videotape studio. If he prefers and pays the additional $100 charge, they can retire to a specially designed, lavish private studio with a hidden camera, which records the events on a videotape cassette that he can take home as a memento.

Everything finally agreed upon (and occasionally for a steady customer who earns very little, a discount price of $7.50 suffices), the girl leaves him to undress while she registers the fee, turns over the money (everything is paid for in advance), or fills out the Master Charge form for his signature and checks the validity of his credit card. Obviously, often additional parties are added during the spontaneity of the moment; these are paid for later. If any man reneges about paying, there are the security guards to confront him, and if he continues to refuse, the local sheriff can be called, just as he would be if a customer refused to pay a hotel or restaurant bill. Margie has the same rights as any other innkeeper.

These protections raise some interesting issues and legal problems, which I later delighted in passing on to my law students at the University of Utah Law School. Immediately prior to my visit the commissioner of human rights for the state of Nevada, a black man, had filed suit against one of the houses. Even though there are black and Chicano girls who work the line, no black or Spanish American male is allowed to cross the divider from the barroom to enter the parlor. Third World men are permitted to use the bar, the billiard tables, the pinball machines, but not the girls. They can't even get to see them.

The rules are such that each girl has the right to refuse to service any customer who turns her off, so to speak, or who wants a party that she doesn't wish to give, such as "going down the old dirt road" (meaning anal intercourse), but in the instances of men from these groups, the girls are not given the opportunity to say, "No, I'd rather not." The house rules negate any such choice.

Consequently, the commissioner filed a discrimination case on civil rights grounds. As an exercise, I instructed my class to write the opinion of the judge. It is a given that public places can't refuse to serve anyone because of ethnic or racial background, but does this guaranty extend to include that a woman must under the circumstances of working in a whorehouse be required by law to be intimate with everyone? The fantastic irony of civil rights, but *whose?* I never learned what the real judge ruled, but the uptightness and seriousness of my rigid, idealistic, clean-shaven, cropped-haired Utah students, facing the complexities of life, perhaps for the first time, was meaningful in and of itself.

Now back to the complexities of getting bedded in the whorehouse, which is definitely much more difficult than grappling in the back seat of a car on lovers' lane.

The John has chosen his girl, they have agreed upon the party, she has collected the fee and turned it over to the management, he has undressed, and she returns to the room. Is sex next? Of course not.

She now "milks" his penis and prostate to see if there is any weakness or "strain," as it is called. If there is a discharge, then all is off; he dresses, and his money is returned. Logically, why didn't she check before collecting the money? Because, realistically, a man might just get "his rocks off" when being tested or milked, and so he pays before she touches. There must be some validity to all this because in the six years Margie's has operated, there has been only one case of venereal disease. Naturally, crabs also make the man unacceptable, and if found, the girls therapeutically "Kwell" him before he leaves. Furthermore, if the whore suspects venereal disease, she fills out a Nevada Health Department card, and the man must seek treatment privately within the week or he will be visited by a state public health worker. The girls work closely with the health department and personally are checked weekly by the local doctor.

Assuming the man has no strain, additional precautions are *still* taken; his genitals are scrubbed with Phisoderm (surgical soap) and then painted with Betadine (surgical iodine).

Oh romance!

Several times during my interviews later in the evening the bells would ring and the girls would leave to go on the line-up. Each time all would return but one. It was hard for me to integrate what was happening all around me. I was amazed to learn that many of the girls were in the midst of extension courses at different schools: in real estate, investment banking, commercial art. When the bell rang, they would hastily put their books away to run off to make a winning impression.

Conclusion: No violence, no damages to the woman, no reneging on payment, no victimization of the female by the male, no fear, no disease, and always the hope and actualization of saving sufficient money to leave to build a different kind of life. It's better than the system we have in the rest of the country. Nevada permits no juveniles (those under twenty-one years of age) to work in prostitution, while in New York the streets are filled with teeny-bopper, pill-popping thirteen- to eighteen-year-old girls, many of whom are killed in shabby hotel rooms, brutalized by sadists, and drugged by pimps and pushers. It is a fact that of the nation's 1 million annual runaways, over 150,000 reach New York, with the largest single group, according to New York City police reports, being fifteen-year-old white girls, mainly from the Midwest. Michael has performed autopsies on more than one of these bewildered, unfortunate children. Many were themselves victims of sexual abuse usually at an early age. In December 1974, the Odyssey Department of Social Research studied every female patient in Odyssey's treatment programs. Of the 118 women, 44 percent have been victims of incest, 75 percent before they were twelve years old, 45 percent before they were nine, and in 25 percent of the cases, the mothers knew and did not protect their daughters. Little wonder these children run away only to find a different type of abuse on the street—and frequently prostitution and drugs.

In the Nevada houses, no drug use is permitted either by the customer or by the girl. After my visit I realized that government control and supervision is better, even though we must never condone such dehumanizing activities as sex for sale. However, since prostitution cannot be denied, it should be made as safe as possible, affording the maximum protection to the girls and their lonely customers.

Recently a very attractive young black girl who had worked one of New York's better-known "massage parlors," told Judge Justine Polier and me of a new kind of abuse. Though she was a cocaine addict, she had had no prior arrest record. Yet she was told when she was hired that part of her job would consist of taking her turn being arrested periodically, about once every six weeks. This was necessary because the police needed to meet their quota in order to appear as if they were doing their job. The officers didn't even have to bother to frame or entrap her. It was simply that on certain days when the police would be waiting to take her to the station house for booking and processing she was told to report earlier to work—say by 2:00 P.M. She had to be early enough for bail to be made by her employer in time for her to return to work by 6:00 P.M., when there was a heavier influx of customers. Everybody profited: the owner stayed in business without being raided at peak hours; the police met their quota; the Johns were never embarrassed; and the girl didn't lose any earnings. But her arrest record got longer and longer. Some day it might weigh heavily against her if she were ever arrested on other charges or if she wanted to seek legitimate employment.

Also, in my experience, there is scarcely a girl who is arrested for prostitution or another crime who has not had to submit to sexual advances from law-enforcement personnel. Shades of Joan Little. Certainly, while I am in favor of strict law enforcement, I cannot agree that saying "no," even if you are a whore, is what is meant by "resisting an officer."

All women must insist that all other women have the right to their own bodies. Until the most successful woman realizes that her standing and rights are affected by the treatment accorded the lowest of women, because she *is* a woman, full personhood and dignity will be denied to us all. It is basically for this reason that I want to share my experiences among the whores with you.

During this period of my growing awareness, 1971–73, I wrote to President Nixon about an article I had read in *Newsweek*. In fact, I had read two pieces in the same issue. The first concerned a brief anecdote: a reporter asked the President, while he was out golfing, what he thought of a recent well-attended feminist demonstration in Washington. He replied, "It's like watching a burlesque show, highly revealing at best." I politely wrote to inquire of our President if, in order to be consistent, he would also compare Martin Luther King and his dedicated workers in the civil-rights movement to a minstrel show.

The second story told of Nixon's concern for our brave soldiers in Vietnam. He had cared so much that he had personally sent his wishes along with the topless go-go dancers who were to do their thing in Saigon. My letter continued by asking if it would be possible to send naked men in trench coats to expose themselves to the Waves and army nurses. I suggested that the nation, under his able leadership, should launch a "Tat for Twat" program. He didn't answer my letter.

While it's impossible not to be intimately horrified and emotionally outraged by the symbolic rape and degradation of the female, which daily surround us, epitomized in the celluloid strip scene vividly portrayed in *Nashville,* keeping a sense of humor is often the only way to cope. For instance, I remember being interviewed as to my reaction when the New York Playboy Club opened. The reporter was an earnest, braless young woman, devoid of make-up and sincerely seeking to define herself as a person. She trusted I would give her guidance and profound insight.

My psychiatrist-lawyer-churchgoing-wife-mother self contemplated the affront of the Playboy Club, especially since J. Densen-Gerber, J.D., M.D., F.C.L.M., had been sent an application to join as a charter member; the alphabet soup always causes the incorrect assumption of maleness.

Finally, the *words* came to me, the wisdom of the ages: "Let's form our own club, the Jock Rabbit Tearoom."

With all these conscious and unconscious thoughts swirling around in my head, I walked through the second glass-beaded doorway, through the large dining room, past several girls eating, drinking coffee, doing their nails (both finger and toe), into the kitchen and breakfast alcove. There Margie was waiting for Suzybelle and me.

Margie was a stunning woman, not yet thirty-five, with the jettest black hair I have ever seen, the longest false eyelashes both upper and lower, bright make-up, and a slinky, knit tubular dress which did its job well in revealing a superb figure. Her legs were stockinged and her narrow feet in skyscraper mules. Long fingernails, well turned ankles, and educated speech completed the picture.

She began by interviewing me as to whether or not I was

appropriate and worthwhile enough to interview her girls.

Finally I passed her scrutiny, and we walked back to the parlor and through yet another glass-beaded doorway. My time had begun.

Selections from within a Whorehouse — I

DR. D-G: Margie, how did you get involved with this?

MADAM: I don't even really know myself. It was about twelve years ago, when I was twenty-two or -three. I had a friend in Reno who was a prostitute, and I got to talking to her about it. I needed some money and needed it fast. I'd gotten myself a little bit over my head. I guess we all know how that is. So, my friend said, "Well, there's a spot open where I work," and I said, "Fine. Can you get me in on it?"

DR. D-G: You came in as one of the girls?

MADAM: Sure did.

DR. D-G: Were you single, or married, and did you have children?

MADAM: I'd been married three times before but without children.

DR. D-G: You were married three times before you were twenty-two?

MADAM: Uh-huh. So, anyway, I went up to the place where this galfriend of mine was working, and she showed me the things that were necessary for me to learn in order to work in a house, which is much more specialized and demanding than working on the street.

DR. D-G: Can you fill me in, because I know absolutely nothing about this.

MADAM: A house girl learns that there are four parties that she has to master in order to please a customer: a straight lay, a good half-and-half, a good blow job, and a good sixty-nine party. These are four things that she's got to get down pat.

DR. D-G: What's the difference between a sixty-nine party and good blow job?

MADAM: A sixty-nine party is where both do it together; a blow job is where only the woman goes down on the man; and a half-and-half is where the woman goes down on the man and they finish up vaginal. Those are the basic four parties. But before a girl in a house even turns a trick, she must examine him. And I mean she pulls the foreskin back, looks underneath the penis, all around underneath the balls, checks through the hair and everything else for things like crabs, warts, any kind of an open sore or cut, anything like that. And then she milks him down for signs of the clap or for any type of strain. As the girl does this the end of the peter usually comes up; she pulls on it until it secretes juices to form a string, like when you're making taffy. The juice that comes out must string, for if it doesn't string, the house rules are that the girl must turn him down, for that means there's something wrong. Anybody could have a strain without any sickness just from being a truck driver, or lifting a lot of heavy merchandise or somethin'. But if he has an open cut or warts or anything, he's what we call a loser. She'll explain to him,

"Honey, I don't know what it is. Maybe nothing's wrong at all, but there is a possibility, and in my line of work I can't take any chances that there is. You wouldn't want me to have taken a chance with the guy before you, would you? So I'm sorry, not tonight. Come back after you have been checked and treated by the doctor." She always gives him a Health Department card which she has in her room. Then we send a duplicate to the Health Department. Often we refer him to the doctor in town to check him out.

DR. D-G: With all these precautions, do the girls often catch a disease?

MADAM: No, very seldom, because the girls are very careful —they do this routine for every customer, every time. It doesn't make any difference if the girl had stayed with the customer ten minutes before, if she brings him back out into the parlor and he decides that he wants to go to the room again, then once again she goes through the same procedure. And then, after a girl turns the trick, has given the gentleman his party, she washes him off, and she cleans herself out. She does this every trick without exception.

DR. D-G: Which differs from what's done on the street.

MADAM: Definitely. On the street they don't even bother cleaning or washing the men or themselves before or after, and they certainly don't bother checking for any disease at all.

DR. D-G: Furthermore, a street whore doesn't have much chance to say "No," anyway, to anyone or anything. If she does say "No," and the guy says "Yes," she has a problem convincing him no.

MADAM: All she has to do here is turn around and walk out of the room.

DR. D-G: I've seen some pretty badly beaten girls who couldn't walk out.

MADAM: That's why I've never worked the streets. I

	couldn't see myself in a bar, or someplace like that picking somebody up to go to bed with. I couldn't do it; it's much too dangerous.
DR. D-G:	In what sense? Because you don't have the protection of the rest of the girls or the house management? Or what?
MADAM:	Well, for one thing, when you pick a customer off the streets, when you want to check him for disease, he is highly insulted. Then there is no protection, none whatsoever. For instance, if you're a call girl, when you're booked into a hotel by one of the bell captains or desk clerks, they don't give a damn what happens to you in the room, just so long as you come up with the 40 percent of the amount that you earned that you owe them. They don't care if you get the shit kicked out of you or not. It makes no difference to them. But here I have security guards that are right in the house. And if a girl tells a customer "No," and the customer gets nasty about it—why, one of my maids or myself goes back to talk to him. If there is still trouble, we get the guards.
DR. D-G:	How many men do you have working here?
MADAM:	Three security guards, and that's exactly what their job is—security. They're not seen; they stay completely out of sight.
DR. D-G:	And the man who opened the door for us?
MADAM:	He's the bouncer.
DR. D-G:	And then there's the cook.
MADAM:	And he just cooks, but if something did happen, he could also help. That makes five men in the house, plus several who work the landing strip. You're right though; the girls feel much safer here.
DR. D-G:	The girls in my therapy groups repeatedly talk about the overwhelming fear they experience each time they trick because of what might happen to them. They fear even being killed.

MADAM: When a girl's on the street, what's she got? Nothing! But when she works a house, she has the protection of the house, and the law, as well. If something went wrong, I'd call the sheriff without hesitation.

DR. D-G: Have you ever had to call the police?

MADAM: No. But I know if I ever had to call the sheriff, he'd be down here to take my side rather than the customer's because this is a legal house, not because I'm paying off the sheriff or anybody else.

DR. D-G: Even where you're paying off, the law-enforcement people can't openly take your side, or someone would suspect. Anyway, in spite of the payoffs, it's illegal and unprotected—all you pay for is protection not to be busted. By the way, what can a girl expect to earn on the line, say, in a year's time?

MADAM: Approximately $100,000 a year, but it varies with different girls. It depends on the girl: how good her hustle is, how good she is at being able to talk money out of the customers, how good she is at being able to deliver the party that she is giving, how many customers there are, and how good business is in general. For most girls the range is between $1,800 to $2,500 a week, and the house keeps a like amount. We split everything fifty-fifty.

DR. D-G: Is there competition among the girls?

MADAM: Some, but not much; there are always enough men to go around.

DR. D-G: Are you limited to the four basic parties?

MADAM: No, oh no—definitely not. These are just for openers, the ones every whore must know; you know, the different tricks of the trade that we learn. A good whore learns to give different types of parties or to use the same party but give it a little bit more exotic twist.

DR. D-G: How do you check on the amount of money each girl takes in?

MADAM: I trust my girls.

DR. D-G: Incredible. Are room and board free?

MADAM: Oh yes, food and lodging, plus protection and the right to say "No." In addition, there is a week off each month, plus workmen's compensation and other insurance—even unemployment. We provide the same benefits to our employees that they are entitled to if they work in a nightclub or in any other kind of entertainment or service profession. In fact, every girl is licensed as a cabaret entertainer.

DR. D-G: I have treated girls who have been in illegal houses in Michigan. There the basic charge is $5; believe it or not, $2 is for the house, $1 is for the manager, and $2 is for the girls, and I am referring to fifteen- and sixteen-year-olds. You can imagine the workload just to make ends meet, so to speak, particularly if she has a $100-a-day habit, in addition; the situation becomes unimaginable, intolerable.

MADAM: No one here is permitted to use drugs or to be underage. We have to be very careful and strict or the licensing authorities would close us down. In fact, the very room you are going to use for your interviews is free tonight because I fired a girl yesterday when I discovered that she let her John use a "popper" without calling the guard to remove him.

DR. D-G: I imagine many men, especially if they are aging or homosexual, want to use poppers, or amyl nitrite, when they come here. They believe it gives them an extra sexual kick which helps them get and keep it up for a while. Mostly folklore and in the head—not reality. Do you have many Lesbians here?

MADAM: We haven't ever had bisexuals or Lesbians working here. Occasionally, a Lesbian customer has come to turn a trick. Actually, when the D.A. called to arrange your visit, I thought it was a cover for some high-placed woman who wanted to do her thing but didn't want to come right out to arrange it herself. It is all right with us, but we charge extra for that special party. More often a man wants to get turned on by watching two of the girls warm each other up even to the point of coming, and then he'll do his thing either alone or with one or both of them. Rarely men will bring their wives. That is really a trip; then all variations occur, often with the wife participating. The human being is truly a sexual freak.

DR. D-G: In most of my experience, the girls I treat prefer Lesbian contacts. They are sick and tired of male sexuality. They feel another woman understands them better, is kinder, gentler. Margie, I have found that most prostitutes are desperately lonely, confused people who seek a loving, caring relationship with another warm person, just like anyone else. You want the stability of commitment; yet there is a reactive contempt for men which prevents the resolution of the tremendous need to be held and comforted. In psychiatry, we call this pregenital love, but I've always referred to this need as litter love. I mean the kind of closeness that newborn kittens or puppies have. Indeed even with Michael, who is my husband, by the way, one of the loveliest parts of our relationship is waking up together or having his warm back at the service of my cold feet.

MADAM: None of my girls working tonight are Lesbians. In my ten years in the business I have only met one or two. Of course, we do many things for money that are not our cup of tea, but then, most times we are usually far away, tripping out during our working relationships. Often we don't even remember what happens.

DR. D-G: That also is a well-known phenomenon to psychiatrists. Frequently, when things get too unpleasant, people protect themselves by amnesia or fugue states, but there is a shorter, more momentary version called disassociation. It is as if you are not there but are an observer outside of your body, watching. Disassociative states protect us from a lot of pain and unpleasantness.

MADAM: That is exactly it. Often I felt as if I was watching a movie, not as if I were participating. I used to playact that it was happening to someone else, not me. As far as Lesbians, I've already told you, an occasional one patronizes the house or chooses this line of work, but most of the girls don't want or need any additional contact besides the tricks, who are as many as twenty a day per girl on a good day. However, each girl has her own vibrator if she is tense or frustrated.

DR. D-G: I remember one of my psychiatry professors telling us that when we were faced with patients guilt-ridden because of masturbation that we should share the motto with them, "God helps those who help themselves."

MADAM: How true. Doctor, you'll be quite amazed at many of the things you'll learn tonight. For instance, one of the girls you'll chat with has returned this evening from her week off—which, by the way, happened to be her honeymoon.

DR. D-G: Her honeymoon? You mean she just got married?

MADAM: Yep, but I leave it to her to tell you the details. Last Monday, we all went to her wedding. I closed the house for the morning. Didn't lose too much money, either.

DR. D-G: What's the entire price list?

MADAM: Ten dollars for a straight lay, fifteen for half-and-half, twenty for a blow job, and twenty-five for sixty-nine, and from there the prices just add on and on . . .

DR. D-G: Why is it more for sixty-nine than a blow job?

MADAM: Because two people participate. It takes more time and effort. We are paid on the basis of quantity, quality, and kinkiness. For instance, we charge more for S/M or B/D.

DR. D-G: Does the girl both give and receive sadistic pleasure?

MADAM: No. In a house a girl is not permitted to receive it, only give it, and during the party we always station someone outside her door. Even though the customer is usually tied up and submissive, there is the possibility that he might get loose and try to turn it around. He could become violent. The shock and realization of someone opening the door immediately stops any nonsense or danger to our girls. In my nine years running this place there has been very little trouble.

DR. D-G: How did you get off the line, into management?

MADAM: When I first began I had made up my mind exactly what I was going to do; I had no intention of staying on my back all my life. I planned to stay on the line only until there was enough money to get out. I banked almost all my earnings, bought stocks and bonds, which I later sold to buy the land to build this place. I had grown up in the kind of background that encourages long-term financial planning. My father is a real-estate investor, my mother is a dentist in southern Florida.

DR. D-G: Fifty thousand to $100,000 a year to invest is a hell of a lot of investing. Is it income-tax free?

MADAM: No. We pay the taxes, plus social security and the like on all our employees except the girls; as entertainers, they are considered subcontractors or self-employed; so they have to pay their own. There is no withholding.

DR. D-G: How many girls do you have?

MADAM: I have twelve. They and the customers come from all walks of life. Mine is an exceptional ranch. Not all of them look as good as this one. And not all of them have the extracurricular activities for the girls like I do.

DR. D-G:	Such as?
MADAM:	The girls go horseback riding every day. I do a great deal of riding myself. In the summertime we all get out there and really enjoy the swimming pool. In shifts the girls can take hikes and walks as long as the house is covered. Here there is no confinement; you don't have the feeling that you want to climb the walls.
DR. D-G:	Do any of the girls keep cars out here and drive in for shopping, movies, and so forth?
MADAM:	No, because when they're here, they are expected to be on the premises for three weeks straight, except for the weekly check-up at the town doctor. Before or after the doctor's visit, they are given an hour or so to shop or do other personal things while others are examined.
DR. D-G:	How are they treated by the public?
MADAM:	Very, very well. You must realize that to these small towns the girls bring a tremendous amount of income. That's all that counts in the long run.
DR. D-G:	How many hours a day is the ranch open?
MADAM:	Twenty-four hours a day, every day. There are no days that we ever close.
DR. D-G:	I have been told that peak hours occur on Saturday and that Sunday is your slow night.
MADAM:	Both Sundays and Mondays are pretty slow. Sunday is slowest. It gets really superslow after midnight—that's why I let you come here late tonight. But then again, I can never really know when the peak hours are going to be. I have had some Sundays and Mondays that were absolutely fantastic and a lousy Friday or Saturday. In no service industry can you always predict.
DR. D-G:	Where do most of your customers come from?
MADAM:	Out of Las Vegas.
DR. D-G:	Why Las Vegas, when there's a hooker to fall over every other step?

MADAM: Mostly because a man knows that when he comes here to the ranch there is going to be no *involvement*. He doesn't have to worry about his marriage being broken up or contracting a disease so that his wife will find out. Our girls are clean, and he knows that he'll be checked to see if he is clean. He can rest assured that he will not be knocked on the head and rolled only to later wake in an alley with his wallet stolen. Nothing unexpected or embarrassing can happen, like being raided. Whereas on the street . . .

DR. D-G: There is an unbelievable cleanliness here, both a physical and an emotional cleanliness, a total, absolute sterility. A world washed in Phisoderm and painted with Betadine. As antiseptic as surgery—free of involvement and commitment. It frightens me for different reasons than I had anticipated.

MADAM: Here there are no hang-ups. It is just a business, purely a business transaction.

DR. D-G: What is the age range of the girls?

MADAM: That all depends. But no one is underage. I have one girl working now who is forty-five years old. She is a damn good hustler and still looks good. She refuses to save money, always spends it on some no-good old man. The customers are all ages, but we don't serve an obvious teen-ager unless he is a son brought in by his father. Many men want to bring their sons for their first sexual exposure and training, to learn the right ways without fear. I think it is a good idea. The men are all classes—millionaires to blue collar workers. About 75 percent are steady customers and churchgoers from the area.

DR. D-G: Not mostly tourists?

MADAM: No, but we do get a great deal of tourist trade, both on their own and with organized conventions and junkets. Of course we have our own airport for small planes. We have people coming in from

	Japan, Hawaii, New York, Chicago—everywhere.
DR. D-G:	I gather you are glad that you have chosen this life and think it should be legalized everywhere. Why?
MADAM:	First, it is the best and easiest way—for me, for almost any woman—to earn large sums of money, and I *like* money; but another major reason is because I like *people*. I enjoy being around people and still offer a public service, particularly when I know that it's a good service I am offering—and I feel it is. In answer to your question, why would I like to see prostitution legalized everywhere: it would cut down on the disease factor, give physical safety to the girls and the customers, and it would keep a lot of the shit off the streets—raping, beating, that kind of thing. House-trained girls are taught to cope with perverted types, to handle them in a way where they—the girls—are in complete control.
DR. D-G:	Can you give me a specific example, because many straight people wouldn't understand what you're talking about.
MADAM:	Take the everyday masochistic type, one that likes to be beaten. You pick one up on the street or in a B bar and go up to the hotel room and you ask him what he wants. You don't have any of the equipment to tie him properly or anything else. Everything has to be improvised and therefore is never as good or satisfying to the client. Furthermore, you haven't any protection for yourself against his jumping up and kicking the shit out of you instead. That's the type of thing I have in mind. As for sadists, the dangers of being alone with them are obvious. Also, once prostitution is legalized, it will be simply another business and the girls can be good wives and mothers when they are not on the job. Most of my girls are mothers, and many are married.
DR. D-G:	Would you have any objection—if and when we

	legalize prostitution across the United States—to legalizing male prostitution, as well?
MADAM:	No, I guess not, though I haven't thought about it. I don't really see how male prostitution could be as profitable as it is for a woman. Most women don't want to buy sex.
DR. D-G:	I don't mean with women, I mean men with men.
MADAM:	Men with *men*?
DR. D-G:	Men with men, tremendously profitable.
MADAM:	I don't have any objections to it. They're entitled to earn a living, the same as we are.
DR. D-G:	I would only approve of legalization across the board. I can't see one attitude for women and another for men—but I can never see allowing activities that include children, such as the Lolita prostitution rings which are so common and, unfortunately, profitable at this time in so many places. But how does your husband feel about all this? Is he in business with you?
MADAM:	No. He has his own business, but I really don't want to talk about him. I believe in keeping my marriage and career totally separate. However, he has no objections to my line of work and often comes here to spend the night. We have our own separate quarters on the ranch because I must spend long hours here, often weeks at a time, but we also have our own home in a different town. To run a good house is not an easy job. Management needs to be constantly aware and involved. In addition, I am alone much of the time because my husband's business takes him all over the continent. One day he might be in Palm Springs; the next day, he'll tell me, "Honey, I'm on my way to Canada." In fact, he runs operations similar to this all over. Just because things are illegal doesn't mean they don't exist.
DR. D-G:	Do many men run houses?

MADAM: There are quite a few of them throughout the state, but they always have women managers. The girls prefer having a woman in charge. They trust her better, and she can keep them under control. There is a vast difference between running legal and illegal operations. Everywhere, because my business is legal, I am treated with the same respect as any other community business leader or bigwig.

DR. D-G: In other words, there is no personal loss of self-respect?

MADAM: Absolutely not. For example, when our present governor had his kick-off campaign party and dinner up in Virginia City, my husband and I were both invited. Everybody there knew exactly what business we were in and everything else. There were no hang-ups. We were treated with no animosity and no whispering, "She owns a whorehouse," because it's a common thing. In Nevada, it's a business.

DR. D-G: How many houses are there?

MADAM: Throughout the state, I think there are thirty-seven houses.

DR. D-G: Do you think that the loss of self-respect and low self-esteem which I see again and again in all my patients come from the illegality rather than from the nature of the operation itself?

MADAM: I would say so, yes. But also a great deal stems from other reasons, such as using dope or having to do anything and everything without any choice because you need the buck. That is slavery. Here the girls are drug-free and not slaves. They always have the right to say "No." That is the essential difference.

DR. D-G: Then, you don't think the problems stem from having one man after another?

MADAM: No, I really don't believe so. We consider it all in the day's work.

DR. D-G: That's something that will take me a long time as a woman and a psychiatrist to digest. I personally feel and was professionally taught differently.

MADAM: Well, for example, take what happens when a girl wants to leave or change her pimp or operate without one. In Nevada if the girl and the pimp don't get along, he doesn't kick the shit out of her, et cetera, and say, "You're mine, and you're going to stay right where you are," as he does in other states. Here they just say, "Hey, we're just not making it. I'll go my way, you go yours." And that's all there is to it. In fact, many girls don't keep pimps in Nevada, since they don't need them for protection or to make bail. The girls have each other, plus the structure of the house and society's laws behind them. It's a different scene. Men can't touch us. We're the ones who are protected. We're in full control all the time.

DR. D-G: That's a tremendous difference. The women own and control their own capital resources, so to speak.

MADAM: No one here is at the mercy of any man. We probably feel more in control than most wives. For instance, if a girl and her customer don't hit it off and she realizes they are just not going to get along, the girl very likely will tell the man, "I'm sorry, honey, but you and I have a personality conflict. Let's avoid an argument or a hassle. Anyway, you're not having a good time, so why don't you just go out and pick one of the other girls that you'll groove with a little bit better." The girls always have a right of refusal even if the man ends up being alone.

DR. D-G: That reminds me; isn't it a fact that black men can't be serviced sexually? I assume such a blanket refusal on racial grounds is probably unconstitutional.

MADAM: Of course not; the right of sexual refusal is the

intrinsic right of every woman. There are laws on rape. You better believe it. Even though the Nevada Equal Opportunity Commission has filed suit, they cannot get the houses on this, and I'll tell you why: my bar and my parlor are separate. There is a door that is immediately closed and locked when a black man comes in. When he enters, the parlor stops working; no bells ring. He can stay in the bar, he can drink as much as he wants to, he can shoot pool, talk to the bartender, and everything else, but he cannot come in and screw one of the girls.

DR. D-G: While he's here, do you close the door to everyone?

MADAM: No, but the other men are quietly shown around the back way.

DR. D-G: That must be unconstitutional.

MADAM: No. I am not refusing them—the girls are, and the girls are individual agents. It's up to them to decide whether or not they want to fuck that particular man, and if they don't, I'm surely not going to force any one of them. Certainly, the constitution is not going to demand that a woman give her body to every man because she is willing to sell it to some men. A whore can be raped! It would be horrendous slavery if she were forced to fuck everyone. All my other employees, such as the bartender, serve them. Black men get service and acceptance, but they are very politely but sternly told if they go to the parlor door, "Boys, I'm sorry you cannot come into this part of the house, but you are more than welcome to go into the bar and have some drinks and shoot pool."

DR. D-G: Can they use the swimming pool the way your white customers can?

MADAM: No, only the bar is a public place. The girls contract on their own and pay us a percentage, like an agent's fee. We don't negotiate with the customer

	or decide what will or will not take place. The party is their own affair—a party in the swimming pool is planned with the individual girl.
DR. D-G:	Lastly, how does your family view all this? I know your mother is an accomplished woman—a dentist.
MADAM:	My parents don't know what I do. Perhaps my mother would understand, but I believe it would kill my father if he ever found out. So I haven't told anyone for fear he would find out—not even my older brother nor my younger one. They suspect that I'm in some kind of borderline racket, but they think it's gambling. They have no idea it's whorehousing.
DR. D-G:	Do your parents visit you from Florida?
MADAM:	Of course, but I always have them to my home in Las Vegas. Because I'm bosslady, I can arrange to stay at home the whole time they're here.
DR. D-G:	Don't you feel this indicates a conflict within you about your present life style?
MADAM:	Not really, no. I do it to protect their feelings and ways of believing, not my own.
DR. D-G:	What is the reason you decided against having children?
MADAM:	I love children, but I don't feel that I myself could cope with children, particularly running this kind of business. How would they explain this to their friends? There would be too many secrets. So I opted not to have any, since I wouldn't ever want my children to be ashamed of me or to have to make excuses. Furthermore, both my husband and I are away so much of the time, and it's hard to get good help to take care of children these days; I couldn't and wouldn't want to bring them to work with me. Bringing children into whorehouses is against the law in Nevada. It was simpler all around not to have any. I chose a career.

DR. D-G: I think you made a wise decision under the circumstances. In Salt Lake City, Utah, we have a facility for the treatment of addiction. In 1971 of the first thirty-four patients we admitted, seven of them, all males, grew up in houses of prostitution in the West. As adults they had become junkies. I believe the early environment was a definite causative factor. Even now at twenty-eight to thirty-five, these young men are still unable to adjust to their mothers' life style. A whorehouse is no place to spend your childhood, but I wonder if that's due to American society's attitude or if it is inherent? I am beginning to think it is more cultural, because children have been able to grow up relatively intact in France and Sweden with this type of input. Being here raises more questions for me than it gives answers! Where do you see yourself ten or twenty years from now?

MADAM: Sitting at home, retired, living off the income of my many investments.

DR. D-G: And very rich! By the way, since most of your customers are married, why do they use these facilities on a regular basis?

MADAM: Doctor, our service helps and maintains many marriages. Many husbands come here to get something that either their wives are afraid to give them because the women think it's sinful and dirty or because the men have a particular hang-up that they would not even ask their wives to participate in. Here, they can have it performed without any problem, question, or side-glance. You would be surprised at the number of men that come here because they desperately fantasize and want a simple blow job. Their wives are too insulted, embarrassed, or scared to give it to them. Absolutely petrified! Some wives are even frightened to touch *it.* Sex is one of the most beautiful things in the world and certainly should be between two people

	who are married, but sadly, that is not the case.
DR. D-G:	You don't have to tell me. As a psychiatrist, my business, too, is people's hang-ups in the sexual area. I was amazed to learn when I was teaching law in Utah that a man is serving time in prison there for forcing his wife to perform fellatio. A man should not be allowed to force a woman to do anything, but since a husband can't be held criminally liable for raping his wife (the courts have held a woman has no right to refuse sexual access to her husband), then I think divorce would be a more appropriate remedy than jailing for fellatio. Many states still provide for criminal penalties for consensual acts between a husband and wife.
MADAM:	I could never understand why sex is such an ugly-not-to-be-spoken-about-hidden activity, but that is part of what keeps my business flourishing, the difference in sexual needs of the husband and the willingness of the wife.
DR. D-G:	Is it true that whores never kiss the customers because they want to keep a part of themselves private, not for sale, withheld—only to be given to the men they love?
MADAM:	That is true; none of our girls nor any hookers I know would kiss a client. Kissing is much too intimate.
DR. D-G:	More intimate than intercourse or sixty-nine? To me, you all have a half-assed, backward viewpoint. As a mother, I hope kissing at sixteen is still more common. When I attended a sexual exhibition on my honeymoon in Macao, off the mainland of China, I remember my amazement that the girls would not uncover their breasts no matter what the men offered to pay.
MADAM:	Why was that?
DR. D-G:	It's the whores' custom. It's the one thing they are allowed to keep to themselves. In China, there is no breast contact between customer and girl. The

Americans at the exhibition kept yelling, "Take it off, take it off" and throwing dollars at the girls. The performers got more and more upset and threatened to leave. I guess the Americans wanted to see the breasts because our culture is a breast-oriented one. Chinese culture is not breast-oriented. Everyone needs to preserve some dignity, and so the girls are usually permitted to wear a shirt or some such cover.

MADAM: I imagine that all over the world sexual customs differ. I've never really thought about it. But what were you doing watching an exhibition on your honeymoon?

DR. D-G: Michael and I have always had a very sharing and doing-together relationship. In fact, we met on a blind date in the New York City morgue. His roommate was my classmate in law school while Michael was a second-year medical student interested in legal medicine, so he asked to meet me. He was very poor; to save money, he invited me to the morgue. It was Memorial Day, 1957, the first big auto-killing weekend of the summer season. I even remember the body we met over; her name was Mary, and she had died from burns in a fire. I was horrified at her total fat nudity, the impersonalness of it all, and the Railway Express tag tied to her big toe, identifying her name and box number.

I guess I must have looked good to him, either in the absolute or in the relative, because after that we saw each other almost every day. We were married, a little over a year later. Michael wanted us to be married in the morgue chapel; he felt the place should have at least one happy event, but sensibly, my family would have nothing to do with that idea, so we compromised by having a formal church wedding and reception with a honeymoon following—visiting the mortuaries of the world.

MADAM: When I married my present husband I wanted to wear white and all that jazz even though it was my fourth wedding and I had been on the line. We all need tradition. I'm glad your mother prevailed, but still, how did you get to China and the exhibition?

DR. D-G: Before we were married Michael arranged a medical fellowship for our honeymoon trip. Then we found ourselves with four months to go everywhere but no money to pay for it so Michael decided that we should go on Johnny Carson's "Do You Trust Your Wife?" They wanted us to be married on the show, but Mother nixed that, too, for which in retrospect, I am very grateful. The Monday after we were husband and wife, we went on television. But—would you believe it?—he never trusted me or thought I was smart enough to answer any questions. He felt it was his male role to win the money to pay for the honeymoon, and he did win for five days straight. It was quite a successful trip. Everywhere we went, tragedy preceded us, so that the morgues were filled: cholera in Japan, smallpox in India, revolution in Thailand, mummies in Egypt, and assassinations in Iraq. Indeed, in Japan Michael took me to a leprosarium, where he wanted to spend the night. I was terrified and seduced him back to the hotel; blowing in his ear did the trick. However, the next day I retaliated by making him spend it with me on my professional turf, a woman's prison. We were having quite a honeymoon. By the time we got to Hong Kong and Macao, where the exhibition took place, we had joined with several other American couples. All the men wanted to see an exhibition, but their wives had the good sense to back out. But I was a starry-eyed bride, and if Michael wanted to see it, naturally I expected to accompany him. I was the only woman on this excursion, but I wanted to be sure that there was little else Michael could be involved in besides looking. I wanted him all to myself. Today I would trust him, but then it was all so new. Seldom had I heard from my Mother or any other women about a man who could be trusted. Infidelity was a way of life which had been familiar to me from earliest childhood. I believed that when a woman was available or easy, no man said "No." So, well programmed to consider all men potential rapists and sexual animals and armed with my commitment to myself that my marriage was going to work and be forever, no matter what adjustments I had to make, I met my first challenge. Less than one month married, I was off with my husband to the not-so-neighborhood whorehouse in China. I have to confess I was a wee bit curious.

It was far from a good idea in many ways and yet extremely good in others. I was shocked, ashamed, humiliated, aghast, at the way sex and women were presented and treated. The exhibition was in a fleabag hotel room—dirty, smelling, and dingy, with a bed in the middle covered with sheets spotted by former users and gray from infrequent washings. This bed was surrounded by a ring of straight-backed kitchen chairs. A cracked washbasin with a leaking faucet highlighted the romantic mood. To this day I remember sitting on the edge of the chair transfixed as my countrymen yelled "Take it off, take it off," meaning the flimsy, dirty, torn T-shirts the girls were wearing, which seemed to afford them the only dignity they had left after exposing spread beaver—labia majora, minora, asshole, and so forth—and after having all kinds of objects, such as double-donged dildos, jammed up every available orifice while sucking off one man or another in the audience as others masturbated and ejaculated all over them.

Fear exuded from every pore in their bodies, and their eyes pleaded with me until I finally cried out, "Gentlemen, lay off—leave them alone." It was beyond imagination. Mercifully, Michael took me home. I left there; I could take no more. We spent the night on the ferryboat shuttling us back to Hong Kong from Macao. I have never been seasick, but that night I threw up over the side. For many nights thereafter my dreams were troubled. It was several weeks before I could join in love with Michael without painful images emerging and postclimactic tears following. The good thing was that both Michael and I were left keenly aware of how easily the special beauty that is shared between a man and a woman can become ugly; he promised me then and there that such things would never, never be part of his, mine, or our realities again. He is terribly worried about my coming here tonight. Maybe I'd better take a break now to go phone him and reassure him that I am fine. He won't believe it when I tell him that some of the things you have shared with me are causing me to reconsider my former adamant position against legalizing prostitution. But before I call Michael, there is a question he wanted me to ask you. What is your opinion on the Equal Rights Amendment?

MADAM: For men or for women?

DR. D-G: For women, equal pay for equal work, et cetera. In other words, should women have the same rights as men?

MADAM: Definitely not.

DR. D-G: Michael said all of you out here would say "No." I thought you'd be for the ERA. Why not?

MADAM: Because in the first place I can't see a woman digging a ditch. I can't see a woman doing any of the menial-type labor that some men have to do to get started. A woman should stay mainly at home.

All women don't have to be home all the time; some can handle an office, say a secretarial job, or something like that, but they must stay within their feminine ways. A woman's job is to always be feminine and maintain herself and all her feminine tools for her man. What man wants to come home after both he and his wife have worked all day long to find that he is expected to get home an hour before she does so that he can fix dinner for her? No self-respecting man would put up with that! And then she comes in from working for the Department of Sanitation and the sewer detail, with her new equal rights, I ask you, what man wants to have his wife come in smelling like a whole bunch of shit? I wouldn't; if I were a man, I definitely wouldn't. Furthermore, if she wants to stand up like a man, it will get her the equal chance to stand up and fight like a man. I never want to have a boxing match with my husband. Believe me, I don't believe in it. It is just not right. It is against nature. What do you think? How can equal rights be better for the country?

DR. D-G: Obviously, I don't agree. But it is understandable that a person such as yourself, whose life's role is defined primarily in sexual terms, feels threatened by equality. It is a tragedy that so many women who are not whores are misled to define themselves in the same way as you do and have organized to keep down women such as myself or Suzybelle, who desire to be defined as full persons. I wonder if Phyllis Schlafley and other Stop ERA women realize they think as you do and often for the same reasons, economic security and protection, plus fear of new, unknown ways of relating. Women should not be servants to men, rather equal partners. Strange bedfellows, causes and houses make! I should get to the phone now. Where is it?

MADAM: I'll take you down the road to the phone. We are not allowed to have one here. It would make us too accessible to the general public.

A Phone Call Later

DR. D-G: Marianne, I am Judi, and Margie has already told you why I'm here. Can we start by my asking how old you are?

MARIANNE,
1ST GIRL: I'm thirty.

DR. D-G: You have two children?

1ST GIRL: No, just one, but I was pregnant twice. The other child was stillborn.

DR. D-G: This is my eighth pregnancy, but I only have three living children. My second daughter was a Mongoloid child who died. Her birth and death changed my life; it was why I decided to become a psychiatrist.

MADAM: I had a Mongoloid nephew who died at nine months. He was a beautiful baby.

1ST GIRL: That's an interesting pin you are wearing. Are you a Libra? I am.

DR. D-G: No. It is a combination of the symbols of law and medicine, the caduceus and the scales of justice. My husband, Michael, designed it as a gift for my graduation from medical school. He is very proud of my completing both law and medicine. But tell me a little about yourself.

1ST GIRL: I grew up in Minnesota. We weren't rich, but my father had a nice job. Mom didn't work but was a good housewife. She did a fine job of cleaning, cooking, budgeting—you know, all the things women are supposed to do, she did well.

DR. D-G: Does she know what you do?

1ST GIRL: The whole family knows.

DR. D-G: How do they feel about it?

1ST GIRL: My mother feels it's all right if you do it for only a few years to earn a lot of money, but you must get out of it when you're still young. Mom's got a bad conception of this business because she read Simone de Beauvoir's book *The Second Sex*. In the chapter on prostitution, Beauvoir says that prostitutes die at approximately the age of thirty-five. Now, that book was written years and years ago; it's a fantastic book but no longer exactly right because it was written too long ago to be real now and furthermore it was written about the prostitutes in Paris. Then they were dying of syphilis and all kinds of things. Also she thinks my pussy is getting extremely big and that I'm falling apart inside.

DR. D-G: No matter how much you use it, it'll never get as big as the stretching from childbirth.

1ST GIRL: Mom's had eleven pregnancies. You'd think she'd know that.

DR. D-G: There's not a penis in the world as big as a baby's head.

1ST GIRL: Once she saw the size of my diaphragm, and she said, "Isn't that awfully small for someone like you?" Now that I've switched to the pill, she probably thinks prostitutes need larger dosages. My mother has finally accepted it. My sister even tempts and encourages me, she constantly asks me to buy clothes, et cetera, for her son; he is eleven. I guess my money makes me good enough to be in the family. Her husband tells her not to speak to me because he thinks I'm horrible, but he still lets me buy things for his kids. *C'est la vie.* My dad just found out.

DR. D-G: How'd he take it?

1ST GIRL: It was really quite funny. He is a very strict Catholic; so he told me I'm in the gutter. I said, "No, Daddy, I *was* in the gutter. I was in the gutter before I got into this business, being poor and all that, but now . . ."

DR. D-G: Would you say that your self-esteem is better now than before?

1ST GIRL: Absolutely.

DR. D-G: Why?

1ST GIRL: Because before I got into this business I didn't have anything. I didn't screw that much before I became a prostitute, but I ran around with all the guys. I never had many girlfriends. In my whole life my dearest girlfriends are the girls working here now. I have nothing for women, and that includes me, too.

DR. D-G: I don't agree with you. That's a myth perpetrated against women, a kind of female self-hatred men use to keep control. One of the accomplishments of the sisterhood is to get women to talk to and learn to like one another. Women run the whole gamut of personalities and abilities, just like men do. I am always suspicious and turned off by a woman, no matter how successful she is, when she tells me that she enjoys the company of men better. Good company is not sex-dependent.

1ST GIRL: You're talking about educated women, with common sense and logic. I haven't met many of that kind. The only women that I can really trust are here.

DR. D-G: There is a strange kind of honesty in this life style. Certainly, no pretense.

1ST GIRL: This house is fine, but I have worked in others that aren't the same.

DR. D-G: Is the difference Margie?

1ST GIRL: Sure is. She knows *how to approach it.* She treats us like people—part of the team that makes everything go. She respects herself and us. For instance, the prices up north—say, in Reno—are different. For ten dollars up north you can get almost anything, and for fifteen it's around the world and back, whereas down here fifteen is next to the minimum price. The girls up there are worked to death. Most have been in the business a lot longer than the girls here. They seldom say "No" to anything or anyone. They're hypertensive all the time and competitive, grabbing out, knocking others down. It's hard for me to explain—they're just vicious. Maybe it's because there are fifty girls to a house. Fifty women together can't get along, especially in this type of situation, being so closed in, in such tight quarters, with little privacy. It is not what we have here.

DR. D-G: Where do you see yourself ten years from now?

1ST GIRL: Ten years from now I hope to have my own interior-decorating company. I draw well. I'm going to work the line about four more years.

DR. D-G: How do you feel about the line-up? That constant confrontation with acceptance and rejection would bother me.

1ST GIRL: It doesn't bother me at all. It's a challenge. Sure, there are times when a man walks in and makes you feel like you're hanging on a meathook, because . . . I'm sure you've experienced this: one man looks at you, and it's very flattering, and yet the man standing next to him looks at you and you feel like you're naked. It depends upon the man. Some, you look at and pray you're not picked. They simply don't appeal to you, but it's not enough of a turn-off to say "No." After all, Margie would get annoyed if you turned away too much business. You have got to do your part. Occasionally I've experienced a feeling of rejection when I'm on a bad run, but I get out of it by realizing it's my fault because I'm not standing up there looking like I want to be picked. A man will pick you if you put yourself forward. It is a question of sending the right vibes.

DR. D-G: Do you just stand there?

1ST GIRL: We stand there, looking as pleasant as we can at the customer—if he's the type you can look pleasantly at. It is a bit awkward, but it's your job. It's as much a challenge for a man in a whorehouse as

	it is for him to pick up a girl at a bar. Suppose she says "No" even when he's willing to pay? That's a terrible put-down.
DR. D-G:	Are many customers very self-conscious?
1ST GIRL:	Oh, sure. They come in all fidgety and everything. Many of them object to the line-up and want to know why it has to be done that way. They don't understand if we didn't stand up, then they'd complain, "We can't see what the girls look like. Could they please stand up?" Like any other business you can't please everybody all the time. When the house first opened, we sat down in the parlor when the customers came in. Margie would introduce us, and we had a visit together first. But the men complained about that procedure; they wanted a better idea of our shape and height than was possible for them to see when we were sitting down. They were embarrassed to ask us to stand. So Margie started the line-up; we girls preferred the impersonality of the line-up. It's harder to be rejected once you have talked to a man. Also, the line-up gives us more time in our rooms to do our homework, studies, personal things, et cetera. We don't have to be in the parlor unless the bell rings.
DR. D-G:	Are you allowed to drink with the customers?
1ST GIRL:	If he pays for your time and wants to, but we are forbidden to be high on anything, even alcohol. Margie is very strict—straight-laced—about how a lady is supposed to appear.
DR. D-G:	I gathered that. Tell me, what does a guy get for the ten-dollar minimum?
1ST GIRL:	He might as well make a hole in the bed and do it there. He's got to get his hard-on by himself. There's no playing, it takes only a few minutes. There's nothing to it. Some of the girls describe it as a party for kids and jackrabbits, not for somebody who enjoys sex, because it's nothing. He might as well jerk off in the shower. It's cer-

tainly not worth the drive from Vegas. But there are some very good customers who can afford to spend only ten dollars three or four times a month. I can put up with that if that is all his budget allows, but the cheapskate who travels all the way from California, only to spend ten dollars and who games to get more out of the girl than he has paid for—*him*, I just give a hole in the bed.

DR. D-G: Since most of your customers are married, what do you think is wrong with American marriages and wives?

1ST GIRL: Nothing, really. Every man needs more than one woman. I don't think there is a woman in the world who can totally satisfy a man in every respect.

DR. D-G: Nor can a man totally satisfy a woman in every respect, but I would hope most partners in a marriage love each other enough not to act out to hurt the other. Do you think every woman needs more than one man?

1ST GIRL: No. She can find security, enough security to make her feel safe and happy with one man, when she finds the right one. Not everybody is going to be able to find the right one. Sometimes you hit and miss three or four times.

DR. D-G: Do you have a boyfriend on the outside?

1ST GIRL: Now? No. I went with a fellow for quite a few years, and we broke up about six months ago. But Jeanna here has a boyfriend.

DR. D-G: How does he feel about this life style?

JEANNA,
2ND GIRL: Pretty much the same way I do. That it is just another job. All in a good day's work, and the pay is terrific. More than I could earn doing anything else. I'll clear over $100,000, and I didn't graduate from the tenth grade. I'm from Houston.

DR. D-G: Does your mother know what you do?

2ND GIRL: My mother is very happy in her sixth marriage. She thinks and acts pretty much along the lines her present husband tells her to. He and I don't speak. He drinks a lot and once made a pass at me. They keep my son for me, though. Here's his picture. He goes to military school in Texas. That's him in his uniform.

DR. D-G: He is very handsome. He is about thirteen?

2ND GIRL: No. Fourteen.

DR. D-G: Does he know what you do for a living?

2ND GIRL: No.

DR. D-G: Are you going to tell him?

2ND GIRL: Yeah. Someday he'll find out, anyway, so it would be best coming from me. But I'm not quite ready yet.

DR. D-G: How are you going to tell him?

2ND GIRL: He's a groovy kid. I think he'll accept it. He might not like it, but he'll accept it. There won't be much to tell him. At the rate our society is going with its permissiveness, he'll understand it completely and probably be proud of me.

DR. D-G: To sum it up, both of you seem to have come to terms with your life styles. It's very interesting to me because the prostitutes that I deal with are unbelievably straight-laced and ashamed of what they do.

1ST GIRL: Really, Doctor, I think we are both straight-laced. But we accept that a woman is supposed to be a lady in the parlor and a whore in the bedroom. We're just whores in the parlor, too.

2ND GIRL: Take pornography, for instance, a lot of average people enjoy it, and I for one don't think it is wrong; everything has its place.

1ST GIRL: Who does it hurt? Some guys come in and want to be beaten; this helps them make it; all's well and good. Sometimes dirty pictures turn people on; so what? Pornography turns me on sometimes. It's your body, it's your soul, it's your mind—what you

	want to do, you should be able to do, as long as you're not violating the law or hurting anyone else.
2ND GIRL:	Violating the law—that's funny, because why should there be laws about sex if no one is hurting? Laws they should pass are things like the equal-rights thing. I think women should have the same rights as men. Isn't that part of our Bill of Rights?
DR. D-G:	Unfortunately not, but let me share a delightful story about our second president, John Adams, who very much loved his wife, a very intelligent, respected woman, whose son also became a United States president. Her name was Abigail Adams, and she wrote John a letter while he was attending the Continental Congress. Let me paraphrase for you what passed between them. She said, "If you are going to raise a fuss about the Negroes, why not mention something about us? Why not put in rights for women and let us be free partners in America, too?" He wrote back and said, "Abigail, my love, the world is not ready to consider female persons people. You'll have to wait. The country must come first." We are still waiting.

An Interlude during the Line-Up

The bell rings, and the two girls file out for the line-up. Suzybelle and I talk for a few minutes in the interlude. She has sat silently, listening, during the interviews. We wonder, she and I, if the madam and the girls are putting on a front for us, pulling our legs, so to speak. And then we decide it doesn't matter because we are learning. We are seeing women in a sexual caricature, clearly illustrating, in hyperbole, the base reality between men and women in America today. Sad, lonely, dissociated, monetary, fantasy, struggle, acceptance, rejection, exploited, momentary—jumbled words, tumbled feelings, overwhelming.

And then Suzybelle tells me the following story. Often she cries, and I comfort her.

> I was ten years old; we had always lived in the deep South. My father was the president of the local college. He was a tall, quiet man, good to everyone but very reserved. However, I always felt safe in the knowledge that he loved and protected all us children. There were four of us, three brothers and myself. I was the baby and the apple of his eye, as you can well imagine an only little girl would be.
>
> My mother was a gentle, flighty, wispy southern belle, best described as a sort of magnolia-blossom person, busying herself with church activities or being the overseer of the mammy, baking cornbread. She still is the kind of woman on whom even the asparagus decorating her hat to the wedding of the year is home-grown. Most of her life she never had to face any problems or adversities. When I was ten, she was almost forty and Daddy was closer to fifty. I slept in a back bedroom that had a screen door. One warm summer night a young black man unlatched the door, entered my bedroom, and told me if I screamed or resisted, he would cut my throat with the butcher knife I could see in the moonlight streaming through the lace eyelet window curtains. He then repeatedly raped and sodomized me. He left as the dawn broke. I remember as if it were today; I remember lying in bed, afraid to move, terrified of even the sound of my own breathing, and confused as to whether or how I could tell anyone. Finally I heard Mammy in the kitchen. It must have been 6:30 in the morning. She was hustling (what a strange word to use!) and bustling, preparing Mommy and Daddy's breakfast. I got up, looked at the bloodied, soiled sheets and then at my stained thighs. As if moving in a dream, I went to the bathroom and washed the blood and scum off, threw my nightgown in the wash, changed into my prettiest pinafore—it was yellow— combed my hair, put a ribbon in it, and went to the breakfast room.
>
> Only Mamma was up. I told her: "Mamma, a man, a black man, came to my room last night, and he held a knife to my throat, and, Mamma—"
>
> "Oh, my God!" she screamed and ran from the table

toward my room. Mammy followed, and when I caught up with them they were standing over my bed, crying and wailing, staring at the sheets with the stains and all. Mamma and or Mammy—I can't remember which—held and rocked me, and sometime she—no, they—looked between my legs at the slit, I guess to see if I was hurt or something. I hadn't had my period yet, so I guess they weren't afraid of pregnancy, and I guess Mamma didn't know too much about disease.

Shortly thereafter Daddy came down for breakfast. Mammy composed herself and left to give him his breakfast. I heard some excuse as to where Mamma and I were. My brothers had gone fishing. I heard him yell "Good-bye, I'll see you at lunch." Mamma and I yelled " 'Bye" back.

Mamma told me it was a terrible thing that had happened to me, and I must never tell Daddy or anybody else or they would think I was damaged. She told me I must never think about it again and it would always be her, my, and Mammy's secret—something only we women would know.

I never said a word again, but I always felt that she told Daddy something, because he never held or kissed me the same again. Judi, you're the first living person I have told this to. Tell me, Was I damaged?

She cried and I held her until the first and second girl returned. They and a third girl had not been chosen. I learned her name was Betty.

Selections from within a Whorehouse—II

DR. D-G: Betty, how old are you, and how did you get involved in this?

BETTY,
3RD GIRL: I'm twenty-three. I got involved a long time ago. I was seventeen when I started prostitution.

DR. D-G: How old were you the first time you had sex?

3RD GIRL: Sixteen.

DR. D-G: Where are you from?

3RD GIRL: Las Vegas now, but I'm originally from St. Louis, and I began prostituting there before I was seventeen. Once I began to screw, it didn't take me long to realize it was silly to do it for free. I wanted the nice things money could buy and other girls had.

DR. D-G: Are your mother and father together or divorced?

3RD GIRL: They've been divorced about ten years, since I was almost thirteen. After the divorce Mom had to go to work. She wasn't trained for anything, so she became a laundry worker. It was terrible. She aged twenty years in two. At seventeen I knew I didn't

	want to do what Mom did—slave in a hot laundry for under two dollars an hour. That was not for me. A friend told me about this; it's high-paying, easy work. So I like the idea. That's all there is to it.
DR. D-G:	Have you ever been busted?
3RD GIRL:	Yes. That's why I came here. It's safer. One bust was enough for me.
DR. D-G:	Any children?
3RD GIRL:	No.
DR. D-G:	Ever been married?
3RD GIRL:	No.
DR. D-G:	Do you want to get married and have kids?
3RD GIRL:	Oh, sure. When I'm ready, probably after I get out of this business. I'm working toward establishing a business so I can retire and be independent. I don't want to marry because of money and for all that security stuff, like my girlfriends in high school in St. Louis did.
DR. D-G:	What kind of work are you interested in?
3RD GIRL:	Oh, probably a boutique store or something like that, anything that makes money. So I don't have to work. I don't want to be poor like Mom. What's she got out of life? Beatings from my father, eight kids, and a seventy-five-dollar-a-week job at most, never having enough to make ends meet. And just one good dress for church. Is that life? She doesn't even own a dress to go dancing in, not that she would dance.
DR. D-G:	Are you Catholic?
3RD GIRL:	Absolutely not. We couldn't afford to be Catholic. Mom is a Holy Roller, a Pentecostal.
DR. D-G:	Does she know about your present life style?
3RD GIRL:	Yes, she does. She doesn't approve, as far as her doing it, but that is because she doesn't understand it; still, she accepts it and me. She says if that's what I want, it's my life. The whole family's attitude is: "Whatever you want to do is okay as long as you pay your own way."

DR. D-G: What about your father?

3RD GIRL: He doesn't know. I don't communicate with my father too much. I don't go back home too often to visit, but if and when I do, I'm not going to bother mentioning what I'm doing—why should I? He really doesn't want to know, and he doesn't have to. Anyway, I don't know if I could find him. When he cut out ten years ago, that was that. He was always drunk, hollering and beating Mom. A lot of right he's got to have a say in my life. We're all better off without him and his opinions. Men—

DR. D-G: How do you feel about this kind of life?

3RD GIRL: It's all right for people who like to do it.

DR. D-G: Do you like to do it?

3RD GIRL: Well, it's not exactly the greatest thing in the world, but for people that want to do this and their head's ready for it, I think they can. It's not the best thing, but it's not the worst, either. I would rather do this than slam hamburgers for thirty-six dollars a week and never end up with anything.

DR. D-G: How did you get arrested?

3RD GIRL: I was sort of in a bind at the time; I was looking for a job on the square, and things got kind of tough. I didn't do it because I had to but because I wanted some extra money. I knew this cabbie, and it was easy. Only I think he got a payoff because no sooner was I in the room with the John when he turned out to be a cop. I had only hooked a couple of times, and that's how I got caught. More men—

DR. D-G: You're not very lucky.

3RD GIRL: I wasn't too smart.

DR. D-G: What do you think about legalization?

3RD GIRL: It would be the worst thing in the world! It would ruin the illusion for the men who come out here. Legalization would—

DR. D-G: What do you mean, "ruin the illusion"? It's legal here.

3RD GIRL:	The illusion that these places are exotic. The customers come from towns where whorehouses are not legal. Men come all the way to Nevada just to come here. It would ruin it, the whole thing, if it was legal everywhere. Besides, I know it never will be, and if it was tried, it would just ruin it for everybody. You're not going to change anything for us, are you? I have got to think about my benefit first, right? We, in Nevada, have it made.
DR. D-G:	I don't know, Betty. I am trying to decide what my stand on legalization should be. I think your way is better for the girls involved, and I care a lot about women and women's issues. I will let you know when I make up my mind.
3RD GIRL:	I haven't got enough, like you, to worry about others. Please don't ruin it for me. I need this. It's no more sinful to sell it and get the money than it is to tell your husband, "If you don't buy me a washing machine, I'm not going to ball you tonight." It's the same thing. Every housewife is a prostitute, one way or another.
DR. D-G:	Not every.
3RD GIRL:	Well maybe not every woman, but all I've known think as I do. A little more here or there and buy me this or that. There are little ways women have of getting what they want out of men. Wives do it to their husbands all the time.
DR. D-G:	There are a lot of women who don't use sex as a commodity.
3RD GIRL:	Doc, stop fooling yourself. What did you get for that belly of yours? What lies did you tell yourself? Our way, it takes away the red tape; it's strictly business. We call a spade a spade.
DR. D-G:	Personally, it's hard to imagine having contact with ten or fifteen men day and night and not, to say the least, getting a little annoyed at them after a while.
3RD GIRL:	Well, it's not all peaches and cream. Some men

that come in aren't exactly the greatest dreams walking, but when it's strictly business, you know, you can be nice to people; you're nice to some people you work with even if they're not your cup of tea because you have to, and so I do, too. Put myself out? I don't have to as much as square women do, but it's helpful and more pleasant if I am nice.

DR. D-G: You see this strictly as a job.

3RD GIRL: Strictly as a job that I'll do for a couple of more years, if that long.

DR. D-G: That's another amazing difference, this feeling most of you have that someday you'll be able to leave. Most whores in the street feel trapped in it for—

3RD GIRL: Sure, on the illegal side, they probably feel that way, but theirs is a different work style. Those girls have a different outlook on it because they don't get regular vacations, and everything is so . . .

DR. D-G: Would you want this kind of life style, say, after you've married and had kids . . . or, say, for your daughter?

3RD GIRL: If I felt that that's what she wanted and she worked in a place like we have here. If it was legal, why not? If that's what she wanted and understood where it is at, but I wouldn't suggest it to any and everyone who is simply looking for work. You need to be fairly well adjusted to do this, and to understand where the men are coming from. Prostitution is only for people who discover it for themselves; certain girls definitely couldn't handle it mentally.

DR. D-G: What goes into being able to handle it mentally?

3RD GIRL: Being able to respect yourself even while doing it and not having guilty feelings deep down after doing it.

DR. D-G: How do you explain your not having any guilt feelings? You grew up in a Fundamentalist reli-

3RD GIRL: gion with its ideas of sin and that whole business. You simply have to throw those thoughts out of your head. You have to change your attitudes and appreciate that this is a business, just like anything else. You have to develop a healthy attitude towards the whole thing. It surely beats being a Porto-San man or ladies'-room attendant. I prefer it even to scrubbing pots and changing diapers. The hours aren't bad, and vacations are good, one week out of every four, and pay equals $100,000 a year. Can't beat that even if it is a bit messy at times or occasionally a customer has B.O. You've got to learn to ride with the punches, don't you?

DR. D-G: I guess that is one way of looking at it, but what about men who buy women? Do you have any feelings about that? Isn't buying a woman revealing weakness? Don't you have contempt?

3RD GIRL: No, I feel only sadness. All men who come here need to, but I feel that the weakness stems from whoever they're married to and whatever they need—otherwise, they wouldn't be here.

DR. D-G: Do you consider it to be something inherent in their marriages, their wives' fault as much if not more than theirs?

3RD GIRL: If they're married, yes. They shouldn't have any reason to be here. They should be happy. Of course, there are a few men that will always fool around regardless to whom they are married. I guess that's natural, just like women, but I really think that most of them come here because they can't get exactly what they want at home. That's why they pay for it. Because they can't get it. We keep many marriages together. We perform a kind of public service. What, Doc, do you think is the reason why we have so much business?

DR. D-G: There are several definite reasons. First, poor sexual—

3RD GIRL: I think that if you ever decide to run for political office, should you also decide that it is a good idea to legalize prostitution (which I know you probably won't ever do because of the way you've been raised, never having been a prostitute), you'll never make it. You wouldn't make it even if everyone admitted and knew that when prostitution was legal, the country would be better for it, because it would keep all kinds of sex maniacs off the street and prevent many horrible things. The square women would still turn against you because whores cut into their game, so to speak. They would probably say, "Oh, she used to be a hooker, too."

DR. D-G: I doubt that. In New York, where I am from, we have forty thousand prostitutes on our streets; people are asking questions and looking for answers. That is why I am here.

3RD GIRL: Prostitution in New York City is much worse than anywhere else because it is connected to so much violence, crime, and drugs. If you are supposed to find out what you can do for the girls in New York, I can give you the answer. For the prostitutes, *nothing!*

DR. D-G: I think legalizing it might be better. Some might clean up from drugs. Did you ever use any drugs?

3RD GIRL: No, I can't truthfully say I've ever tried anything. Where I came from, I didn't know about anything except marijuana. I never got involved because, like I said, I started working in this business very young and I have spent most of my time trying to make a success of myself instead of being out running around using drugs.

DR. D-G: Do you have a boyfriend outside?

3RD GIRL: Over the years I have had several boyfriends, but I'm not interested in meeting any now because I have something that I want to do for *myself.* Becoming a success takes time, dedication, and all my energies, and besides marriage isn't my imme-

	diate goal. Someday I'll marry and have kids, I suppose, but I wouldn't get married merely because I want to have children. Marriage isn't a necessary happy ending.
DR. D-G:	If you get married and have children, would you tell them about this—
3RD GIRL:	If I thought it was necessary, I would tell them, but I probably won't; but I will tell my husband. I wouldn't hide it from him. That's a long way off. I'll worry about it then. Oh, here comes Star. Star, this is Dr. Judi. Dr. Judi, Star.
STAR, 4TH GIRL:	You'll have to pump me. I don't talk too much.
DR. D-G:	Just tell me a bit about yourself. Anything you want, so I can get to know you. I'll ask questions. Relax and don't worry.
4TH GIRL:	I have my own home in Vegas, a car, and three German shepherds. What do you do?
DR. D-G:	I am a psychiatrist, and Suzybelle is a nurse. I'm from New York, and she lives here in Nevada.
4TH GIRL:	When I was younger if I could have afforded to go to college, I'd have studied to be a psychiatrist, but I was lucky to get through high school before I had to work full time.
DR. D-G:	How were your grades?
4TH GIRL:	They were always good. I liked school. But there wasn't enough money for college, not with all them kids. We were twelve kids in Little Rock.
DR. D-G:	Suzybelle, I see the same things that I see causing addiction: lack of opportunity, striving to better oneself . . . The girls are like the many black dealers who never had it . . . but have a tremendous amount of ambition.
3RD GIRL:	Too bad everyone isn't born rich. Maybe instead of buying a business right away, I should give school a whirl. It's kind of a late start now, but—
4TH GIRL:	By the way, did I hear you say your parents were divorced?

DR. D-G: Yes, why?

4TH GIRL: Because mine were, too. Did it bug you when your mom and dad got a divorce?

DR. D-G: No. I was delighted.

4TH GIRL: I was, too. I thought it was the best thing my mother had ever done. Do you think that has something to—

DR. D-G: Yes, almost every girl I have talked to so far has had divorced parents. Most prostitutes and drug addicts I treat come out of bad family settings—fighting, drinking, abuse—

4TH GIRL: Most people these days are divorced. Nothing matters any more. My mom is only forty-five. When I was home, she worked in a beanery with a forty-dollar-a-week take-home. All twelve of us kids watched the television always showing all the luxuries you could have if you could only afford it. It hurt so bad; our family was a bummer.

DR. D-G: Approximately what are your earnings here? I promise not to report you to the IRS.

4TH GIRL: I wouldn't answer that question even for the IRS. But if it was forty dollars a week, I'd sure as hell get out of here, go somewhere else, and be out in the free world all the time. Twenty-four hours a day, out here in the middle of the desert, is a bummer, too. That's the only thing bad about this; it is a bit confined and I hate feeling trapped.

DR. D-G: Have you ever worked in any other house but this one?

4TH GIRL: Yeah, two; two years in each. Before that I worked the hotels. This one's a lot nicer, the clientele's better. In Reno it was more work. We had to do more volume to get the same money, since it served a different class of people. They get a California trade, which isn't quite as well-to-do or as gentlemanly as the tourists who come to visit Las Vegas. Tourists have nothing but money to blow and don't mind spending it. The Californians are

	average workingmen, taking care of a necessity and not on a holiday spree. But you never can predict what someone will spend—you just have to play it as it comes. Doc, how did my mom and dad's divorce affect my becoming a prostitute?
DR. D-G:	Star, you've probably never seen a good marriage. I suspect you are cynical.
4TH GIRL:	You think so? A girl that works here said that to me just yesterday, but I didn't agree. Maybe she is right. Too many men that come here dig for the reason in my past as to why I turned to prostitution. They always ask, "What is a smart, pretty girl like you doing in a place like this?" They make me sick. Square people, even men, want to find a cause to explain it all—my early childhood trauma and all that jazz. I'm doing this because I want to. Not because my mom and dad got divorced.
DR. D-G:	You may want to because of the divorce. In other words, this may be an acceptable life style for you because you were disillusioned at an early age.
4TH GIRL:	I'm not disillusioned by their divorce—and why I'm doing this . . . I know exactly why! Because this is a means to an end. I can get where I am going faster here than working a square job, because I didn't get to go to college and do some of the other things I could have done, because there is no other way a woman can make more money except by doing what I'm doing now; so this is it, lady. No forty-dollar-a-week jobs for me, no, ma'am, and I get the best tips of anyone in the house 'cause I give damn good service. You know what, Doctor? I never made below a C in school. Sometimes B's, and I remember an A in history. And I used to be the best cheerleader in school . . .

The bell rang, and Star was picked. Her vibes were right-on! The hour was drawing late; dawn was already breaking. Margie excused Virginia from the line-up. She had just returned from her week's honeymoon, and Margie wanted me to experience her.

VIRGINIA,
5TH GIRL: Doctor, there's one girl who refuses to come in, she said she has nothing to say.
DR. D-G: Which one is that?
5TH GIRL: The little one. The Mexican girl.
DR. D-G: The heavy one in the purple stretch suit?
5TH GIRL: Right, the short, squat one. She's my best friend.
DR. D-G: Tell her I don't bite.
5TH GIRL: I know you don't, but she says she doesn't really have anything to say. She told me to tell you she doesn't want prostitution to be legalized, and that's that. She doesn't appreciate people coming to gawk and ask questions.
DR. D-G: There's a black girl, too. Won't she come to chat? All the rest of you have been white.
5TH GIRL: Oh, she doesn't talk to anyone. She's always angry and alone, but I'll talk to you. I like to rap.
DR. D-G: How old are you?
5TH GIRL: Twenty-two and from Vegas. And you?
DR. D-G: Thirty-eight, from New York. Where did you pick up the southern accent?
5TH GIRL: My husband's from Texas, but I've always lived in Nevada. I guess from living with him, I started to talk like him.
DR. D-G: How long have you been married?
5TH GIRL: Seven days, ten hours, and twenty-five minutes, to be exact, but he and I have been making it for a long time.
DR. D-G: No children yet?
5TH GIRL: No, a four-year-old stepson, that's all.
DR. D-G: Does he live with you?
5TH GIRL: No, but we intend to get him in December. His mother is going to give us custody.
DR. D-G: I certainly never dreamed I'd meet a new bride

	here. What does your husband feel about you returning here to work after the honeymoon?
5TH GIRL:	He thinks it's great except for the long hours I work. We miss seeing each other so much it hurts, but Margie's real swell. She gives me every Sunday off, plus my week each month. I guess being newly married, we need more time together than other couples.
DR. D-G:	What kind of work does he do?
5TH GIRL:	He's a security guard in a strip nightclub. He used to be a deputy sheriff in Texas. He is older than I am by about twenty years.
DR. D-G:	How long have you been in the business?
5TH GIRL:	Well, I turned my first trick when I was fourteen. I had wealthy parents and everything, but I hated asking them, always feeling I owed them and all that. One day I wanted a dress, so I turned a trick.
DR. D-G:	You did?
5TH GIRL:	I could have had the dress from them, but I'd rather get it on my own. Home was a nice two-story house. Dad was a wholesale distributor. He earned over $30,000 a year. There were eight kids—seven girls and one boy. I grew up Catholic but became Christian Scientist when I decided to marry my husband. He is, you know.
DR. D-G:	How old is your brother? Is he the youngest?
5TH GIRL:	Yeah, he's four. I have a twenty-eight-year-old sister, one twenty-six. Then I come. The next is eighteen, then thirteen and seven, and one would be six, but she is dead. She drowned in a neighborhood pool right before I wanted the dress—wanted it in fact to wear the Christmas after her funeral. The pool was down the street. I was watching her, and I told her she could go swimming the day she drowned. Sometimes I feel bad but I don't want to talk about that. My parents are still living together.
DR. D-G:	There's twenty-four years between the oldest and

the youngest child. Are your parents still happily married?

5TH GIRL: They live together.

DR. D-G: What do you think is wrong between them?

5TH GIRL: Us kids.

DR. D-G: What do you mean? Too many kids or what?

5TH GIRL: No, it is a typical modern marriage; I never remember them happy together, always yelling and snapping and fighting, but they stay together because of us kids, and they are always making more kids. It never ends. My father doesn't like women. *He doesn't.* His mother was a prostitute.

DR. D-G: Your father's mother was a prostitute?

5TH GIRL: Sure. Why are you so surprised? There were prostitutes before tonight, but that's why I can never tell him where I am. My grandmother was a prostitute, and Dad was the product of one of her tricks. It was back in Baltimore. Grandma had eight children that way.

DR. D-G: How do you know this? Was this something that Mom and Dad discussed?

5TH GIRL: Yes, quite a bit; Mom would yell at Dad, "You whore's bastard!" Those were happy times. Other times when my father and I clashed, he would tell me I was one of the reasons that he didn't divorce my mother. In fact, I *was* the reason.

DR. D-G: How come?

5TH GIRL: They were planning to get divorced even though they already had two girls. Dad had left Mom and come to Vegas from Idaho, where they were living. He was going to start a new life, but when Mother found out that she was pregnant again, she refused to give him the divorce. My father always said I was the one who kept him from getting away and having a good life.

DR. D-G: Now I understand. What about your grandmother? Did you know her?

5TH GIRL: No, never did.

DR. D-G:	And she never married but had eight trick babies; didn't she know about birth control?
5TH GIRL:	I never had the chance to ask her. I simply know there were eight kids in my father's family. I guess it was 'cause she was Catholic, she couldn't protect herself. Birth control is against the Catholic religion, you know.
DR. D-G:	So is never marrying but having children by tricks. Crazy! What about your mother's family?
5TH GIRL:	I don't know too much because Mom was adopted. It was a very freaky type of situation. My mom was being watched by the woman I later called Grandma Josette, and one day her mother just left her there and never came back to fetch her.
DR. D-G:	Her mother wasn't married, either?
5TH GIRL:	Yes, she had parents who were married, but they simply left her with the babysitter and never came back to get her. Mom was just a little kid. She wasn't big enough to walk. Josette raised her from then on. Josie's dead now, too.
DR. D-G:	Your mother never found or knew her real parents?
5TH GIRL:	Right. My father never knew his dad, either; didn't even know who he was. It is a freaky family. I started screwing around at nine.
DR. D-G:	How come?
5TH GIRL:	I was raped.
DR. D-G:	By whom? Did you know him? Was he caught and punished?
5TH GIRL:	Sure I knew him, but I never told anybody until I was fifteen because the man is my brother-in-law. Of course, the family never took any action—by then my sister had four children with him. Therapists tell me I am a psychiatrist's dream. My parents sent me through group-therapy sessions and one-to-one with psychologists because I was really fucked up in my head.

DR. D-G: Was it a single time that he raped you, or did the relationship continue?

5TH GIRL: After the first time, I sort of liked it. We did it regularly until I was about sixteen, at least once or twice a week. Most of the time it was only fondling and rubbing each other, but occasionally we'd go the whole trip. He would tell me, "If you tell anybody, it will hurt your sister; they'll put me in jail, and your sister will have to take care of the baby (and later babies; she has six now) all by her lonesome. You don't want to cause the break-up of our marriage, do you? Anyway you send me signals. I can't resist you, you sexy bitch." So I never told anything. The time I was first raped, my sister was pregnant. This is how come she married at fifteen. He was thirty. But she knows now. I told her one day when we had a fight.

DR. D-G: And she's still with him. What's wrong with her?

5TH GIRL: She claims she loves him and I should stay away and not entice him. Anyway, she has kids by him; she's knocked up now.

DR. D-G: After you were raped by him, who was next?

5TH GIRL: Couldn't tell you. I had a whole crew before I was fourteen and started tricking.

DR. D-G: Why did you do it? Did you want sex or need to feel someone's love, being wanted, or what? Or you just didn't give a goddamn?

5TH GIRL: I didn't give a damn, I guess. I was very, very, very promiscuous. I'd tell my mother I was going to babysit, but I'd walk down the street and get picked up, just to get balled.

DR. D-G: Do you like to ball?

5TH GIRL: I guess so.

DR. D-G: Do you?

5TH GIRL: Yeah.

DR. D-G: You don't have to; it wouldn't bother me or surprise me if you didn't. You probably are doing all this screwing for reasons other than "fun."

5TH GIRL:	Actually, Doctor, I really don't like sex; it is always disappointing. It's as if I want something, and afterwards—every single time afterwards—I feel empty and sad. I guess I'm like women they write about in magazines—frigid. But the men all go after me like flies to honey. They always have—I've got a reputation for being a nympho. I never say "No."
DR. D-G:	How do you feel about men? I don't mean your husband; let's talk about other men.
5TH GIRL:	I don't know. For a while as a teen-ager, I went to several psychiatrists so they could diagnose and perhaps help me. I'm sounding like a textbook case. I'm not trying to impress you with my words or anything like that, but they simply said that I was promiscuous because my father never loved me and so I wanted love and acceptance from other men. Always searching, never finding. They told me I was always looking for the father I never had. I sure hope I found him in my husband. He is twenty years older. I go for older men. Even my brother-in-law was twenty-one years older. I guess you shrinks may have something to all your nonsense; I simply don't know how I really feel about men. I know I don't hate them.
DR. D-G:	How about your husband and his letting you do this? How do you feel about him?
5TH GIRL:	I'm afraid of him; I don't want to get pregnant again. I don't want to live like Mom.
DR. D-G:	How many times have you been pregnant?
5TH GIRL:	Just once.
DR. D-G:	Did you have an abortion?
5TH GIRL:	No, a miscarriage, which I wanted 'cause I was only fifteen. I couldn't handle it, and I didn't know who the father was. That's when the family started sending me to psychiatrists. It was then that my brother-in-law stopped out of fear that I'd tell. Doc, you know the doctors tried to treat my head,

but nobody told me about birth control pills or stuff like that. I could have gotten pregnant anytime again. I was lucky, I guess. No care but no "knockee-uppy," either. Sometimes I wonder if God's going to punish me by never giving me any children. I cry about that often. I don't want to be sterile. I turned twenty-one two months ago and was eligible to work here. You can't work a house underage. Margie and the other girls fixed me up with birth control pills, sent me to the doctor in town, and all that. Those other men doctors, they didn't care or think or understand. For all they knew or cared, I was an easy lay; I was looking for a father, being pregnant and all. I bet they joked about it; more than one of them used to pat me on the ass, but no one got down. I guess they were afraid of my being underage. What's the saying men have? "Keep 'em barefoot, pregnant, and in the kitchen?" I guess all men are no-good bastards. When I first met my husband and we started living together, he took me off the streets, since he had connections in the hotels. Hotel work is easier than the street, but a house is the best ever.

DR. D-G: Now I'm going to ask you a naive question coming from my naive bag: how come he's not jealous? And how do you feel about his not being jealous?

5TH GIRL: He trusts me. I am a very trusting person too. Too trusting at times. He knows I don't love these tricks. You don't love tricks. You don't even let them kiss you. He's the first man I've ever loved.

DR. D-G: I don't understand how you can love a man after all this nonsense. I would have guessed all hookers would feel contempt for men at best but more probably hatred but that's beside the point.

5TH GIRL: He is a . . . hell, it's hard to explain. He knows where I am coming from; my husband is very, very jealous but not of my working here. I'm working here for us, because I have to get up the money so

	that we can adopt his son. I have to get up money so we can get married in the church; that's why I came up here in the first place.
DR. D-G:	The Christian Scientist Church?
5TH GIRL:	No, the Catholic Church because my parents are Catholic and they wouldn't consider us married unless the ceremony took place in a church. Anyway, I was raised Catholic. I converted four years ago. Furthermore, I always dreamed, since I was a little girl, of being married in a big, white formal gown and the whole . . . so here we are.
DR. D-G:	Incredible—marriage in white, cream, ivory. Oh well . . . I am confused. Aren't you just married and returning from your honeymoon?
5TH GIRL:	That was only the civil ceremony. We are married in the eyes of the law but not yet God. My parents wouldn't let me back in their house if they knew I'm living in sin, and I like to visit and eat dinner at home. They don't know anything about my present job.
DR. D-G:	Did your father totally reject his own mother?
5TH GIRL:	He doesn't like women. He has no respect for women.
DR. D-G:	How about your husband?
5TH GIRL:	I'm the first woman that he's ever loved. He's lived with quite a few, but he's never trusted or loved any. I'm the first one he married. After forty years of being a bachelor and fathering six kids. I hooked him. I mean, I got his name and all. Just thinking I am Mrs. Johnston makes me feel good and goose pimply all over. Jim (that's my husband's name) can be jealous. He is, when we go out to dances. I love to dance, but he can't dance so I dance with different guys; if they come and ask me, he'll tell them, "Get the hell out of here," but if I go over and ask them to dance, it's all right. He can be very jealous in social situations. He's very big, with lots of muscles. I don't like to get him

	jealous because then he gets mad. Not at me but at them. I don't like fights or violence or anything. Being here is different; I'm working for us, for my dream.
DR. D-G:	To get married in church?
5TH GIRL:	To get married in church.
DR. D-G:	Religious church weddings, long white cathedral gowns and trains, like sugar plums dancing in my head at Hiroshima. Do you think this life style is sinful?
5TH GIRL:	This is not sinful. I hook decently; it is open and honest; I'm not ashamed of what I do. All our friends know and accept it. I'm also working to make a home for Jim's kid.
DR. D-G:	What about his mother? Why does she want to give the boy up?
5TH GIRL:	Oh, she said we could have him for $6,000.
DR. D-G:	She's selling him?
5TH GIRL:	Yeah.
DR. D-G:	She must be a lulu.
5TH GIRL:	You better believe it—she likes money real well. I've got her letter in my room. Do you want to see it?
DR. D-G:	No, that's all right. But nobody would believe this. Even I can't, and I'm sitting here. Twenty-two years old, on her honeymoon, raped at nine by her brother-in-law, hooking at fourteen for a dress, pregnant at fifteen, and now working to pay for a church wedding and to buy her stepson.
5TH GIRL:	I'm a very sentimental woman.
DR. D-G:	When's the wedding?
5TH GIRL:	In June, of course.
DR. D-G:	Will you come back and hook in the summer?
5TH GIRL:	Sure. Summertime is a good season. I'll make that six grand in the next seven months; then I will stay home, be a good mother, and have my own kids. I'll even bake my own bread, like I've always dreamed.

DR. D-G: Is six grand all you'll make in seven months?

5TH GIRL: I know I'll make at least six grand. I'm not a very good hustler. I never can make a guy pay and pay and pay.

DR. D-G: I expect you'll make more than that. I see you are wearing a wedding ring. Do you wear it when you work?

5TH GIRL: You bet I do now that I've earned it. No guy's going to make me take it off. Anyway Jim says it turns some men on to think they have some other guy's woman. Others, I tell it's an engagement ring and I never got married . . . It's none of their business. Usually, most Johns don't even ask. Anyway, it is not a band; it's my engagement ring. Jim hasn't given me my band yet because we haven't gotten married in the church. He's going to give it to me then. This is only what he put on my finger when we got married in the civil ceremony.

DR. D-G: Are you going to tell your children?

5TH GIRL: Yes. I'm not ashamed. If I was, I'd hide it.

DR. D-G: What do you think is the difference between working the strip or here? In other words, whether you're hooking illegally or legally?

5TH GIRL: There's not as much respect for a woman on the street. You have to hustle, hustle, hustle. You get continual temptations to steal. There have been times when I've felt like stealing, but I've never done it. For instance, a guy has got a couple hundred dollars laying out on the dresser and you look at it when he's in the bathroom and you're dressed; you sure are tempted to take it. It's an honest living here. You work honestly.

DR. D-G: That's an absolutely beautiful statement. Do you think prostitution should be legalized?

5TH GIRL: Not all over the country.

DR. D-G: Why not?

5TH GIRL: Because for one thing, there's . . . it's too easy a living. As honest a living, say, as painting walls, whatever . . . but much easier; therefore, if it were legal, many women would question going to college or bettering themselves, particularly if they can make more money in a house. Why stand up when you can lay down? A girl won't use her potentials if there is this easy way.

DR. D-G: Why didn't you use yours?

5TH GIRL: 'Cause I had to have money quick, and it's hard to get it. CPA's start . . .

DR. D-G: Are you going back to college?

5TH GIRL: I never went. I was going to, but I don't think so now.

DR. D-G: How did you do in school?

5TH GIRL: I graduated with a 3.8 average.

DR. D-G: What's your I.Q.?

5TH GIRL: I'm not exactly certain, but it's high. And I have sure been tested by all those docs. On those percentile type of things I get from 94 to 99 percent scores. The lowest I ever got was 94 percent.

DR. D-G: That's over 130. Why do you suppose a smart cookie like you from a wealthy family is here?

5TH GIRL: Because I'm not with my wealthy family any more. I'm on my own. I'm working for my old man, my husband, to get what we want. Margie did the same thing; she empathizes with me; I guess that's why she hired me. In fact, my husband got me the job. He knew Margie from the old days. I guess I like this work because I'm a nymphomaniac. At least, that is what my shrinks said. All that balling even before fourteen.

DR. D-G: When you say "nymphomaniac," do you mean you come every time?

5TH GIRL: I've only come three times in my life that I can remember—with a man. I can come by other stimulation.

DR. D-G: Do you like women?

5TH GIRL: Of course, I have had women. I do have slight Lesbian tendencies, but I don't enjoy women any better than men. It is all the same. I climax only through oral sex. I came one time with intercourse ... That was the night I got pregnant; ever since, I can't.

DR. D-G: Do you believe orgasm and pregnancy go together? You can get pregnant without ever coming, and you can come without ever getting pregnant.

5TH GIRL: I know that now. I used to think differently. One of my psychiatrists cleared that up.

DR. D-G: A lot of women don't know that, though; they still think they both have to be together. Did you ever use a vibrator?

5TH GIRL: Sure. We all do.

DR. D-G: Don't you come with it?

5TH GIRL: Oh, autostimulation, sure, or oral.

DR. D-G: That's positional, you know that. If you turned over, face down, and put a pillow under your pelvis you'd probably get enough clitoral stimulation to come when you're having intercourse. You probably have a highly placed clitoris.

5TH GIRL: I do. Very highly placed.

DR. D-G: That maybe is what it is. I suggest that when the man has intercourse with you, turn over, put a pillow under your pelvis, and you'll come, face down. It's called doggy position—or *à terre,* from the French.

5TH GIRL: I never tried it. I'll let you know if it works before you go. You're easy to talk to. Leave your address so that I can write you. I had one man, a wealthy older man, whom I was dating pretty regularly when I was fifteen. He was the only one who could ever make me come orally; he was the first man that introduced me to it. My husband's only made me come once. Only one time! Often I use (did you ever read this month's *Playboy*—I mean *Penthouse*—well, in the "Dear Madam," she mentions something that I've done for three years; it's the quickest way that I come and I have no frustration through it) a stream of water from the bathtub jet against my clitoris. Often when my husband's there, I can't come because he's there, I get frustrated and I cry and everything else. He also comes too quickly. Can I ask you questions, too?

DR. D-G: Definitely. Go ahead, shoot.

5TH GIRL: I don't know if it is important or of any interest, but I'm very masochistic—very. I like to be tied, then dominated, but not by a woman, only by a man. I like to dominate a woman and be dominated by a man.

DR. D-G: When you say dominate a woman, you mean you like to tie her to the bed and beat her?

5TH GIRL: I'm not a beating type, but dominating. I don't even like painful masochistic things, rather just to be controlled or in control. If my partner is a woman I want to be in control, and if a man, then I want to be controlled by him. I tie her hands down and make her beg for me and all that jazz, but even with a man here, when I am working, I can't get into the position where he's in total control. Like when I'm blowing him, I have to be on top. I panic if my head isn't free to move up and down; or if my legs are up over his shoulders and I can't move, I feel as if I am going to die. I need air and freedom. I can't take the chance of somebody I don't know dominating me and holding me down. Now my husband, I can let him control me; he's got the bed all rigged up.

DR. D-G: But you still don't come?

5TH GIRL: But that's because he likes . . . I'm a weird chick. I'm definitely weird. I like to get fucked in the rear. I like anal intercourse better. I don't enjoy normal intercourse. It used to hurt, but I'm the only girl here who does it. My husband has trained me how to take it the back way. Margie says we don't have to do it, but if the guy is going to pay $200, $300,

	for it, we can do it if we want to, and I do. Margie does not like us to do it because it can put a girl out of commission for several days; that is why the fee is so high. But I am stretched by my old man, so Margie lets me do it 'cause I don't get sore and lose days.
DR. D-G:	Do you have anal intercourse face up or face down?
5TH GIRL:	Usually face down, kneeling on my hands and knees.
DR. D-G:	Not flat?
5TH GIRL:	Sometimes flat if I'm tied down on my back. I've never told anybody about my sex life before. My husband yeah, but . . .
DR. D-G:	When you get your stepson and you get out of this life style, you should go for some therapy.
5TH GIRL:	I'm crazy, right? I've got a lot of fantasy when I masturbate, and I love being turned on by pornography. I come easiest by myself.
DR. D-G:	I don't think you're crazy at all. *Crazy* means you don't have any reality testing. There is nothing wrong with your reality testing, but you have a few neurotic quirks. You should move sex out of your anus and into your vagina. It's really much more practical.
5TH GIRL:	Yeah, I guess so.
DR. D-G:	There's nothing wrong with masochism, but it can get dangerous.
5TH GIRL:	Jim doesn't like to be sadistic. He's a very large man, not fat; he stands 5'11" and has a 50-inch chest and 18-inch arms, and he can't walk through the door straight. He's a very large man.
DR. D-G:	That's one of the reasons you're attracted to him: the power.
5TH GIRL:	Yes, I like large, tall men. He's not really tall, but I like very, very big men. I always have. My favorite John stands 6'5". However, he's as skinny as a broomstick.

DR. D-G: Of your five sisters, have any of them become involved in this kind of life style?

5TH GIRL: No.

DR. D-G: How come they're so square and you're not?

5TH GIRL: Because they were all virgins when they married, that kind of stuff. It probably had to do with my father. I don't know. He's never told me he loved me. I was always treated differently. He never held me or hugged me or said he loved me once in my whole life. Mom loves me, but it never seemed enough. I'd like you to meet my family. Can I send you an invitation to my wedding? It should be soon—by June.

DR. D-G: Do write to me, but I doubt that I can travel, as my baby is due the first week in July. But I'd love to hear from you. Best of luck.

5TH GIRL: Thanks. There's another bell call. I guess I better go on the line. Need those bucks! It's going to be the biggest church wedding in Vegas.

it's all how you look at things

a snail
was talking
to a crab
in a tide pool

asked the crab
to the snail
why
do you walk
so very slowly—
is that the thing
for snails to do—
or why?
you can easily be
overtaken

replied the snail
i really have no choice
i was born this way
and intend
to stay it—
anyway
it is better
to be able to go slowly
in a world
of rushing madness—
the slower you go
the more of the earth
you can see
there are many
beautiful things
the world has
to offer
and why
do you
rush about
sideways
quite madly—
is that the way
of the crab or what?
it seems very odd

like you
i have no choice
i was born like this
and as you
i really don't wish
to change it
anyway
it is more fun
to see things
from a different
point of view
than most other
living creatures

so both of them
feeling quite content
with what they were
left it at that
and walked off—
one going slowly—
the other going
sideways.

>Ellen Harrington
>Grade 6

a young friend of mine.

. . . and now to the world of square women.

Bridges to Part II

On reading what I have written, I cannot help but ask myself, "Where am I going? In what direction am I walking?" In the four years since I first conceived of writing this book I have experienced many changes of position.

Though many of the twelve successful women I interviewed three years ago have become friends whom I admire and respect, when I read their tapes, they pale in contrast to the twelve gals—five of whose interviews I shared with you—caught up in the world of whoring. And yet both groups are mouthing stereotypes, rationalizing behavior, and justifying their existence. The twisted, distorted concepts of whoring in order to pay for a big wedding are not so different from being unable to ask for a wage commensurate with the copy boy at the TV station because you are a woman and must remember your place even if, like Jackie Nokes, you are the anchorperson on the "Midday Show." I was pleased I could aid Jackie by speaking on her behalf to the president of Bonneville Television, in Salt Lake City. She subsequently became vice-president in charge of community affairs for KSL at a much more appropriate salary. Many of us have experienced good happenings in the years since I began this book. I recently read a lead article in *New York* magazine. It begins, " 'Tighten your vaginal muscles,' said Dr. Penelope Russianoff, addressing the first class in her female assertiveness-training workshop. This unexpected exercise turned out to be more for the mind than for the body. The muscle-flexing, according to Dr. Russianoff, helps women find their central core of identity and balance—first step in assertiveness."

Yet I have trouble believing that vaginal muscle-tightening and -flexing is in some way going to increase my concept of "who I am" and enable me to become more. I see women in many roles and relationships that have to be defined, developed, and integrated into a functioning, happy whole person who is above concerns such as whether or not it is her balls, boobs, or guts that she has to put on the line to move ahead in a positive, constructive direction. She should put herself forward, and that should be sufficient.

But how do we, as women, in a society constructed to undervalue our complete personhood as equal to man, feel that we are total, complete, not defective? How do we create a world not defined by penis envy or womb jealousy? Power versus creativity! How do we simply begin to be?

I pondered, getting more and more troubled by the ludicrous need to pay for assertiveness training to go from pussy to panther in six weeks, by the silly platitudes and the magnitude of the desperation that leads women to seek, seek, seek. And yet it is all part of womanlife.

How would *I* write a "how-to" book? Do I even know how to? I pondered and read on in *New York* magazine. The writer, Marsha Dubrow, continues, "I come from a long line of women—like all of us—who were raised to think it is inappropriate to assert ourselves. We were taught to be ladylike, and ladylike means compliant, agreeable."

I started to sob, dried my eyes, and went to wash my face with cold water. "Oh, hell," I muttered to myself, "it's the damn premenstrual tension—the 'day-before blues.' " I asked myself, "When are you going to be old enough to have control over those raging hormones, the ones Dr. Berman attacked Patsy Mink about in their encounter over the democratic platform and women in careers way back in 1970? You are forty, after all, and you did take a diuretic last night." I concluded: "Behave yourself."

Once again I felt sudden love for Michael, and the mood lifted. I remember telling Patsy during the taping of her interview about how Michael had written the following letter to the New York *Times,* dated on his birthday, July 27, 1970. It was his very special present to me from him on his day.

The remarkable aftermath of the letter on the following page was the twenty or thirty proposals of marriage he subsequently received. Women desperately searching for a man who respected them. I remember his sheepish grin when he handed me the first one and said, "Judi, you better answer this and tell her I've been reserved for you for a long time, only for you."

But I knew my sobs were not basically hormonal in origin but more maternal. From the time I could toddle, I remember my successful corporation-lawyer Mother telling me again and again that the most important quality for me to develop was to always be a lady. No matter what happened, I was to remain ladylike and feminine. I could succeed, achieve, create, I don't know what, as long as I remained feminine and was considered a lady. If I weren't a lady, then she would be ashamed no matter what the accomplishments. And yet I never *felt* like a lady. I didn't even know what it entailed or what were the qualities that should differentiate my personhood from males I knew. Mystically, it seemed based on not comprehending or using four-letter words or having an awareness of sexual matters—but if that was the price of ladylike respectability, my Mother was fucking right: I'd never be one. There was nothing I expected or wanted Michael to know that left me out. Our relationship was a shared togetherness, and sometimes expletives made the point better than saying, "Once again Mother is absolutely correct."

Did "being ladylike" mean that when I went to Washington

OFFICE OF CHIEF MEDICAL EXAMINER
520 FIRST AVENUE, NEW YORK, N. Y. 10016
Telephone: 212-684-1600

July 27, 1970

The Editor
The New York Times
229 West 43rd Street
New York, New York 10036

To the Editor:

I share Congresswoman Patsy Mink's concern for Dr. Edgar F. Berman's charges that the "raging hormonal imbalance" of the menstrual cycle and menopause disqualifies women from key executive positions (News story, July 26).

Women do have periods of depression, but so do men. Suicide is one measurable manifestation of depression. In New York City, where the Medical Examiner's office investigates more than one thousand suicidal deaths a year, the suicide rate among women is lower than among men. Indeed, the incidence of suicide among female executives is much lower than among male executives and much lower than among women in general. Much of the depression that women experience is probably due to indoctrination of the "scientific truths" of physiologic, psychologic and physical inferiority, as expressed by Dr. Berman. Career women who overcome these prejudices may be much better able to handle their mood changes than men, or women who reluctantly accept housewife status.

At autopsy, men in middle life have much more arteriosclerosis of the blood vessels of the heart and brain and more damage to these organs than women of similar age; this, and the increased life expectancy of women, is largely due to their hormones. Is there not advantage in training a woman for a high position in which she may be able to function for many more years than a man?

If Dr. Berman means to point out that there are hormonal differences between men and women, I would raise no objection. But I cannot accept his <u>non sequitur</u> conclusions that, of the many factors affecting ability to perform in our complex society, female hormones per se prohibit women from assuming positions of great responsibility.

Sincerely,

Michael M. Baden

Michael M. Baden, M.D.
Deputy Chief Medical Examiner

to testify on the Drug Education Bill for Senators Williams (N.J.) and Javits (N.Y.), the important thing was what I was going to wear, not what I was going to say?

Did it mean that in fantasy life I would someday be planting flowers, decorating the White House, and playing the first *lady* because there was no way as a girl child I could imagine being president, but even less could I define the role of my husband "the first gentleman"? The tasks presently assigned to the president's spouse fit no healthy man's image.

Or did it mean—? I remember my last analytic session, long ago, when I was still a psychiatric resident in training. I was on the couch, decrying the foolishness of governmental research spending on asinine, esoteric projects while patients need direct, immediate care. I had just read a medical-journal report on a project done in the Veterans Administration Hospitals that had cost over a quarter million dollars. The doctors had attached balloons to the anuses of 100 patients and discovered over a period of several months that a healthy human has to pass 250cc of obligatory flatus each day. One could, of course, pass more but never less.

My Mother had always told me a lady never passes gas. I had always secretly known no matter what I did, I could never make it as a lady because—. Suddenly I sat up on the couch and looked the doctor straight in the face. I was thirty-two years old, and I repeated, laughing and crying, again and again, "Doctor, my Mother farts—yes she does—she farts, she farts, she farts." I was finally free of the stereotype which denied me even the most basic of human needs. It was a denial which condemned me to the pain of knowing (even if it was only my secret) a sense of ever present failure. I had been unable to live up to her expectations and had suffered subsequent paralyzing guilt.

What is a lady? Why, someone who passes gas. I have long since realized that honesty not conformity, truth not rationalization, freedom not status, being not belonging, is the beginning.

Let us begin. I see myself and all women in the following way:

First, woman faces herself. She must define herself and know who she is, not in relation to externals or to others. She must touch and feel that intangible uniqueness that is her person, and she must like that person and be friends. If flexing the vaginal muscles begins the journey—so be it. As for me, I seek self in relation to the universal—to my God or absolute purpose.

Once *being* is defined, then *becoming* can be understood. Next, woman faces her mate. She must define herself in relation to her sexual partner, for he is her next-best friend. Third, woman faces her children. Woman must define herself in relation to her progeny, as reproduction is an intrinsic part of her destiny. Fourth, woman faces her career. I am person, wife and mother; these are intimacies more intrinsic than doctor, lawyer, or professor; the latter definitions are outer-directed and of a vastly different import. The Mormon Church has a teaching written by its late President, David O. McKay, which embodies this for both men and women: "No other success can compensate for failure in the home." I deeply adhere to this construct. It fits just right for me. I hesitate not for a second; if my child is sick, then a million-dollar contract waits for signing or finds its way to my child's bedside.

Fifth and last, woman faces her sisterhood. Woman must define herself in relation to other women; because, until we respect and demand for one another by joining hands together, none of us will ever truly succeed. Tokenism is personal achievement without being truly accepted and respected.

Simone de Beauvoir writes of her emerging consciousness by saying that in her early years she always felt complimented when her father introduced her with great admiration, saying, "This is my daughter Simone; be careful, she thinks like a man." At forty Beauvoir realized that there was nothing wrong with thinking like a woman, and she requested the compliment to cease.

I accept that my personhood is female and my actions are valid and competent within all frames of reference without my denying my womanlife.

I recently did therapy with a young Orthodox Jewish girl, who was a Lesbian probably as a reaction to always being told that she was to marry the rabbi or the doctor, not that she could *be* the rabbi or the doctor. I had prescribed the wearing of phylacteries twice a day, but instead of saying, as men do, "Praise be that I am not born a woman. Praise be that I am not born a woman. Praise be that I am not born a woman," she took out the *not*—the negative of life—and praised her womanhood. It's all in one's attitude.

Jeanette Picard—the first woman in space, who joined her husband, the famous balloonist Jean-Jacques Picard, in his stratosphere flight in 1934 because he did not want to have an experience so close to the divine celestial being that she, his wife, did not share—has waged a painful struggle for sixty-eight years to become an Episcopal priest, to serve the God she has been so close to. Now that struggle culminates in her quasi-legal ordination in her eightieth year because she fears waiting any longer. Jeanette relates that a prerequisite for being properly ordained is that the bishop certify that the candidate for priesthood is a perfect man, namely that he hasn't been castrated or had one testicle removed or undescended or had the whole thing fall off or get lost or something. This practice dates from the third century.

Of course, this creates great problems, both theoretical and practical, for the woman who wishes to be ordained. Picard claims definitively that she is "a perfect man of the atesticular species."

I am reminded of the recent problem of the young girl who had sued (and won) to become a member of the Little League. On her first day of play, the umpire insisted that she conform to the regulations before she be allowed on the playing fields. One of the rules required that she wear a protective jockstrap with a metal cup. Overcome by surprise, her father initially consented, but on thinking it over, he filed yet another suit to waive this requirement or to permit the wearing of a specially designed female protector pant. I shall rejoice on the day when the only balls required to play in the Little League will be baseballs, but that joyful day is sadly still to come.

Jeanette remembers the night almost seventy years ago when her mother came into her room: "The lights were turned off. Mamma sat down and said, 'What do you want to be when you grow up?' and I said, 'I want to be a priest!' She burst into tears and *ran out of the room.* Now I know that I was supposed to answer that I wanted to get married and have fifty (no, it was actually eleven) children, just like she did."

I then countered with: 'But, Jeanette, don't you feel she ran out of the room because in 1905 your dream was not possible?" Jeanette quietly responded, "It was a monstrous dream. It was something terrible. And how could she go into telling me about the birds and the bees after I told her I wanted to be a priest?" I asked, "Were you outraged that it wasn't possible?" She continued, "No, then I really didn't believe her, but I thought . . . I didn't know girls were limited and defined by men as less in God's eyes. Over the years the feeling of resentment has grown. It seems completely unreasonable now. There are no women priests yet. Union Theological Seminary opened its doors to me only in 1972."

Several months later, in 1973, the Synod that Jeanette so desperately prayed would approve the ordination of women, refused. In 1974 eleven women were ordained by retired bishops. The challenge had begun. In 1975 Bishop Nolan flew from New Orleans to New York to convene with other bishops to discuss the threat posed by these women and the fact that the Canadian Episcopal Church had agreed to accept women clergy. His plane, Eastern Airlines flight number 66, one I had taken the week before, crashed, claiming 119 lives. Michael autopsied his crushed and charred body. Strangely, the bishop's huge gold and amethyst cross and clerical ring were never found. The following week Bishop (Right Rev.) Frederick Barton Wolfe, of Maine, wrote, publicly demanding that the women repent, for it was their ways that had killed Nolan.

Jeanette and the other women are tired of the games men play. It was easier to soar the heavens in 1934, to be closer to God, than to enter the pulpit in 1974.

Two stories which appeared the same day in the Dallas *Morning News* of October 9, 1975, point out by their very juxtaposition the problems facing the women's movement. The first reads in part as follows:

> The ordination of women as priests is not the most pressing issue before the Episcopal Church, the denomination's leader insisted before this week.
> "Ordination cannot be the major question for this denomination," said the Most Rev. John M. Allin, presiding bishop of the church. "The church needs to be concerned with pressing human needs, such as world hunger, prison reform and distribution of decision-making powers."
> In Dallas for the triennial meeting of Province VII of the church, Bishop Allin admitted the rights of women are important questions.
> "But for too long," he said, "the ordination of women has blotted out more pressing issues."
> The issue has dominated the last two biennial General Conventions of the denomination and is expected to be the overriding decision facing the 1976 convention.
> Several women were ordained this year in "irregular" ceremonies conducted mostly by retired bishops. Alluding to this, Allin said the ordination of women is "no decision for me or retired bishops to make alone.
> "People in the General Conference make decisions on what the churches shall do," he said. "They will decide on who will be in what order in the ministry."
> Insisting that ordination of women has nothing to do with their capability, the prelate said, "Look at 75 percent of my work. Many good women can do it as well, some probably better."

The bishop went on to discuss a *real* urgent need—that of world hunger—and the joining together of all churches in agreement on this matter.

The second article reads:

> NEW YORK (AP)—The FBI and two of the nation's biggest police departments are investigating reports of pornographic films in which the actresses are actually mutilated or murdered.
> New York City police detective Joseph Horman called the high-priced sadism "the ultimate obscenity."
> Horman said that "reliable sources" reported two

> months ago that the 8 mm. 8-reel films called "snuff" or "slasher" movies had been in tightly controlled distribution for a month.
>
> They have reportedly been screened here, in New Orleans, in Miami and in Los Angeles, where that police department is also probing the reports.
>
> The difficulty is that no law enforcement officer has seen the films, which Horman said were made in South America, possibly Argentina.
>
> An FBI spokesman said the agency was conducting an active investigation to determine whether the films exist and whether, if so, there has been a violation of federal law.

Bishop Allin, the most urgent need facing humanity is not world hunger but building a world of values in which all human beings have the right to be equally close to God. Solutions to other problems will flow from this realization and acceptance. Move over, Bishop Allin, we are all here—all God's children.

And unless we are here, the mandrake alternative is to be so little valued that the ultimate obscenity is celluloid—but real —murder.

Jeanette shared with me another vignette of the strange ways in which the world of men organizes itself. In the 1950s, when she had to be cleared for a NASA consultantship as a space expert she listed on her clearance questionnaire that she was both a natural-born and naturalized citizen. The computer kept rejecting the form, consequently she almost didn't get the job.

Even though Jeanette was from a prerevolutionary Vermont family, when she married her husband, a Swiss natural, she lost her citizenship. Though her three Swiss sons were born with the right to be Sons of the American Revolution, when Jeanette returned to live in the United States, she had to be naturalized in order to vote. She deeply resents not being a person enough in her own stead to have been able to remain an American.

The relinquishment of citizenship by a woman on the occasion of marriage to a foreign national is no longer required. But I remember what happened in 1972 when I went to get a reissue of my passport. I was scheduled to go to Geneva to represent the United States at a World Health Conference. I filled out the information, including the blanks concerning my spouse. The clerk informed me that I needed Michael's written permission, notarized no less, to be able to retain the use of my maiden name. First I sputtered, trying to explain that Densen-Gerber was my professional name and the one I always used and the one I would register at the conference and the one most people knew me by and the one by which even my husband refers to me—and then my apologies and explanations turned to anger. I asked if Dr. Michael Baden needed my permission to keep his name to get a passport.

The clerk in all his bureaucratic magnificence looked at the crazy lady he had facing him and said, "All right, lady, just move along. You fill it out as I say or get his notarized permission, and that is all there is to it. Now move along, lady. There's others waiting."

His supervisor agreed with his interpretation. The conference had long passed, without my attendance, before the attorney general of the United States personally untangled the mess and sent Densen-Gerber a passport in her own name.

To me the keeping of one's name is extremely important. One of the first and major attitudinal changes that our society must make is that little girls must know from the day they are born who they are and what they will be called throughout life with the same authority and continuity as their brothers.

People often wonder about my name Densen-Gerber. My Mother was an early Lucy Stoner, who did not professionally take my Father's name, but in marriage she was Mrs. Gerber. They both gave me the hyphenated last name. I knew I had married the right man when on the day of our wedding, my Mother suggested to my bridegroom that we both adopt the name Baden-Densen, and adeptly Michael postponed the decision-making discussion to this day.

For many years, I compromised the whole issue by being Judianne Densen-Gerber a/k/a Judianne D. Baden. However, during the time I was organizing my thoughts for this book and was a-growing my youngest, Sarah, a profound change occurred. I was me, and that was Judianne Densen-Gerber. In no way did I experience a change in my being greater than Michael's the day we married. There was a continuity of my being before and after my marriage just as there was for Michael. There was also the sad possibility that I might outlive him and marry again. My life should not be divided into parts called by the names of the men with whom I share a legal relationship. The fact that there might be more than one marriage for either of us mitigated against our combining our two names. We each kept our own name, but I, along with my J.D., M.D., F.C.L.M., had added an a/k/a to mine.

When Trissa was born the birth announcement was printed as follows:

Trissa Austin Baden
July 6th, 1959

Dr. & Mrs. Michael M. Baden

The same format was used for Judson and Lindsey's announcements. But when Sarah arrived my secretary attempted to order the announcement on the facing page.

The clerk wouldn't accept the order; it appeared scandalous, as if we were not married, or worse yet, as if a *ménage à trois* had hatched Sarah. Explanations such as those given pass-

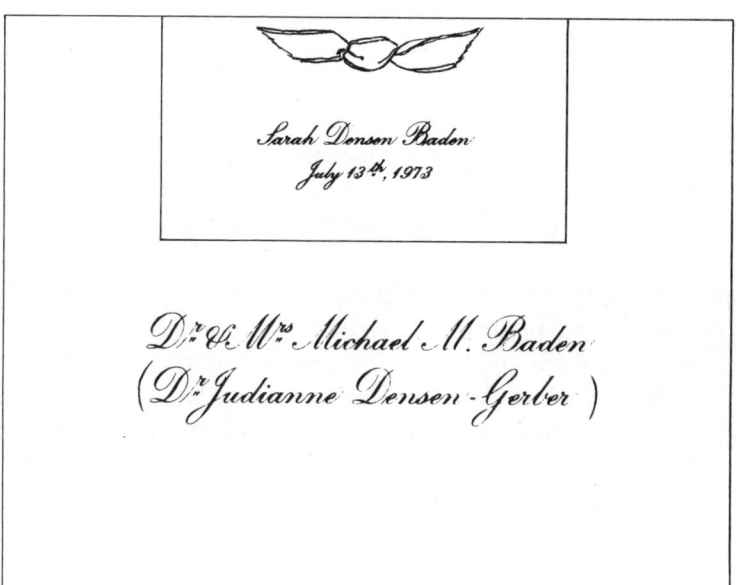

port clerks were no longer my style. The president of Tiffany, Mr. Farnham Lefferts, delighted in accepting my request and indeed wrote me a warm congratulatory note.

Looking at the two announcements concretizes how I have grown in fourteen years. Differing from my Mother, I do not need my children to carry my name. I love their father, and if our customs pass the lineage through him, I am delighted. Trissa and her siblings also love their father and delight in sharing his name: Trissa Austin Baden; Judson Michael Baden; Lindsey Robert Baden; and Sarah Densen Baden. Sarah carries Densen, too, after my Grandmother, and Judson stands for Judi's son.

I demand continuity to my being, and to be defined by myself, not by my relationship to my mate. My daughters, like my sons, shall always have the privilege of knowing their names. They will not wait to redefine themselves. When asked in college what they intend to do or be or have, they will not be waiting for a husband for the answers.

Tragically, so many of my Bryn Mawr colleagues molded in

the time of *The Feminine Mystique* waited only to become dissatisfied and questioning now. I remember being incensed at the letter accompanying my invitation to my fifteenth college reunion. It said, "Let's get together to share what we hoped to accomplish and didn't. Our unfulfilled ambitions and dreams." We were the class of 1956, and it seemed to some that we had been a series of failures. I didn't feel like one, and differing from the thesis of Radcliffe's Matina Horner, I was not one of those women who feared success. I thrived on it, and so do my children.

None of them stumble when they introduce me to their friends: "This is my mother, Dr. Densen-Gerber." They have the same tone of pride as their father does—only he especially delights whenever we register for a together-bed in our separate names in hotels because more often than not, the management sends flowers to us assuming we are lovers. How right they are!

Part II

Woman in relation to Her Self
Woman in relation to Her Mate
Woman in relation to Her Child   =   WOMANLIFE
Woman in relation to Her Career
Woman in relation to Her Sisterhood

Woman Faces Herself

An Interlude

The issue of equality and personhood is vastly complicated by religious concepts. It starts with Adam and Eve. It starts with the symbol of woman as the sinner, destroying through her curiosity, through her basic feminine essence, and then being punished by having to bear in pain forever after, while man, her mate, is blithely smelling flowers, roaming among the animals, and skipping. *She* was always getting into mischief; *he* was the innocent victim. Travail for her and death for both were the consequence.

    Yet change the attitude, look at the story another way, interpret differently. Adam is walking around like a complacent dodo bird, very bland, asking no questions, making no waves, but Eve wants to know why and what. By nature she isn't as much a team person as he, if one properly can characterize Adam and God as a team. No, Eve simply isn't a team person; most women back away from hierarchical authority structure as alien to their nature and tend to see themselves as peers or equals. The sisterhood is replete with large steering committees. And so what probably runs through Eve's mind as she looks at the apple hanging on the tree of knowledge, forbidden by God to both her and Adam, is: "I am going to look God right in the eye and ask him, 'Why can't I take that apple down?' and if he doesn't tell me why, I'll just shake that apple down. I'll see for myself what all the fuss and bother is about."

Eve wasn't the type to obey or follow orders without good reason. Her mother had never taught her to behave. She intended to find out where it was at.

Knowledge, understanding, curiosity, commitment, not blind adherence to authority, are all qualities we praise in men today. Why didn't we praise them in Eve then? And furthermore, isn't the serpent a universal phallic symbol?

Amusing at best. Humorous. Laughable. Tongue-in-cheek. And yet one of the earliest symbols shared in our culture. Sad, unfair, condemning . . .

A Speculation

It is the nature of the human to blame-assess, and it is often the weaker, those different from ourselves, who are scapegoated. The ancient men writing the Biblical stories had to blame someone in order to explain why man was not God but rather mortal, suffering, and shivering in the wake of the mysteries of the universe. Woman was the ready target; for she had the mysteries of life secreted within her body, the biology of beginning and birth contained within, not hanging down flopping without, vulnerable, and exposed. Usually she is physically weaker than her mate, and through much of her life span, she, pregnant and/or nurturing her young, is dependent upon him for survival. Both her own and her young's dependency and need make woman easy prey in the struggle to avoid blame. And blamed she has been in almost all cultures. Forget not Pandora.

Following in the footsteps of Voltaire, Dr. Homer Smith, the famous urologist-philosopher who claimed that the seat of the soul was within one's kidneys and urine was its tears, wrote that if God had not created man in his own image, then man would have so created God. A relevant construct, for in our stories—the ones we tell one another and more important, tell our children—we find the symbols that reflect societies' attitudes and influence our thinking.

The world of primary process—the unconscious—is the world of symbols. Lessons are taught and heritage passed through symbols. They people our dreams.

We must carefully inspect our symbols and guard against their misinterpretation. Man feels his symbols; they are concretizations of whole patterns of thought, and they feed back into feelings. They are the bridges between emotions and thoughts. We must cherish and purify them.

Our anxieties and fears are embodied in our symbols, and no little harm is done to our black peoples when we fear the dark or make death black and glorify the light and the purity of white. From earliest childhood evil is black and goodness is white. Black then unconsciously becomes a bad thing, and to be feared. It happens in other instances too numerous to mention, but that it *profoundly* affects the reality of womanlife is indisputable and omnipresent.

Man was first, and woman was created second, out of him. And then she was uncontrollable and disobedient. Punishment awaited her—God's wrath expressed as pain in childbirth (which is in reality the moment of her greatest glory) and the uncleanliness of menstruation. Menstruation, in almost all primitive societies, continuing even unto today, as an earlier story showed, makes women taboo.

No longer in modern society are menstruating women banned to crouch over leaf-lined pits alone, naked, and shivering in specially constructed huts away from the rest of the village, but there is a mass market (and a fortune made) in advertising ways (often proven harmful to the user) of eliminating that "special feminine odor"; douches, feminine sprays, powders, vaginal deodorants, and so forth continue to be promoted, when truly, an ordinary routine of cleanliness and bathing is as effective for us as it is for our brothers. The need for these special items is little more than a carry-over from past taboos, having truly symbolic, not scientific, basis.

Changes in language portray changes in attitudes. It always fascinated me that my Grandmother Sarah called menstruation *the blessing* because in her day, before birth control, it meant you weren't pregnant and soon to be saddled with yet another responsibility. My Mother used the euphemism *the curse* because to young women beginning the struggle for equality and the vote, those facts which made one different from men were abhorred and rejected; breasts were bound, clothes man-tailored, and hair short. To me, the term *the period* was most commonly employed; we were neutral, noncommittal, distant, and euphemistic, pretending no one understood. I was well into my thirties before I did not write a long grocery list of items into which I slipped sanitary supplies, hoping they would be supplied but not noticed. I still have more difficulty than Trissa letting anyone know I'd rather "sit this one out" because I am "unwell." She is nonchalant, accepting, and scientific about it all. It is a fact of life no more embarrassing than a sneeze, and she blithely states, "I am menstruating," if and when such a statement is relevant. What a long journey it has been from the blessing—the curse—the period—to menstruation and an even longer journey from the total incapacitation of the squatting in the menstrual hut—to the bulkiness of rags and diapers needing to be washed and boiled—to the discomfort of belts and external sanitary napkins—to the ease of internal protection.

Attitudes, symbols of womanlife itself.

The ways in which a woman and her society view menstruation and biological changes seem to me to be central symbols of woman's acceptance of herself and her societal place. When I read Phyllis Chesler's *Women and Madness,* I was horrified at the concept that menstruation is the blood sacrifice that society or nature demands of women and that equality can never be realized until we all have hysterectomies and stop making that sacrifice. Symbolic, I hope, to Ms. Chessler; and yet I have consulted on and treated several women—most in their late thirties—who were in the throes of the middle-age identity crisis. They were seeking elective hysterectomies to "get it all over with and to be equal and able to compete with the men without all that bloody nonsense." I counseled them strongly that surgery would not help them find answers or happiness.

I believe that woman will never be at peace with herself until her biology is accepted and integrated—indeed, not until she rejoices in her specialness. To indulge myself in a bit of romanticism, menstruation is like the tides or the seasons, a cyclical expression of nature within one, a oneness with nature's processes. Menstruation could be interpreted as the tears of the body because, that month, a new life was not begun.

Recently *Playboy* magazine did an interview with Erica Jong. *Playboy* asked the question: "Wouldn't you say there is rather a lot of emphasis on menstruation in your writing—your novel and your poems?"

Ms. Jong answered as follows:

> A lot? Every twenty-eight days. Why not? I just think that for a woman it's a very very important thing, that rhythm of menstruation. It's a kind of connection with your own mortality. Maybe it's hard to conceive of one's own death, but I don't think it's that hard to conceive of aging or menopause. And one thing that's absolutely finite is your childbearing capacity. So every time a woman has a period, she knows that she is twenty-eight or twenty-seven or whatever number of days closer to the end—menopause, aging, death. It's a kind of biological time clock, a constant reminder of mortality.

Michael was always with me during the labors and deliveries of each of our babies, asking for aspirin for his headaches, releasing his tension by bugging the nurses and doctors with endless questions, counting for me, helping me with my breathing, always gently rubbing my back, and in the final moments taking movies as the head and body emerged so that in later years that child could understand the facts of life by viewing how he or she first saw the world.

After Sarah, our last, was born, Michael asked me to share

with him my thoughts and feelings at the moment of birth, for it was an experience forever denied to him—the sadness of maleness.

I wrote, "At the moment of pushing the child out, it is like 'The Hallelujah Chorus.' It is an ectasy beyond anything. There is myself and the baby and eternity and immortality and religion and earthiness and spirituality—all fused. As that baby's head is born, there is pain and there is pleasure. There is a total sense of one—whatever one can be one with—a oneness in the Buddhist sense."

Hallelujah! A sense of glory—a child is born. It is the ability to have this experience, which is denied to the male, that I believe is the root of the basic hatred and subsequent subjugation of women. Womb jealousy is more a reality than penis envy. In other words, since women can create and bear life, all else, especially power, shall be denied them—that is the price women shall pay for the very special privilege.

This is the punishment for the sin of Eve. In an emotional sense, this is the meaning behind the symbol of the pain of labor. But in reality labor is not painful, and with understanding and love of ourselves as women, fewer and fewer of us enter the delivery rooms with moans but rather with cries of joy and praise. And yet our mates can never existentially share, and the punishment is aloneness in this glorious experience. The male can never physically know this symbiotic integration—hence his basic core jealousy of the female—and she accepts the penalty of remaining in the background because she has the satisfaction of giving life.

Of course, this is a generalization. There are many women who hate childbirth, who elect not to have children because of their own insecurities or inabilities to cope, and many who don't feel it because they are not sufficiently self-actualized to permit experience to overtake and flow through them—just as there are many people who can't appreciate a work of art or a piece of music. Lack of appreciation doesn't invalidate the reality of the situation. Orgasm and mutuality exist even if much of the world is frigid and alone.

On Becoming Self-Actualized

In the past five years I have frequently preached in pulpits across the nation. Each time, I entitle my sermon the same way, by using the following quotation from Camus: "If we don't help ourselves, then who else will help us?"

Then in a different manner, appropriate to the setting, I describe the *who* that we are "who must help ourselves." The following is a compilation of those thoughts from several sermons. It will preach, but that is the business of sermons.

Now to go one step beyond the Camus quotation: who will care, and what is behind much of our doing and the human search for becoming; let us go on to our search for being. I will talk about the "who" in the identity crisis: "Who am I, what am I going to become, where am I going?" Each of us in these very difficult, chaotic times—in which we, like our children, are sadly without believable leadership—feels extremely confused. We have to begin to look for role models, and everywhere we turn, unfortunately, we are not finding viable ones. We are not being role models for our own children, and our leaders are not being role models for us.

We must build ourselves by building each and every one of us. This is the essence of what we do at Odyssey House. We have a concept of actualizing our potential; we become adults. To take responsibility upon oneself, to govern oneself, and to expect others to govern themselves is truly the diameter of being adult. There's very, very little of this, ladies and gentlemen, happening today.

What does it take to actualize self? It takes a great many things but really very few things. We have to realize that each of us, to my way of thinking, and I am very existential, is divided into two parts: that of what we *are* and that of what we *do*. In existential philosophy we call this the essence and the existence. There is a difference in being and doing.

Historically, Western civilization, epitomized by this great nation, values great doers; Americans spend very little time, as do other people, such as the Japanese, dwelling on being, finding out, and knowing exactly what kind of people we are. There is very little feedback between what we do and what we are, and they're not always the same. We do many things, often crowding the day in order to prevent awareness of ourselves, awareness of how we feel. Our doing, our action, our existence, has a very limited time frame. Our being or our sense of self has a natural history over time.

In America we are going through an identity crisis to see if we have time to be: time to be ourselves, time free from constant activity, time for meditation, time for reflection. We are also asking a very important question, and I refer to it only tangentially: we are asking, "Is *being* necessarily stereotyped?" Is *being* tall, short, Christian, Jewish, Moslem, rich, poor, white, black, male, or female? We are asking these questions, and that is what I think the human liberation movement is about. I believe *being* is not so limited.

When one talks about being, one is referring to the soul, but to speak of soul is a twentieth-century malapropism. Yet I still shall forge forward to ask, "Does one's soul have a shape? Does it have a cultural limitation, or can we relate to one another all as parts of the human condition, prism reflections of God?" Unfortunately, very few of us accept other people as pure from all of these transcultural definitions. For example, tremendous stereotyping exists between the young and the old. This is a nation which has no place for either its young or for its old, it only has a place for its middle people.

Unfortunately, the human liberation movement contains an awful lot of ventilation, an awful lot of yelling, "Don't box me in; let me be free!" These noises tamponade the quiet search of many for a beginning to development of self and accomplishment. We continue to judge one another tremendously by actions and status rather than by the quality and rhythm of the human being we are facing. Every one of us is completely unique. You know that without my telling you. Every one of us is a product of our life experiences and the world around us. Often, we don't realize how much, based on our individual experiences, we can differ from one another. Dr. Abraham Maslow guides us on how to become, as he puts it, a self-actualized person—a person who is aware of self, aware of other selves, aware of moving in a positive direction; in summary, a conscience-directed person. He lists fourteen characteristics to be developed. I find twenty. I modify his fourteen and add six of my own.

Maslow writes that an individual, in order to be a self-actualized, conscience-directed person, has to be: *One,* realistically oriented. *Two,* he or she must be able to accept self and the real world for what it is. One can not live in an idealistic fantasy, but must come to grips with the reality of self and the reality of the environment. *Three,* the self-actualized person has to be spontaneous, but *four,* must remain problem-oriented or -centered, rather than self-centered. *Five,* the self-actualized person maintains an air of detachment and a need for privacy (which I think is extremely interesting in view of the young people finding answers involving communal living). A certain need for privacy, a need for quietude, is essential. *Six,* such a person is independent, and *seven,* he or she possesses a quality of some mystical or spiritual experience. *Eight,* he or she identifies with mankind, and *nine,* experiences intimacy with few but has deep love for them. (In this country we value ourselves usually by how many friends or acquaintances we have, but we truly make very few deep and intimate relationships. We're very afraid of intimacy. Maslow's emphasis on intimacy, as well as the need for privacy, is a very important one. One can be a private person and still be capable of forming deep relationships.) *Ten,* he or she lives by values and attitudes which are democratic. *Eleven,* creativeness is indispensable. *Twelve,* there is an absence of confusion of means and ends. *Thirteen,* a sense of humor must be present which is philosophical rather than hostile. And, *Fourteen,* there's a resistance to conformity.

The six I add are as follows: *Fifteen,* competition is allowable only with oneself, not with others. *Sixteen,* a self-actualized person possesses an ability to grow and to accept the capacity for change. *Seventeen,* there has to be a structure within the individual, but the ability to be flexible must be maintained. *Eighteen* is a commitment to honesty and integrity as the basic foundation of personality, rather than diplomacy and compromise. I mean the kind of honesty which gets things done, not the honesty which we sometimes use to channel and ventilate hostility. *Nineteen,* there is an integration of the human condition with its great paradox of our individual insignificance to the world at large but our absolute relevance in our own scope of functioning. And *twenty,* one must have the ability to truly like oneself.

That is the "how to." More than that, I cannot tell you.

From whores to lady preachers—a strange book, but all part of the diversity of womanlife. I wish I knew how to list things, one, two, three, four. So many of my colleagues seem to be able to, but I do not see life that way. I see it as a series of "doings" with only the thread of being as the continuity and orderer of endless wisps and wishes. I ask you to keep traveling with me in my shoes as we share being and becoming. I would welcome your writing to me if this list doesn't explain itself or you feel more is needed or if you just want to write so that we share a moment in time together.

An Intrusion into My Being

Existential loneliness and the questions of life and death have possessed me throughout my consciousness. I define death as the greatest affront, the final joke that God plays on man and the one fact man spends his life denying, rationalizing, and trying to forget. Most of the power games we play are to ensure, albeit falsely, a sense of immortality; yet it is only through giving life that any semblance of immortality is even remotely possible. All the pyramids and Taj Mahals are meaningless in the face of atomic bombs or the ceaseless erosion of time. So is life itself, but somehow within the consciousness of history and the lineage of the race, permanence emerges.

Oh, to be an amoeba! How often I have had that thought as I watched this one-celled animal dividing in two to be half-sized, identical-daughter versions of the mother that is now no more. Theoretically, the amoeba is immortal and endlessly reproductively duplicable.

Life—defined by its strange paradoxes—is made up of parts sometimes opposing, sometimes interfacing, sometimes complementary, sometimes bilateral. Always the whole embodies more than one force. Our task is to harmonize these forces: Yin and Yang, good and evil, black and white, male and female, right and left, electron and proton, life and death . . . Therefore, I believe that one can not live completely until one accepts the eventuality of death and indeed incorporates the daily choice of suicide. Until, without fear, one integrates suicide as an elective possibility each and every day and then affirmatively decides to live, to grow, and to enjoy whatever is, one is never free. Living for mankind is only possible when there is no fear of dying. Survival is not the highest value; being at peace within self is. Acceptance of nature's ways, glorying in one's self and being, facing the fallibility of humanness, are the beginnings.

The symbolism of the Christ story is of maximum importance to me. Whether it is completely true or not is irrelevant. Its lessons and values have absolute relevance as I construct a path to walk along. I shall never believe in the virgin birth; to me it is an intolerable story, born out of the need of fourth-century men at the Council of Nicaea in A.D. 325. It came from the minds of a group of men who hated the closeness and beauty of the sexual relationship; men afraid of the intimacy of man and woman. Without reason, without love, mankind had moved from the sin of knowledge to the sin of conception. That which happens between man and woman should be a good thing, and when it begets another, it should be a *very* good thing.

I can relate only to the adoptionist theory of Christ, which is found in the oldest gospel, that of St. Mark. Of the gospel writers, only St. Mark knew Jesus personally. His book is the simplest and easiest to understand, straightforward and folksy, with none of the mysticism of St. John's. I can understand St. Mark.

St. Mark begins with the Baptism of Christ in the River

Jordan by John the Baptist. Christ's adoption at age thirty by God as His Son signifies Christ's acceptance and realization of his oneness with God and the universe. The attainment of a personal and universal peace within the chaotic human environment constitutes that which is meaningful to me. It is what we all seek. It is the purpose of life, the finding of Nirvana. Therefore the adoptionist theory is tremendously relevant—not only because of what it doesn't imply about the relationship between men and women but also because of what it does say about each of us. If the journey or process for all humans is the same and Christ is our role model, that is, the person to emulate and follow—the symbolic one who has made it—then we have to start out protoplasmically the same. It is futile for mortal man or woman to try to attain this oneness if Christ embodies the mystery of the Trinity: God, Man, and the Holy Spirit. If we are to hope to be one with God, as Christ was, it is imperative that Christ be born as we are, that he earn a special place, and that therefore he is adopted by God; I can comprehend and trust the idea that another human being is so good and attuned with the processes of the universe that he is harmonious with Nature and becomes one with God. In a sense, God adopted Christ because of what Christ did; his life is a model, but not unattainable by other mortal human beings. This principle of role modeling is the same one that I believe works best in rearing children. Man is but a child to his parent, God. The good parent is naught but a good role model. The parent must be approachable and understandable to the child. The parent must be believable and worthy, possible of imitation. And so must be our religious constructs if they are to be relevant. No other symbol system will work.

To me life is a journey to harmony, which comes only through the acceptance of the many selves that make up each unique personality within the world in which the person called *myself* lives. I remember a young schizophrenic boy who was a patient of mine. He used to wake each morning, lying on his back in bed, and say, "Good morning, head, neck, chest, arms, belly, and legs. I hope you're ready because it's time for us all to get up."

Though I have never expressed my feelings that way, each day my child self, wife self, parent self; my intellectual self, physical self, spiritual self; my tragic self, indifferent self, comic self; my person self, doctor self, lawyer self; my warm self, distant self, own self; my multifaceted, complex myself faces the day. When they are all working together, then I am at peace and liking myself. It is difficult, but essential, for each of us to accept the many parts that make us up without fear and without guilt. It is the facets of a diamond that catch the light.

Of course, life is a process toward this goal. It is essential that we be persons of integrity. Process continually flows through us, shaping us, and unless we guard against corruption, we find ourselves inevitably destroyed. Never do the ends justify the means. Means and ends are inextricably tied together. No one who has experienced the Watergate fiasco and the demise of an American president can question this. I remember a funny story.

A Funny Story

Years ago, retired Supreme Court Justice Arthur Goldberg came to Odyssey House. It was the beginning of his campaign to run for governor against Nelson A. Rockefeller. It was the hope of one of his senior campaign aides that attitudinal training might help him increase his awareness of Third World ghetto peoples and his ability to speak to them more effectively. I agreed to try. So on a hot summer night, he had journeyed down to the Odyssey Mother House, located in the polyglot East Village, in a building which used to be Temple Emanuel Brotherhood. The Brotherhood was the first stop for many immigrant Jews after their initial processing at Ellis Island. Then it became a yeshiva, and now it was a therapeutic community halfway house for drug addicts.

We sat on the second floor back terrace, under our banyan tree. The top of this great tree traveled two floors from its roots in the tiny New York City yard, surrounded, as if at a grand opening, with banners and ribbons. Only our banners were many-colored clothes, strung on clotheslines from one tenement window to another. It was difficult to hear as we sat around on wooden folding chairs—Mr. Justice Goldberg in shirtsleeves, myself, and all hues and shades of assorted Third World citizens—because of the blaring of the rock music coming from open windows, the live playing of Latin congo drums, and the singing and yelling of the neighbors as they called from house to house. It was dinner time, and the cooking smells were as oppressive and stifling as the summer heat itself. There was no doubt that we were not in the cool Waspish quiet of the Adirondacks.

Abruptly I began, "Mr. Justice Goldberg, before I vote for you, tell me why my impression of you as a latter-day King Solomon is wrong. That is how I see you. The only difference from Solomon is that you would cut the baby in half on principle—the principle of negotiation and compromise. Tell me, what are the issues of integrity upon which you stand firm?"

Quickly and angrily he responded (though I cannot remember the exact words) to this effect: that I was impertinent and disrespectful to so address him.

I wondered if he was aware that good manners and etiquette are not uppermost in the minds of those who are deprived and hungry, those who feel disenfranchised and unheard, those who live in rat-infested tenements on substandard incomes, those who live in neighborhoods, such as the South Bronx, where a third of all deaths are unnatural. So I pushed on by saying, "Tell me, now, why I shouldn't consider you a bad parent who won't allow a child to say what he feels? At this moment I'd never go into that voting booth and pull the lever for you." At this point Mr. Justice Goldberg left the group. He went on to one of the greatest defeats ever recorded in a New York gubernatorial election.

But before his defeat in early fall, I received a call from one of his senior aides who asked me if the reference to compromise and integrity in conjunction with King Solomon cutting the baby in half was original with me. Laughingly, I assured him that it was, wondered why, and was told to pay no mind. Within the week, the New York *Times* quote of the day was Mr.

Justice Goldberg asking John Lindsay if he was King Solomon . . . re the Consolidated Edison plant in Astoria. What a clever saying for Mr. Justice Goldberg to have originated.

Like most of the nation, I yearn for good leadership. I trust much of it will emerge in female form. New and different input is desperately needed, and the priorities of women are often different from those of men. Women tend to think over generations—more in terms of what is best for their children and less in terms of competition or who will win whatever game is being played. Planning over generational time spans, rather than two-, four-, or six-year terms of office, is necessary. Human ecology and concern for our children must be primary considerations in our decision-making. Otherwise, no civilization will survive.

Another Story

I have always been moved by the plaque of the praying hands with the saying *God, grant us the serenity to accept the things we cannot change, the courage to change the things we can, and the wisdom to know the difference.* The acceptance of our humanness, our fallibility, without a reactive feeling of total helplessness or apathetic cynicism is imperative.

An extreme example, but one which is familiar to all of us in medicine, is the confrontation of the doctor with the dying patient. It is the same for family members. Too often lies are told, more to protect the tellers than the listener. Death is an integral part of the life process. It is time people grew up and accepted reality.

The physician withdraws usually for two reasons: first, because he or she feels that the patient is making an impossible demand—give me life—and second, because he or she feels that if the patient really loved him or her, the patient would get better—another impossible demand.

If the patient-doctor relationship is a true one between two mature human beings, they understand all that can be expected is mutual respect; that each is doing the best possible;

and much is not within our control. Humility in the face of nature's processes and wonders is essential.

Fortunately, I learned this early in my practice, when I was an intern at French Hospital, in New York. It has carried me through the personal tragedy of eight pregnancies with only four living children, the death of my Grandmother, and many failures both with patients and anticipated accomplishments.

One of my first patients was a beautiful young married Frenchwoman in her early twenties, who was dying of metastastic choriocarcinoma. Her entire body was riddled with this cancer, unique among cancers in that it is made up of tissue from the fetal placenta, namely the baby's cells, which travel and invade the mother's entire body. It is as if the baby takes possession of the mother and literally stifles maternal life. It was an unusual case in that her survival had been long. She had lived four years beyond the birth of the beautiful tow-headed little girl who used to sit at the edge of her bed and whose cells were now out of control, killing her mother.

I often wondered what was understood and what was felt when this beautiful, suffering woman held the hand of her child. Ten years later, when I went into congestive high-output cardiac failure with Sarah, I knew: there is only love, no resentment.

Every third night I had to stick a large needle through the back of the Frenchwoman's neck, up into her head, withdraw some fluid for analysis, and inject highly cellular-toxic drugs into the fluid surrounding her brain, which was filled with cancer. The pain and headaches which follow changes in intracranial pressure are indescribable, and yet she never resented me, though she seemed cold and hostile to her family doctor. With each daily visit he began to stand farther and farther from her bedside until finally he was only sticking his head in the doorway to say, "Hi, Mignonette. All is going well," even though each day the patient was in more agony and becoming weaker.

Even after I was transferred to surgery from the medical service, where she was a patient, I would stop on my way home for a moment to hold her hand and chat. She seemed to need physical touching; she was always extending her hand, and most people would hastily shake it and move away. I would sit holding her and talking.

One day, near the very end, she gave me a little book of French poetry and said, "Doctor, I want you to know that I know I am dying. I want you to have this book because I am grateful that you are the kind of doctor who lets me know that you know it, too. Ours is the only honest relationship—you don't hate or reject me, as my family and the others do, because I am dying, and you don't feel that somehow you have to save my life. God bless you."

I walked out of the room, and through the tears in my eyes, I read the inscription: "To Dr. Judi, who alone holds my hand and fearlessly looks in the face of the dying. Thank you for permitting me to spend whatever moments I have left without blame. Gratefully, Migonette C----."

The need for my visits ended within the week.

A Conclusion

How much energy is wasted in needless struggle for control and game-playing? Physicians learn humility early because in the long run the adversary, Death, always wins. Lawyers play in a different ballpark. Theirs are man-made rules, arbitrary systems which are devised and maintained. Doctors deal with Nature's laws. It is no wonder the two professions are now busy attacking and destroying each other. As long as the frames of reference are so vastly different, law cannot police medicine. Good people can honestly differ and often both be right within their own context. Priorities, concerns, confusion. If our leading professions are confused, what about the sexes?

A Dream

I laughed when my editor described me as totally successful. I laughed because I find myself far from totally successful—rather, bewildered and questioning. Only one of the women I interviewed—Joan Glynn—is successful to the extent that she has never known personal adversity. She is a delight, but at the end of the interview, I felt like pinching her, simply to hear her say "Ouch." It is so difficult for me to feel the texture of someone who has never known great pain. She admits she is a woman of deep religious faith, but she fears she will not know how to cope with tragedy if it does occur. She organizes her life computer in such a way that everything moves in a certain direction and her world falls into place. She is so wonderful a person that whatever befalls her, loving friends and family would certainly be there. She recently ended her job as president of Simplicity Patterns after having been there less than a year. For many years previously she was vice-president in charge of advertising for Bloomingdale's. She began her career as a junior executive for Altman's at twenty-two dollars a week. Strange to meet someone so kind, concerned, and compassionate who has never known adversity; I have always known adversity, usually not of my own making. Early in my life I faced illness and death more than once. Somehow it seems to be good for one's development; it yields a withstanding toughness. When I was five, post–German measles, I had viral encephalitis, leaving me with a left-side residual weakness. Because of this illness I was never good at athletics. I was last chosen for any sport team, always feeling rejection and abreacting with avoidance and dislike for competitive sports. In fact, all competition or jousting in general seems based on cruelty, not fun. My body contains a real, concrete biological Yin and Yang. The left-sided weakness has had tremendous repercussions for me throughout my whole life! It still affects me. All my remembered life, I have had a recurrent dream which occurs approximately once a month:

There is the ocean, and the waves are tremendous. In reality, because of this dream, I never go into the ocean. I am terrified. I love to look at the ocean but have no desire to go onto the beach and seldom do except for social reasons. However, in the dream I'm swimming, and the waves are pulling me out to sea. It is so vivid that I fear I may have had a real-life similar experience which I have expanded upon in dreaming. I am struggling and struggling against the waves to reach the shore, but the undercurrent is winning, pulling me farther and farther out to sea. The right side of me swims, and the left side just hangs there, lifeless. The effect is terror, simple and total. Finally I know I'm about to die—to drown. Suddenly, there's a huge, great seashell . . . a Botticelli seashell . . . and this great clamshell, really a half-shell, stops me. I am caught by the shell, and I don't drown, and I wake up. I am both happy and sad at being saved. I feel ambivalent about living again.

I have analyzed the significance of this dream many times. There is a difference between the right and the left in the collective unconscious—myth, tradition, custom, folklore, and so forth. For instance, in palm-reading, the lines of the right hand symbolize what the person will make of him or herself, and those of the left side what God gives. The left is heredity, the right environment. The left symbolizes man's sinful instincts, his sexuality; the right, ambitions and pursuits. The left side is passivity; the right activity. There is a significant part of me, a half of me, that wants to lie back and let life do what it will. The other part fights . . . Seashells are beautiful . . . and Botticelli's Venus a role model. She is femininity personified. And so I make the interpretation that now I feel my present journey embodies an acceptance and glory found only in womanlife. The dream symbolically deals with life and death principles within us all. The dream tells me that in addition to being active, creative, and able to overcome forces beyond my control, the actual thing which will save me is understanding my own person as a woman, as well as other women. It is a good journey. What I am and can accomplish is specially molded by my femaleness—I rejoice in it. I shall not negate it or avoid it.

A Caveat

Perhaps this is an appropriate time to pause and reflect on how much I should reveal myself. In general, I am a very open and blunt person, allowing myself fearlessly to free-associate, sharing my thoughts and feelings with others. In most of my conversations I permit myself to be unblocked and open. I am really not very afraid of what is thought of me. As Descartes so long ago wrote (in a different context): "I think, therefore I am." I more simplistically write, "I am what I am; so be it." I swing easily with the "so be its" of my existence. My autobiographical book, *We Mainline Dreams*, is edited heavily to protect others. However, in one part I discuss what eating means to *me*. It is a highly personal thing. There is a description of a session in which one of my patients talks about his mother. He graphically describes her attempts to make him suck her tits. I can't take the pain. I run out of the room to devour a whole chicken. I stuff myself. I eat that whole chicken compulsively because eating comforts me. In times of pain, I need to love myself; so I feed myself. I wrote this story to illustrate how I, in my own way, identified with this boy. I had experienced a sterile, isolated childhood with anger and misunderstanding being the major dynamics among the three of us—my parents and me. There had been very little familial closeness. I wrote to share pain with the boy—and the reader.

Later a reporter decided to use my own words to make fun of me. He asked, "What is this big, fat food-addicted woman doing treating addicts? Maybe she should treat herself?" I was hurt, not because he said I am a big, fat food-addicted woman. I say that about myself. I know I eat for irrational psychological reasons. I have unending insight and unbeginning willpower. Weakness is human, and being human and honest and sharing with others doesn't make me unfit to treat the addict; perhaps it makes me more fit.

Mignonette needed someone to care, not just to read laboratory reports. Patients need warm doctors, not perfect gods. When I revealed myself, I didn't expect to be made fun of or to be questioned as to my expertise. I never make fun of people about their pain. I make fun of images, games, and defenses which prevent another from knowing the real person, but I never make fun of the person per se. No matter what the honest pain is, it should be dealt with and helped, not ridiculed. I would rather be laughed with than at. Now that I have expressed that, I shall proceed on my journey, trusting and sharing all, as you walk with me in my shoes.

My Role Models in Reality

Queen Elizabeth I is a definite role model for me even though she was unmarried and barren, because of her understanding of power. She would have had children if she could; she was probably a congenital syphilitic (thanks to Henry VIII) or perhaps she caught gonorrhea on her own. Her ability to say "I want this, and that is what I'm going to have" inspires me. I admire her living her life as she wished, in spite of custom, taking many lovers and insisting on "I'm going to be me." I like her as a person. She's right-sided and active. I don't like Mary Queen of Scots. She's the passivity, the left side of being.

Another woman is Hatshepsut, the female bearded Pharaoh whom I acknowledged at the beginning of this book. When she had to put on a beard to rule Egypt, put on a beard she did —so be it. If to rule she had to pretend to be a man, pretend she did. Another is Pope Joan, history's only female pope; it happened at the time of Avignon. A lack of testicles didn't stop *her*. Personally, I feel the only limitation on my doing is that I can't be a daddy; but then, I really don't want to be: mothering four children satisfies. I won't be a weight-lifter, and I won't be a Walt Frazier. But when it comes to the exercise of my intellect, it's good; it works well; I shall let it take me where it will; there are no limitations on being.

In the story of my black friend at Christmas, I referred to his listening to Nina Simone's record. Often after listening to it he would say to me: "There is probably no pain worse than being young, gifted, and black." I counter with being young, gifted, and female. And then find it is gifted and female. Only in the last analysis, find it is being *female*. Black women have it easier than white women; they are less threatening to the white establishment, the white *male* establishment. The closer or more threatening you are to those who are in power, the less they let you in. The more they look like you or need you, the more afraid of you they are. Association and familiarity may bring understanding and cooperation, but they lead also to issues of control and subjugation. Men *must* relate to their women; therefore they demand control. It is the way to feel safe. I indulge in a tongue-in-cheek pet theory which I share inappropriately at appropriate cocktail parties. I pose the question, "How can women assume their rightful place in society when the higher you go in status the more doglike are the nicknames of the women: Fifi, Ceecee, Boopsie, et cetera?" Another expression of our attitudes. Boopsie can't really be taken too seriously.

Of all possible role models, it is a man I most admire—Leonardo da Vinci. His paradoxes fascinate me. Leonardo was the bastard son of a peasant girl and a wealthy man. I don't have the exact details at my command, but what influences me always is the subjective rather than the objective truth, and that's what I shall share with you. All people act and react more from that which they believe to be true than from what is actually so. When Leonardo was five or six he was taken from his mother, the country wench, to the home of his father for his education and upbringing. His father could never marry his mother because of social differences. Leonardo hated his father for looking down upon his mother. After all, she had been good enough to bed, why not to wed?

Leonardo wrote that the child is never free *to be* until the death of his father . . . free to be an adult, his own person. Unfortunately, that sadness is too often true. Parents must let their children become adults. Yet it is hard when you are an adult to have someone who always remembers when you were a child or a baby in diapers. I understand that better now than ever before—because no matter how old my own children are, they will always be my babies.

Leonardo's world was not limited to any one discipline, and he lived to a very ripe old age. He was an almost asexual being, more probably due to his being so vastly different from other people—so much more gifted and alone. Scholars describe him basically as schizoid. His reputed homosexuality may have stemmed from the same causes as those in Greek society: the women were not permitted to develop, to learn, to experience, to converse. They were molded to be only sexual partners and bearers of children. Little if any emphasis was placed on their becoming companions.

The inability to travel and develop alongside the male constitutes one of the major dynamics of the present high divorce rate. The American value system encourages women to become educated and good companions to men during courtship and early marriage years. This causes men to have certain reasonable expectations and entices them more quickly into the marital state; however, once childbearing and rearing are present realities, the woman's frame of reference shifts—due to cultural stereotyping—to the house and the children. Yet her husband continues to grow through experience. She becomes bored with her life and often hostile. He too is disillusioned. Furthermore, neither knows why he or she doesn't feel good, happy, and contented—rewarded, so to speak—since each has behaved as society demands. Often both seek answers outside of the marriage bond, for even sexuality becomes routine and destroyed. Infidelity, guilt, divorce, and restless searching too quickly follow, without a realization that answers must be found *within* role definitions and sharing. Nothing destroys more quickly than boredom, the phenomenon of time hanging, hanging, hanging too heavily.

The more intelligent and capable the man, the more he expects and needs from his mate. I assume Leonardo had nobody to talk to, particularly no woman. I wish I had known him—a touch of arrogance, certainly, but permissible in fantasy.

My Role Models in Fantasy

I am endlessly entertained by the comic strip "Broomhilda." Someday I hope to enjoy meeting the cartoonist Russell Meyers. There are framed copies of the happenings of Broomhilda in the offices of my friends and colleagues.

I had one adolescent crush, a single case of hero worship. Again, it was a comic-strip character. I fell madly in love with Prince Valiant and the Knights of the Round Table, with all the attendant romantic symbolism. To fall in love with a comic strip is typically me. It permitted endless fantasy, renewed each week, not ending after a certain number of pages, the way a book does, or hours, the way a movie does. It just went on and on and on.

Even as an adult traces of the happy childhood daydreams persisted, and I was distressed when they labeled the Kennedy administration Camelot, particularly in view of its drugs and infidelity. I was even more disillusioned upon visiting the castles in England. They were damp and drafty, without bathrooms. Knights and ladies must have had body odor. So pass all fantasies in the light of reality. It is imperative to keep a small part of self never invaded by truth. Imagination and dreaming rest the weary competitor. Someday I'd like to write a novel rather than tell stories of real events or give advice. Naturally, it will be a novel of a multifaceted woman who accepts and fulfills her many selves; inspirational and moving in parts but also sexy and graphic. She is the kind of woman taken to surprising her analyst by fantasizing mating with Secretariat and having his colt. She sees Secretariat as the symbol of the best, with all that power and speed. The manner in which Secretariat conquered space and time is definitively masculine in appeal. My heroine's mating with him will not be in the model of Catherine the Great but rather like the Platonic definition of the relationship between man and woman: she wants to be *one* with symbols of perfection. Plato imagined that in the beginning of time man and woman were joined and moved and experienced as a two-headed, four-legged animal. Then, as punishment for some transgression, the gods rent them asunder; each half was henceforth condemned to search for the other, for completeness. Personally, I have viewed heterosexual relationships in these terms—equal parts searching for wholeness, for a mutuality of experience, a reciprocity—totally complementary, finally complete.

In my world, I listen to the stories of both male and female patients describing how they can never trust a person of the opposite sex because previously they had been so hurt. In my own life I have never had an interpersonal relationship with a man in which I have been hurt. I doubt that it's because I am insensitive or unfeeling but rather because sexuality for me is always an expression of the deepest of friendships.

The "zipless fucks" of the Erica Jong genre are little more than expressions of the isolation, alienation, and fragmentation of the individual, as is our entire "swinging singles" set. They come from nothing and go nowhere. Zipless experiences are pure present without past or future; no wonder they leave the participants empty. Such relationships may please in fantasy but can never fulfill in reality.

Recently, on an out-of-town Odyssey supervision I was invited to be guest of honor at a party to meet some new people who, it was hoped, might become interested in helping our work. Let me describe what happened as if we are there. The hosting couple, Caroline and Ralph, are in their forties, and as I will later learn my hostess is known as the local nymphomaniac. When I arrive at their home, a swinging party is in progress: the lights are low, flirtation is everywhere; people are feeling each other up; a teen-age passion pit that I had last moved through at sixteen or seventeen. Middle-aged me perceives self as totally out of place. I have journeyed there believing there is work to be done; I am tired; I want to withdraw, to flee to my hotel room, to call Michael and the children, to rest, to relax, and to read, to be alone, to be myself. And yet there I am in Peyton Place, with its three-walled bedroom, like a hayloft, overhanging the living room and the exposed bathroom appliances in the middle of the bedroom. I can't find my balance in the midst of wife-swapping at forty and being additionally assaulted by a large beautifully decorated cake that I know shortly is mine to cut, to cut through the magnificent inscription in multicolored butter cream: "Congratulations and Welcome Dr. Judi and Odyssey House." There is no place for me to hide. I question why people's behavior cannot be more appropriate—a passion pit for marrieds, at our age, combined with fund-raising for charity?

I escape the situation for a moment by remembering an experience Michael and I had on our around-the-world honeymoon. It was the 1958 World's Fair in Belgium. Suddenly Michael grabbed my arm and pointed "Look there." A middle-aged woman crouched by the side of a car, urinating. My husband continued, "Judi, on one level it's marvelous—on another terrifying." We faced the symbol of total freedom to do whatever you want whenever you want, but also the total inappropriateness of unsocialized behavior. Since then I have treated several patients who as children and teen-agers were devastated by their alcoholic parents, most often their mothers, peeing in public. There are lots of people who pee in public. But when I window-shop on Fifth Avenue and have to urinate, I find the nearest ladies' room. Only if I were in the jungle would I squat immediately then and there.

My mind returns to the party and I wonder why people don't behave themselves sexually and not tread on other people's space. My gentle musing becomes anger and frustration welling up within me. A second time, I free-associate to a not-too-distant past episode; thus I am spared once more having to deal with the present. I throw myself into this second daydream.

I am attending a luncheon for the promotion of my last book, *We Mainline Dreams,* the Odyssey House story. It is a warm day in May, and still being very pregnant with Sarah, I am once again sporting that tartan-plaid wool jumper that I wore to the whorehouse. By this time, near the end of my pregnancy I have been in and out of high-output congestive heart failure, with its fast heartbeat (more than 140 beats a minute) and the compensatory fainting spells. My two senior associates, James Murphy and Frederick Cohen, have been trained by Michael to take my pulse and to handle the difficulties that situations of passing out invariably cause.

The luncheon is on Long Island, and I remember climbing the stairs and being told that the local press has a deadline to meet within the next few minutes and therefore I must pose immediately for the press pictures. Feeling trapped but led, we pose, I sitting down at the flower-decorated table with the mayor and local police chief on either side and Fred and two of the chairladies standing behind. I mumble to Fred, "Take my pulse. I think I am about to leave you." I next remember

Fred pulling me by the back of my hair out of the flowers and saying, "Smile, cheese, Judi, cheese," me smiling, and the flashbulbs going off, one right after another. Pregnancy, fainting, smiling, posing, doing my thing—that day was certainly a test of some kind. People make unreasonable demands and . . .

I muse again. Passion pits are a mere nothing. Happily realizing that I'm not pregnant or sick and that all the wife of the town's most prominent citizen—Caroline—expects from me is to cut the cake, I relax and enjoy the freedom to observe everyone at the party desperately seeking the escape from his or her existential loneliness. I ponder why it is assumed that Nirvana is in Caroline's crotch. Sadly, there are whole segments of the population that believe the answer to existential loneliness is in the next passing crotch.

There is no Nirvana there; there is no more Nirvana in your genitals than there is Nirvana or the attainment of the universal harmony in any other game you play. Harmony comes from letting life flow through you, not in doing any one particular act. Obviously, Caroline is the type that says "Let's fool with this one, that one, and the next one" . . . but only she is fooled. Swinging is objectionable not only on moral grounds but because of how it changes the individual. It destroys; promiscuity destroys—as a psychiatrist I am convinced of this. In another way the hippie movement —the flower children—who loved everyone without distinction in truth loved no one. There are many ways to touch one another's humanness besides intercourse. We can feel each other—a sense of togetherness—through all shared human experiences. There are many points in time when we are not cold and alone.

Love is not a universal; it is very particular. Love is a carefully nurtured relationship which is very very special, especially sexual love . . . If you seek Nirvana in the crotch, with its cock or cunt, and that's all there is and it disappoints you, you become angry and hostile. If you want something and don't get it, then you turn against it, you turn against sex. The end of the road is a forked one between pansexuality and asexuality. All is meaningless; there is just nothing left any more, and many people become depressed and suicidal. Sex becomes sadomasochistic pleasure confused with pain. We are angered because we have asked of sex what it cannot give us.

A Bridge to Woman Faces Her Mate

A Story

The women in Afghanistan are working in the fields, and as the army troops pass by, all the women lift their skirts to cover their faces. Even though they wear no underwear, it is still understandable. You can be identified by your face; it is unique and special. It involves human relatedness. Your face should be seen only by your husband, brothers, sons, and father. Everyone's crotch is very much alike. No one can recognize you from just your crotch. So in good common sense, the women of Afghanistan lift their skirts and cover their faces when unfamiliar men pass by; and that is fine.

Two Closely Related Stories

In 1972, in the middle of wrestling with the concepts that were to be this book and at the height of my Aunt Agatha phase, I was asked to be one of the keynote speakers at the first organizational meeting of the Professional Women's Caucus. The tentative title of my book at that time was *Why Not Have Everything and a Little Bit More?* and I had so entitled my speech. The book would have been better called *Peachy Poo*. I had set out with a peachy-poo attitude in all my interviews—a self-righteous well-girls-we-have-made-it-now-let-us-show-the-young-'uns - how - it - can - be - accomplished - with - minimum - but - constant - effort - and - maximum - success - after - all - we - did - it - didn't-we attitude. I should have realized if the interviewer is "peachy poo" or "coochy coo," then it's peachy poo all the way, and that is just what I got back. Dammit, you get what you ask for.

But at this juncture, I hadn't overcome the saccharine-sweet smell of success, and I still was a very-much-engaged believer and evangelist. So I found myself in front of the lectern, facing mature women of accomplishment from all over the country, most of whom had shied away from the women's movement because they felt they had made it in the world and did not believe in most of the shenanigans and foolishness they saw happening. They didn't want to be tarred with the spillover from some of the more vociferous women in pain. Most of us who had made it were not yet aware that many of the outrageous actions were mere reflections of the extreme pain many women are feeling and that it will take extreme measures to free womankind from the stereotyped cages of today's acceptable life styles. Many women of accomplishment have made dedicated conscious efforts to remain feminine, noncastrating, or ladylike, letting the struggle for full personhood and acceptance happen around them. Aggressiveness on a woman has to be worn only as an accessory; the basic dress must still be nonthreatening and appealing to the male.

For women who have most of their lives walked a narrow line between social acceptance and rejection because of their deviance from normal patterning, it is no wonder that cries for acceptance by Lesbian sisters, public demonstrations, negation of make-up and bras, aggressive confrontations, exploration of one's body with menstrual evacuation in consciousness-raising groups, and so forth, are terrifying and threatening. Even in the seventies most women who had made it have done so by both conscious and unconscious capitulation to the world's terms, which are male terms. Indeed, there is not a career woman I know who has children, who at some time during the child-rearing years has not suffered irrational but understandable pangs of guilt. The tyranny of the three-o'clock milk and cookies and the suburban car pool! I myself spent almost a quarter of my first book, *Drugs, Sex, Parents and You,* written with my teen-age daughter, exploring her feelings about my working and leaving her and her siblings alone so much. I stopped this line of dialogue only when Trissa confronted me with the fact that we were wasting too much time on my hang-ups and not dealing with advice to teen-agers, the supposed subject matter of the book. Trissa pointedly taught me then and there that this guilt which I feel and which is never never shared by their father, who is home even less than I, is totally my problem, stemming from my programing. In reality, the children enjoy the excitement of sharing my life and working with me. She told me they have all discussed and evaluated Mommy's irrational guilt more than once but decided that their lives are very much enriched by their Odyssey experiences. They perceive Odyssey as part of their family, extended and caring. They are secure in the knowledge that there are many loving adults to share with them whenever they wish or need. She reassured me that I had been adequate as a mother and that they, the children, were happy, developing persons in spite of or because of my hectic busy schedule. She reassured me so well that I decided to bring another baby into our involved family life style—a decision the whole family appreciates more and more as the years pass.

I had made this decision before the Professional Women's Caucus meeting and so was pregnant for the seventh time. I was to miscarry shortly afterward, in the fifth month.

My speech to the women remained true to the peachy-poo genre, jocular and light. Treating feminist issues with a large dose of humor was the style I had adopted and seemingly befitted my condition; a too-antimale stance certainly would have been both inappropriate and hypocritical. I was being extremely well received by most, including my Mother; I was giving the successful woman's party line: "Hard as it is, we made it and so can you; we succeeded without being masculine, aggressive, castrating, or threatening; we didn't demand, we performed. We succeeded while remaining feminine, sexually appealing women not rejected by men."

I still believe that success and true womanhood are compatible. The change is that I don't consider for even a fleeting second whether I'm seen as pleasantly assertive or castratingly aggressive—to waste energy on such concerns is to divert valuable time to matters that are the male's problem. Let him waste his energy worrying about whether or not I want to hang his balls in my closet. I have enough problems finding the time to hang mothballs to protect my woolens. His balls are of absolutely no use to me. Silly, foolish issues. I have decided to be me, just as men long ago decided—being and doing are enough without worrying. I worry now about what I am going to say, not what I'll wear. That doesn't mean I disregard how I am going to present the subject matter to make the greatest impact, but it does mean that I refuse to compensate or apologize for being a woman and to walk a narrow line in order not to bruise the male ego. I have always felt that it is nice being a woman. Now it is just nicer.

I was about ten or twelve minutes into my speech when a militant young braless female person jumped up, yelling from the back of the auditorium, "Dr. Densen-Gerber, before you go on, before you dare to continue to speak about the feminist movement, take a vow—a vow against penetration. How can you lead us while you still copulate, relate to, traffic with, and are penetrated by the enemy—the male?"

She was sincere, genuine and very braless. I felt sorry for her on one level but annoyed with her on another, perceiving her interruption as a nuisance to my speech. She continued to rant and rave at the violation of the integrity of the female body by male penetration, as if the penis were a knife within the woman, eviscerating her. Many people, both male and female, conceive of the erect phallus as a weapon which conquers and subjugates the female. *Screw* magazine recently had a cover portraying a naked man with a six-shooter for a penis. The association between sex and violence, master and slave, is clearly apparent in instances of rape-homicide. The more inadequate the male, the more he needs to master; the more dependent the female, the more she needs to be enslaved. Several of my male patients have been extremely hostile to women, so hostile that they have had intercourse with a female partner for hours upon hours without losing their erection or reaching orgasm because to do so would render their weapon flaccid, impotent, and ineffective. Sexual relations end in these cases only when the woman begs the male to stop, as it is too painful to continue. Her begging provides his satisfaction. Many women, particularly victims of forcible sexual relations (usually rape but occasionally with men they knew but were afraid to say "No" to) also refer to the engorged penis in terms of a penetrating weapon. Indeed, sadly, too often the bed is a battlefield between the sexes, both in actuality and fantasy.

But at the moment of the young woman's outburst, I had little time to understand her needs. I was a performer concerned about my effort and anxious to be on with the show. Again, humor. I responded, "Young woman, in my obvious gravid condition it would be absurd for me to take a vow against penetration. It is all in one's perspective. Why look at sexual intercourse in terms of penetration? I have always considered my partner enveloped. I'd rather make a toast to all the great envelopes of the world. What say you, ladies?"

Laughter and applause eased the tension in the room. I had won, and the young braless female person, quietly crushed, left the room.

If she reads this book, I apologize.

Several hours later on the same day, on the same business:

I was in my office at Odyssey with several women from the Professional Women's Caucus. My particular expertise is organizational structure, heading as I do a system which I founded of forty-four service units and halfway house-hospitals across eleven states and serving twenty-six states. Odyssey's in- and out-patient load is close to four thousand, with a staff of almost three hundred.

We assembled in my office with the head of graphic design (a male, no less), and I asked the others, what are the elements to be included in the organization? I didn't anticipate any struggle for control, as I had no opinion about who should be where, and wanted nothing personally. I saw my role as simply putting the different factors into a workable structure with clearly delineated authority. The structural form I chose is the one I am most familiar with—a pyramidal hierarchy, with defined roles, responsibility, and decision-making. The one by which I run my own agency:

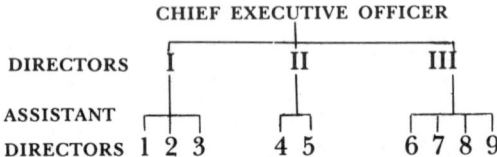

And so forth. In other words, a $\triangle$, a triangle from a broad base to an apex. I was feeling very open-minded and noncombative.

And then Kate Millett, of *Sexual Politics* fame, let me have it. She accused me of being brainwashed by the male model. She stated that a pyramid coming to an apex is phallic in design and is by definition antifeminist. Women can't flourish or operate to the best of their abilities in such a model. She demanded I become my own woman, my own self.

I was confused and annoyed. Certainly, Odyssey has done well and I don't feel annihilated. Once again I tried humor, but I had met my match. "Kate," I said, "just turn it around, in other words, a $\triangledown$ and you have the female escutcheon. We'll simply reverse the whole theory and put the power at the bottom":

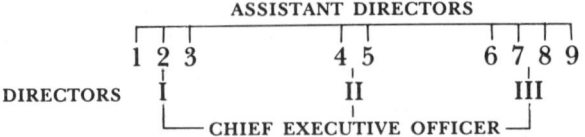

No one laughed. The matter was dropped, and an eighty-perdaughter (female form of person) steering committee was created. It was simply not for me. I still believe that it doesn't matter whether you read from right to left or left to right, whether it be a phallic form or a female escutcheon, as long as decision-making flows, responsibility is assumed, and the job gets done; my feminine being is not on the line, depending on the shape of the charting of authority.

In later years, I have entertained many other shapes—three-dimensional, spokes of a wheel, and now a tetrahedron. But then I got nowhere, and was out-yelled, outvoted, and out-done.

For this one I don't apologize.

A Final Story

Sometimes I have fantasized being Elsie the Borden Cow. I read about her as a child and thought how nice it must be to be lazy and contented, regurgitating my cud seven times and only gaining weight for one time's calories—the endless joy of eating, re-eating, re-eating, re-eating, re-eating, re-eating, re-eating, and re-eating once again. There was Elsie, endlessly ruminating, contented, and stupid. All the bulls except for Ferdinand—who must have been bisexual at best and probably was a latent if not overt homosexual—basically fit my opinion of many *macho* males. The bull charges anything, particularly if it is red and moving, even if he gets killed for the deed. Meanwhile, Elsie is content, giving milk and ruminating, not very bright, and defecating—and with all that milk! There is a basic earthiness, a usefulness, to the cow, while the bull is just a stud, butting his head against everything. Caricatures of us—female and male?

There is wistfulness in my contemplation of this bucolic scene—a merciful escape from being young, gifted, and female in this society. Our minds function on many levels simultaneously; and on one, I desperately seek peace from the restless striving to grow, develop, and achieve. The left-sided me would love to be Elsie. There is this tremendous yearning for peace, quiet, having no questions, canning vegetables, going to church suppers, watching my children at the spelling bee—just being not demanding of life.

Still, there are more and more Ferdinands in the world. Homosexuality is a life style deliberately chosen by more and more young men and women. This is inevitable because there is little if any healthy communication between the sexes; more couples are engaged on battlefields in life-death struggles for control. Unfortunately, fantasy notwithstanding, women are not Elsies. Such a life style leads to boredom, especially since there are smaller and smaller families, in combination with more and more timesaving devices. Women are restless but stagnant, while their men continue to experience and grow within the context of the world at large.

I dearly love my two-year-old, but I would go out of my mind if she were my sole conversational partner for eight to ten hours a day, save for the "idiot box," the television, which tells me once again how to produce a cleaner toilet bowl with less effort than on the day before or shows me perfectly happy, smiling babies who are never colicky and who sit still for the camera.

Soap operas, which stereotype my being even more, would certainly grate on my nerves, but I would welcome the endless tragedy to feel alive again. And what would I have to talk to Michael about when he came home? Dr. Malone's latest case, a cure for African jumping fever?!

And then Michael and I would be trapped at home—strapped to our young; for no longer are there extended families with many hands to relieve the breeding couple for a night out together, nor is there adequate money or people willing to babysit. No indeed—tied we would be to a mewling, puking infant or two. No wonder a night out with the boys and I with the girls would soon replace our sharing together, and we would grow apart in leisure experience, as well, only to seek more and more other sexual partners until we found the newly forged chains were "his, hers, and our" children. One out of every three American first marriages will end in divorce, as will one of every two second marriages; almost two-thirds of the teen-agers who marry will see the divorce courts, and over half are pregnant at the altar.

As there is more and more discontent, parents become more and more polarized, losing respect for each other, bickering, fighting, cheating, abusing, drinking, and tearing the children apart. Disturbed, unhappy children don't just appear; they are molded and developed—over many years. At the time when we had many youngsters protesting the Vietnam war in New York, the *Daily News* ran a picture of a young demonstrator and his hard-hat father. It was one of the days down by New York City Hall that the hard hats were out beating up their young. In psychiatry we are taught that one of the most difficult moments in a person's life occurs during adolescence, when he or she realizes and accepts that his or her parents are not perfect or omnipotent. The awareness of human frailty is painful for even the healthiest, best-adjusted youngster because it involves accepting realities concerning his or her own humanness. During this period of time the youngster must realize and integrate without reactive self-destructive hostility that his or her parents have clay feet. The painful realization from the sixties was that too often our parents and leaders have not only clay feet but clay heads, as well, and consequently they must don hard hats to protect them. The clay-headed Mamma sees her role more and more as protecting her baby (now at least six feet tall) from Dad; and the clay-headed Daddy becomes more and more frustrated and angry until only violence and abreactive homosexuality results, as the boys will not imitate or role-model after these fathers.

Peer men and women must communicate and have time to be together and to grow together. The center of a healthy family is a happy husband and wife. I remember a homey parable, which I gave Michael last Father's Day. It went like this: "The best thing a father can do for his children is to love their mother." The children are derived from that core, and they must be free to grow up, individuate, and then leave to make their own nests.

In present-day America men and women seldom talk together. They have nothing in common except the bed, and that is passing, infrequent, and not terribly interesting, though present-day coed living rooms sound like yesteryear's men's lockers. Personally, I find I am not outer-directed enough to be interested in the size, diameter, and creative ability of Mary Jane's current lover's penis, and truly, one roll in the hay is much like another.

New York is one of the few places where conversation is still an art, at least among the middle-aged. There men, as well as women, consider the ability to converse an attribute to be developed. But when I travel throughout the country, I note that after dinner the men frequently go into one room or group to talk, and the women into another. The only permissible communication is flirtation, and flirtation is really not communication. Flirtation is a prelude to sexuality, and sexuality is the culmination of a relationship. You can't build a relationship on sexuality; it puts ass end first, and it simply doesn't work.

Woman Faces Her Mate

A Recent Happening

It is the evening of Sunday, July 13, 1975, and with family and friends, the Badens have just finished celebrating the second birthday of Sarah. It has been a great day, and I sigh with relief; July is a month of birthdays, beginning with Judson, on the third, Trissa on the sixth, Sarah on the thirteenth, marking the halfway point, Frederick (my colleague and one of Sarah's godfathers) on the twenty-sixth, and Michael, the anchorman, on the twenty-seventh. Only Lindsey and I share November. Therefore, July is always a tiring month of celebration, with its rounds of pool parties, cakes, and summer lunches. This summer in Stamford, where we rented a quiet country property, Doral Farms, is no exception. Michael and I are spending the summer here together, committed to writing our books. At least, I can say I am well on the way; he is yet to begin.

It is shortly after eight o'clock in the evening, and I complete a hypnosis session for the relief of depression with one of my patients. He is a young man, soon to be thirty-five, who has not yet found a woman with whom to share his life. He is questioning if he ever will. The world seems to him so lonely, even though he is highly successful and a very dashing bachelor. He is tired of notching his belt with more conquests, but his search still leads nowhere; he wonders throughout the session how old he must be or if he will ever be sufficiently fearless to give up some of his own independence in order to form a truly meaningful relationship. There is still one more patient waiting when I emerge from the consulting room. I go to momentarily raid the refrigerator; somehow Sunday brunches never carry me through the day the way they do the rest of my family. Afterwards, I start to call the patient who is playing billiards with my sons but I hear the television playing in the TV alcove, and instead I stop. Since I feel cold, having listened the past hour to the loneliness of spending life without marriage, and since I feel warm all over because of Sarah, I give in to the sudden desire to go kiss Michael and say "Thank you" before I continue working.

My husband is sitting all alone in a gray-striped armchair, watching a program about the middle-age blues for men, narrated by Art Carney. It concerns what happens when it starts to be all over, when you are a forty-five-year-old man. I can't believe it; mesmerized, I don't say anything. One look at Michael's face tells me that whatever I have to do had better wait. Michael says, "Judi, this is a program about being old," and he adds, "they're my age." That's all he says in a very wistful, terribly wistful, voice and then: "Come spend it with me," which strikes me as a very funny but appropriate word to use because it's so sexual a word; "come *spend* it with me." I answer, "All right," and am about to sit down in another easy chair, but he motions. "No." Now, I'm not a small girl, but he motions for me to sit on his lap. So here he is in this great big chair with me sitting on his lap, something I haven't done for a long, long time, and he simply holds on to me and we watch the program. The program is a nightmare, terribly done and offensive, absolutely offensive. Art Carney does a couple of jigs in the intermissions to a story which tells of two men facing "going over the hill." Seven years before, the first man had failed in his lumber business and his wife had to start working to help him out. The other is a civil engineer who never "arrived." Both of them claim to be happily married and to have found their major strength in marriage. Both of them have not succeeded to the point they had expected in business, and they desperately cling to their wives in rationalization and depression. The wives seem younger and more together. But marriage is a bondage not a joy. Both families are middle-class with incomes of $20,000 to $30,000. Both men talk endlessly about how wonderful their wives are and how if their wives hadn't gone back to work, they don't know how they would have survived. One needs his wife to supplement the family's income. The other works because of her husband and her boredom; however, he articulates his fears that she may become liberated and leave him and their daughters. Both men allude to casual vacations; leisure seems troublesome and time wasted. Each invites the audience into his home to a party. The parties are sad, worse in their way than the passion-pit scene. One imitates a Hawaiian luau, with people dressed in costume, eating "exotic" foods, making banal talk, and acting as if they are really living it up. They explain to the viewer how other groups might swing but that they are solid people; boredom decorates everywhere. There is no insight, no depth. It is tragic, the saddest middle-age blues.

Michael was to be forty-one in two weeks, and I in four months; this TV program shouts out at us that at forty-five the young ones will pass us by and that we will live within the ever present aura of failure and competition, constantly being threatened by younger men below. We have always felt that forty-five is the center point of our lives; why, we didn't finish medical training until almost thirty-five. We were counting on a minimum of twenty more good years. We would expect the un-heroes of the program to be at least sixty, not our age. I want to telephone Art Carney to protest! "Do a program about the man or *woman* who is a success. Forty-five is only the middle of life. It signifies a roadmark to rejoice at, a place to note where you have been and where you have still to go."

The platitudes and the jig are too much. The overall feeling is that manlife is superficial, nonperceptive, asinine, and composed of immature drivel. After forty-five there remains nothing for them to do but cling to their wives for dear life. It is as if all the strength is stored in womanlife. We sit silently, Michael holding on to me as if I possess some kind of life force. I become confused, not knowing what to do; I still have a patient waiting in the other room. The session before, I have been asked by the patient to guide him in the event that he doesn't find a woman to help him define himself. Through my mind runs the thought "My God, will a major result of woman's liberation be the shattering of male rationalization? Does the male sense of personhood and security depend on supremacy?" I believe it isn't so. For as woman must be taught new ways of relating, so must man. New definitions must replace old. In truth, the male will benefit as greatly as, if not more than the female. Life doesn't have to end at forty-five. There must be a time for every age—prowess in the bed, at the bank, and on the tennis court must not be the measure of male being. Tragic as is womanlife's second citizenry, it pales next to manlife's panic. And I continue to hold on to Michael throughout the entire program, and he shares: "I can't stand watching this. It is too painful, but—I have to, I have to look at myself and other men." He adds, "I don't know what I would do without you. When it's down to the final act, you know most who you are by what your children become." It was terrifying.

For centuries women have defined themselves in terms of their offspring, and now, in the time when women are finding themselves, men are turning to women's ways to find themselves and a deeper sense of satisfaction. In an immortal sense, success is measured by what you leave with your young. And Michael tenderly whispers, "We have the most marvelous children. Thank you."

When the program finishes, I get up to leave, but Michael motions for me to sit and remain held. It isn't even sexual; it is much more—litter love, a protection against the whole terror of being human, against the affront of getting old and dying and death. Underlying is the theme of the danger of competition and being outdone by younger males. It is as if humans are lions or elephants whose place with the females and in their group depends on defeating all younger male challengers. Biological history reigns supreme. Sexual prowess in the male is now replaced by dependency upon the female; as her children grow up and leave her, she replaces them with her husband, a child whose dependency and need increase with each passing year. Even if he doesn't need her in the bedroom, she is needed in the kitchen, laundry room, department store, and office. Decision-making becomes hers, and he is safe—he won't lose her to another male, and for that he will pay any price. And the wives play the same game. The program was really "Three—No, Four—Blind Mice; See How They Run."

The station announces that "The Middle-Age Blues" will be followed by a rerun of an hour special called "Three Women Alone," by the same producer but about woman; Michael gently challenges: "Stay, let's see how it looks for you." I stay.

It turns out to be magnificent. The producer is the same, the director is the same, but the writer is a woman and the three stories are of womanlife: a single girl, a divorcée, and a widow. The first tells of a woman divorced at twenty-seven, now thirty-five, living in Massachusetts with her one son and working as a photographer and writing poetry. She cares about others, teaching photography at a school for the retarded. She is involved in the women's movement, doing special photographic essays on womanlife. She is defining herself in terms of understanding and liking women. I wonder if she is a Lesbian, but I am not sure and I don't care. Sexual orientation to me is a matter of personal preference. I have the feeling that it doesn't matter to her, either. She is beginning to *be;* personhood is emerging. She has a deep relationship with her brother. She talks about how her child has had some difficulties in accepting her occasional dates. The way she speaks about herself, contrasted with the men, leaves no doubt that men and women are facing reality differently. She is sensitive to life. She has the confidence of self and independence. She experiences a joy in living. She feels successful even if alone, while the men are defeated and dependent. She is in tune with nature; she is in tune with her whole life. The men are in tune with nothing.

These portrayals of humanness remind me of the flight of the bumblebee. One female, the queen, leads; thousands of male drones follow, only one destined to reach her and mate. After copulation the suitor leaves his entrails within her, and the shell of what he was falls to the ground. He is no more. She returns to the hive to digest the parts of him that remain within her body for extra energy. They give her strength to lay the twenty thousand or so eggs he has fertilized. The drones who did not succeed try to return to the hive, only to be denied access. They all die shortly thereafter without shelter or food, not having known how to care for themselves. For months previously, the drones have been fed and protected like children by the sterile female worker bees in preparation for the day of the flight. One male succeeds, only to die, and the others are rejected, to fall prey to nature's forces. Only the queen and her barren servants remain with tasks and life flowing through them.

Life for today's male seems as meaningless as that of the drone. Males, too, will grow behind liberation. It will be better for us all when men become more like women rather than the other way around. They certainly haven't created a very nice world. Consider how male were Watergate and each of our recent wars.

The second woman portrayed is a Westport, Connecticut, widow. Hers is a hard and rugged face attesting to her recent bereavement. She has always been defined in relation to her husband, a well-known sports writer, but now he lives no more, though she still does. Currently, she is working for her son-in-law and is defined through him. She couldn't financially manage to keep the large house of their marriage; so now she lives in a small apartment. She often eats alone.

Eating alone is a sad thing. If I am away from home, Michael frequently does without eating. I don't like to eat alone, but I will eat with my children or with friends. Michael eats with me. I define home for him. I am the soil; I am security and safety. Michael comes home to be with me. I come home to be home. Our feelings are vastly different.

I am completely mesmerized by the widow. Her destiny may someday be mine. I fear; yet I accept. In fact, this very Sunday, Michael and I have signed for several life-insurance policies, payable to each other. I have made him promise not to die first. I can't imagine life without his companionship nor can he without mine. Yet I know we could each survive, but with deep grief. The togetherness has been so good for so long. We snuggle, comforted in the knowledge that all the world may put us out to seed but we will have each other. These are tremendously precious personal moments.

We watch the widow trying to define herself without her husband. Her entire status has been derivative. Her whole life has revolved around her husband; consequently, she has made him singularly important. He had to always live up to her expectations; she had to always worship him. She had nothing else, and suddenly she is a widow of fifty-five, with many more years to go. There is still another third of her life to live. She feels empty, but she isn't pathetic; she is overwhelmed with pain not of her own making. A decade later, she is facing age much as her male counterparts have on the previous TV hour. Loneliness and death are difficult contexts within which to define oneself. But she is not weak. The listener is warm toward her. You don't move away from her.

There is a scene at the Westport railroad station, a place where for many years previously she has stood waiting for her husband to return home. Standing there now, she asks, "Where will I ever meet someone else—another man? Are there no single tickets to finding oneself?" And she looks fifty-five. Alone, again and again she walks the autumn paths with her dog—sheer, sharp pain. And you have the feeling that no matter how happy she was with her first husband, she has to have a second husband. The widow searches for another partner. She talks and talks of the loneliness, the continuing loneliness, in terms of the absence of a man; she seems to have forgotten her grandchildren. Death is part of life; grieving is natural. Solace is only found in the continuity of life.

There is an osmosis of the loneliness of this particular woman through the pores of the viewer. There is nothing else. She doesn't even date; there is no way she can possibly date and keep within her very proper concepts. She can't go to a bar, she can't pick someone up, she can't do any of the things that young girls do today. She is not a good-looking woman. She doesn't give the feeling that she will ever experience a brief encounter. She is the most devastating and difficult to accept, but empathy prevails. The divorcée is developing herself—metamorphosing, being born again. The widow, while tremendously competent, has never been allowed to develop; she has been quiescent as a person for thirty years, and now the struggle to become is almost too great. Perhaps it is too late.

The last person, I disliked—the single girl. She is twenty-nine, from Colorado, a young executive in an advertising agency, one of whose clients is Cinzano, another Yonkers Raceway. The camera shows her developing a woman's day at Yonkers Raceway while ordering Cinzano; serving two masters at once. She lives alone. She is successful; she is going to the top—her body moves that way. She is part of everything young, "with it," and swinging. She exercises: stretches her neck, bends down; she is very well put together. She does her thing: if she wants to have a man to her apartment, he visits; if she wants to cook dinner for him, he dines; if she wants to screw, he produces. She gives you the impression that she is a *man about town,* and she bothers me. And when I say "a *man* about town," I mean just that. She is a bachelor. She talks about how marriage would interfere with her career. She talks about how if she wants to clean up her room, she does, and if she doesn't want to clean up her room, she doesn't have to. She doesn't have to moderate her needs, drives, or desires by the concerns of anyone else. She's in the least conscious pain. The divorcée is examining her being and growing—a painful but good process. The widow is trapped by her past doing—her environment—without the know-how to better the situation. The bachelor examines and questions nothing—merely experiencing without integrating or learning. I perceive her as only narcissistically committed, if committed at all. She has no relationships not defined on her terms. She knows no one, feels no one, is nobody! She is as superficial as the men in the first program. She is the most glamorous. She is the one the viewer is supposed to envy. She is the one who finds aloneness a life style by choice. She is the present-day ideal woman as defined by male values. Within my values, she is terrifying.

The Game As Played by Men and Others

Around 1972 one of the magazine houses similar to those that publish *Playboy* and *Penthouse* decided to print a comparable magazine for women. The arrival of sexual liberation made it obvious to various types of entrepreneurs that women are a wholly untapped market for soft-core pornography—witness how well *Cosmopolitan* has sold with its change in format from the homemaking garden-club world of Helen Hokinson to the scene of *Sex and the Single Girl* of Helen Gurley Brown. However, in our current world of scientific technology almost nothing is undertaken without a survey or Gallup-type poll, so our aspiring publisher hires an opinion-taker, or -maker, whichever way you want to look at it, to find out first, if women are ready for such a magazine; second, if they would buy it; and third, what kind of pictures turn women on.

To no one's surprise and everyone's pleasure, the answers to the first two questions are overwhelming "yeses"; it is the third which presents problems. It appears that the majority of women are visually sexually aroused the most by pictures of babies.

It was more than the publishers of a *Viva* or *Playgirl* could handle. They couldn't accept producing a Gerber's baby food brochure each month. They feared being laughed at, and furthermore, they knew that women wouldn't buy what they liked but would purchase what their men told them women liked. Many women prefer to be led by men than make their own decisions or be true to their own desires. Faced by the more dominant male, they trust his judgment before their own even when it comes to their own feelings. It is this problem I had worked through during that fight in the kitchen with Michael. So once again it is decided to transpose and modify the male model to meet assumed female needs—it was decided that the proposed magazine would feature nude men. However, when tried, it simply didn't succeed except with the homosexual subculture; so now many of the photographs are of couples; it seems women plug into that scene a bit better.

The motivation to do this book for my daughter and her generation incorporates in part a warning not to equate liberation with becoming pseudomale but to walk always in women's shoes. Our emancipation, our liberation, our attainment of personhood, will happen by being "ourfemaleselves," not by mimicking the men and certainly not by copying their bad habits. An extremely important question is posed by the widow on "Women Alone": "Are there no single tickets on the journey to find yourself?" In other words, to be self-actualized, can you do it alone?

The crux of this book is that each of us is defined only in terms of relationships: first, with yourself; second, with your mate; third, with your child; fourth, with your career; and last, with the sisterhood. (For men of course the last is with other men or male bonding. These truths are equally applicable to manlife.) You find yourself not in terms of your unique drummer, but *you find yourself in terms of playing with the orchestra.* There is absolutely nothing when you live by yourself; it is an empty nowhere. Narcissus turned God.

Several years ago at Odyssey, after years of exquisitely refining group-therapy techniques to the point where the staff felt there was almost nowhere to go, we decided to try an extremely intensive exploration into self. We called it the OTTIS, or Odyssey Trip to Inner Space. We freaked out when we learned later that OTTIS is the name in Greek mythology for the wanderer condemned to search forever, without rest, trying to find self. It seemed as if there were a common vocabulary, as the Jungian collective unconscious postulates.

The OTTIS is an experience in which five to ten people who are trained therapists enter a room (which has been prepared to have a minimum of sensory stimulation) for a period of thirty-six hours, during which time they wear only shrouds made of terry cloth. You feel naked, alone, exposed to yourself and to life. Powerless, helpless, afraid. At the eighteenth hour each person takes a whirlpool bath to symbolize rebirth. The only permitted food is liquid and semisolid. Pacifiers are supplied to encourage regression. Time is irrelevant; windows are sealed so that not even a division into day and night is possible. There is no dialogue or conversation allowed, though people can talk to themselves and are encouraged to free-associate.

I have experienced the OTTIS twice, in 1970 and 1972. The first time, OTTIS I, was to cope with the fact that Odyssey was growing into a large agency beyond the manageable stages of a family business. The second time, OTTIS II, I was pregnant with Sarah. The OTTIS is devastating. Within minutes the womblike atmosphere produces regression, and the free associations are mostly of death—God, fear, and anxiety. Some people begin to sing, others to quote poetry, some withdraw into hypnotic trances for the entire time. Others assume the fetal position and its freeing sleep. They do not wake even to eat or go to the bathroom. They refuse to take the ritual bath, with its new robes, dividing the OTTIS into two parts: one of purge and one of reconstitution. Some, of course, refuse to play by the rules and talk to one another or organize tasks or play games and tricks on other participants, and occasionally someone will attempt to work through a problem, enticing another to be a therapist. A leader always emerges who disciplines the group back to the ambiance of a severely disturbed ward in our local state asylum, with its attendant primary-process material. All participate, authors of *Marat/Sade*.

My first experience was excruciatingly painful; my second exhilarating to the point of madness. In OTTIS I feelings of being trapped, suffocated, entombed, possessed me; I went into an agitated depression, with accompanying repetitive motions similar to those occasionally seen in schizophrenia or drug-induced psychosis. I began to bang my hand against the draped, closed window until James came over to me and gently said, "Stop or you will cut yourself." Later, Murphy led a raid on the downstairs refrigerator—never has a piece of cheese meant so much. Still later, after I took my bath and felt refreshed, I refused to reenter the group tomb, as I then saw it, but rather I demanded as the leader to be alone—at least, the isolation and alienation of that position entitles me to the privilege. I will not play by the rules; I am not understood; I suffer in my difference.

The OTTIS has a profound message: the more you go into yourself and explore inner space, the emptier you realize it is. The inner core of self is the permanent tabula rasa of the eighteenth-century philosophers. Only relationships define us and make us real, and unless relationships have continuity over time, we become confused, bewildered, lost, void, empty, and meaningless. The OTTIS, beyond any other single experience, made me understand what was so philosophically wrong with the entire hippie drug movement of the sixties: *a journey into self just digests self until there is nothing left.* The healthy ego must define itself through the perimeters of others.

In one type of mental illness there are extreme moments of depersonalization. The patient does not intuit the limits of his or her body. For instance, the patient literally touches the wall with his or her hand to try to find out where the hand ends and the wall begins. There is only terror in this extreme form of not knowing self. I first experienced this during OTTIS I, and being me, I initially withdrew, quickly to realize that only action and relating to others would free me.

OTTIS II can best be described by the words of Oliver Wendell Holmes: "A pregnant woman is doubly precious." I was not alone, and "The Hallelujah Chorus" played throughout. When I finish this book, I shall OTTIS once again if I can find anyone willing to journey with me. It purges the soul, sets one straight, and refreshes.

The happenstance that night of finding Michael alone is extremely revealing of our relationship. Being male, he could not come to me, as I could to him, and say, "Judi, I need you." At all costs he has to be strong, even when his need is so great. This demand on the male always to be in control is one of the greatest tragedies of sex-stereotyping. Men have as many frailties and doubts as women. They need to share human fears and terrors; they, too, are born and die alone. They, too, must be free to cry.

Even though I was busy when I found Michael alone, all else could wait. I was pleased with myself because I had stayed the two hours with him. I explained to my patient, and he understood. I was attentive and untroubled during the session which followed.

Sadly, too often women forget the importance of their mate's needs in the myriad of responsibilities that face them. We act as if talking to one's husband can always be put off until living rooms are vacuumed or the children put to bed or the laundry done. Priorities are wrong; they are for men, too.

Frequently women are immediate-task-oriented, while men occupy themselves with larger work goals. As much energy and time should be spent on one's primary relationship with one's mate. But maybe nature fights against us.

How many women are willing to spoil the roast—burn it, even—to take a break to make love? Spontaneous love in the afternoon can be more delicious than perfectly mashed potatoes.

Defining and Enjoying the Orgasm

Recently Michael and I were traveling together to visit good friends in Corpus Christi, Texas. We expected to combine business—discussing the development of Odyssey Texas—with the pleasant company of Sarah's godparents.

We seldom travel on the same plane, missing many shared times because of our commitments to our children and our fear of a common disaster. Once again, in yet another context, the need for the extended family is apparent. However, on this occasion, because connections were so bad, we were sitting side by side, glancing at the Braniff Airlines flight magazine, and we chanced upon the same article simultaneously. It made us smile and quietly hold hands.

Entitled "The Viejos of Ecuador," it described a village in

the Andes where people live to be the oldest in our hemisphere. We read the following together:

> Señora Mariana Toledo had never been to a beauty salon, never used lipstick, powder, or rouge. But time had not robbed her of an inner radiance and her smile suggested that her husband found her an attractive mate. She was thin, with acute faculties, good vision, good hearing, a clear mind and an excellent memory. She was independent, even-tempered and possessed of a lively sense of humor. She had never owned a clock ("I don't need it," she said), had never seen TV or listened to a radio. Mariana and I talked about airplanes (she had heard of them but never seen one) and flights to the moon (she refused to believe that a man could walk on the moon). Then, with an unabashed simplicity, she talked about the happiness that comes to a woman when she lies in the arms of a man she loves. In her ninety-two years, she said with an earthy directness that was too natural to doubt, nothing had equaled that quiet sense of joy and well-being.

Experiments with cats have been done showing that when a fish is waved in front of two cats engaged in copulation, the male cat continues to fornicate but the female tries to push him off to go eat. Male rats, when presented with females in estrus, fornicate until they die; they take no time to eat or sleep. Female cows continue grazing while being serviced by the bulls.

In some ways this holds true for humans, as well. There have been times in my lovemaking with Michael when his intensity is total but I find myself thinking of a laundry bill or wondering if the front door is locked.

Once, early in our marriage, I looked at him in a tender moment and articulated what was flashing through my mind: "Did you take the garbage out?" That was that. I never did it again. I am sure many readers can recall a similar incident.

Orgasm has no past and no future; it is total present. Once the pleasure area of the brain fires off, the response is absolute. Afterwards there is an obligatory refractory rest period. I have never understood the genesis of the theory that women have multiple orgasms; it must be based on a basic confusion between peaks of excitement and the orgasmic exhilaration.

The pleasure derived from orgasm involves a total firing of the nerve centers in the brain and affects the body in much the same way as a seizure; it obliterates all other reception. The French call orgasm *le petit mort,* "the little death." I delight in fantasizing that death is *le grand mort* and therefore not to be feared but rather eagerly anticipated—an orgasm with God, the universe. It is only during orgasm that one escapes the weight of existential loneliness. There is a feeling of universal peace and, for Michael and me, an experience we affectionately call PCS—postclimactic sleep, a rest that is profound. Biological feelings of closeness, safety, and security reign supreme, and one is content simply—completely—to exist.

Coupling can take many forms, depending upon the level of maturity, the feeling tones, the mood of each individual, and the relationship itself. In psychiatry we divide developmental levels into three stages: first, oral-infantile-narcissistic; second, anal-adolescent-compulsive; and third, genital-adult-reciprocal. Naturally, these are generalizations, but they serve to clarify the different needs sexuality serves.

Frequently, I have referred to "litter love," in which holding, closeness, and the need for another is paramount to genital contact. This is a universal human need. To a child it is a need for the security, warmth, and safety of the parent. It is often confused with heterosexuality. Litter love is basically an oral drive for understanding and acceptance. Much of the present-day emphasis on the importance of good communication (again oral) comes out of this developmental phase.

If we were permitted more deep friendships across the sexual barriers, without jealousy or the confusion of sexual demands, there would be many more happy people. Sexuality is a special kind of friendship; there are many others. We should not expect that all our needs for human contact and security will be met by our chosen sexual partner. That is an impossible demand to make upon any one person. I am not advocating sexual infidelity; what I am suggesting is not demanding of one other person that he or she be all things to you. If one is secure within oneself and secure in the love of one's partner, other friendships can develop of special value. I have my life, Michael has his, and we have ours. I trust him, and he trusts me. The need to possess is not a measure of love but rather of insecurity.

The story of the young girl demanding that I take a vow against penetration indicates one expression of the second, or anal, phase. Here sex meets the power need, the need for supremacy. The bed becomes a playing field, an arena for the battle of the sexes. Notching one's belt, conquest, and performance are the rules. Unfortunately, this is most frequently the level attained by American sexuality. We are more concerned with how we do than with what we feel. Technical manuals are our bibles, and the bed is the proving ground.

Formerly women set the limits. My Mother taught me that any time a woman was willing, no man would—could—say "No." This is certainly no longer true if it ever was. More and more men are becoming sexually mature as a result of the new freedom. Since the female so frequently presents, the male is becoming discriminating; he no longer responds like a rat. Men are demanding meaning and substance. Now too often, sexual freedom equals license, and men find that "going to bed" is an expected part of an evening date, even before the couple know or like each other. Sex has become a matter of obligation. Many times the male feels that his female partner is lying there grading his performance. He wonders if she has a rating sheet hidden in the night table. Does he do well on part one, on part two, on part three (foreplay, actual intercourse, and afterplay)? How many positions can he suggest in the first five minutes? The second? *Is there* a third five minutes? The male really doesn't enjoy getting into bed to be graded. Therefore, many men are becoming extremely hostile and angry. The "Tuesday mate" doesn't want to know if he was as good as Wednesday's or Monday's.

Most women do not imagine that they are being compared to other women in bed, though many have felt they were obligated to go to bed with a man because he expected payment in exchange for meeting the bills. Now there has been a role reversal. Men seek acceptance and love just as women do—to be human, not a dildo. No man can move against the clitoris with the speed and efficiency of a vibrator. Nine out of ten nerve receptors will prefer the vibrator. Is that what counts? Gearing sex to performance makes men more and more anxious.

It doesn't matter who reaches orgasm first. If she does, then he will follow, or vice-versa. An erect phallus is not the *sine qua non* of female satisfaction, not even for all men. It is a myth that sexual satisfaction depends upon such a thrusting object or its rigidity. Neither its size nor its diameter—nor even its color—is important, but rather the person *behind* the stiff prick. Sadly, only too often there isn't much of a person, and that is the problem.

Our culture-created sense of inadequacy is foolish. The chance of simultaneous orgasms is nearly nil and not even very much to be desired, as it is not operationally sensible. When the physiology of orgasm and the pleasure center in the brain are understood, it is quickly realized that each person's electronic nerve endings are firing off at a certain rate which is individual and represented by a unique rate of muscle contraction and relaxation. The best reaction for your partner when your orgasm begins, whether you are male or female, is to lie still and let your pleasure run its course. If he or she moves, it short-circuits the orgasm. If you're firing off at ten muscle spasms, and your partner at fifteen, one's going to interrupt the other. It is similar to a resistance on a wire hook-up; you'll only lessen the impact. The coincidence of two people having simultaneous orgasms with identical firing times is possible only against astronomical odds; this is quite apart from the fact that such a happening could only be appreciated in retrospect; when you are there, you don't care. If you are in the midst of an "attack" of *le petit mort*, then you are unable to appreciate what your partner is experiencing. Why is there a need for both of you to be there at the same time? I see it as a silly need, one of vanity born of sex manuals and pornographic propaganda—another unattainable American goal, designed to frustrate all. There is something nice when you can watch each other reach climax; it is sort of double the fun, a true sharing.

I have never understood the myth of multiple orgasms, either. When you reach orgasm, you are momentarily unconscious, then satisfied and satiated, and then peacefully sleepy. There is no way I can pinpoint the experience clitorally or vaginally. When the brain goes, the whole self goes with it. Wherever the initial focus of the brain-wave firing began is long lost in the pleasure of the total experience. Genital sexuality is loving and doing and being, all together. You become one and explore, tell each other what you like, and combine a healthy body and mind with a full functioning imagination. It is nice, this special happening between a man and a woman who both love and like each other and who know each other by name and personhood.

There are many other myths which confuse us and make us feel inadequate. Do women "spend" themselves, that is, experience "female ejaculation"? Pornography endlessly claims women do. There is no such phenomenon. Lubrication at the beginning, yes; ejaculation at the end, never. Many men will tell you women spend because men see things always within their own frames of reference. Experts, women included, write of multiple orgasms, sometimes eight or nine in a row. How sad to confuse peaks of excitement with the holistic orgasmic experience, after which you sleep and feel at peace and after which afterplay is simply the joy of being together. Women and men are the same in the need for postclimactic sleep. The only reason we have voluminous literature instructing the male on the necessity of afterplay is that the female has not reached sexual satisfaction.

Still another myth is the expectation or demand that every time there is sexual contact, orgasm must result. Occasionally men, and more frequently women, want sexual play without the desire for climax. Often a loving partner's needs are not the same as yours, but there is great satisfaction in delighting the other.

Sexual experiences differ not only between individuals but even between the same individuals at different times. There is no how-to rule book. There is just the many ways of each other. Satisfactory sexual contact can be brief, before catching the morning train, or prolonged, over a lazy Sunday afternoon. It can be intense or casual, but it should never be a testing ground. Performance criteria or outmaneuvering are out of place. The immediacy of a roll in the hay has its moments, as does the poetry of a seaside hideaway. The bed is an expression of tenderness, comfort, sex, sharing, amusement, and laughter. There have been times when Michael and I have made love when we could barely function because of laughter at each other, at ourselves, at the situation . . . Sex is really a funny thing. God must have been a practical joker or temporarily irrational to have approved the mammalian reproductive design. Yet there is a beauty in finding your other half in the Platonic sense.

When Michael was in analysis, his analyst once asked him, "How come you need so few friends?" Michael responded, "Because I have one special friend. Therefore, I don't need many more." Michael echoed one of Maslow's criteria for the truly self-actualized person; he has many acquaintances but few friends. Our being best friends first and lovers as a consequence is the strength of our relationship. Not enough men and women, when they go to bed, do so because they're good friends.

Until you are fully adult, it is difficult to make and maintain meaningful interpersonal relationships. Therefore, the special friendship of sexual intimacy should be one of the last experiences undertaken by the emerging adult. Teen-agers can neither appreciate nor handle the demands of genital sexuality. There is a right time for everything. Even for adults it is difficult to know when friendship is ready to ripen into sexuality. Frequently people are confused and feel that any companionship based on sharing and caring must be headed toward genital contact. Not so. Many of my most intimate friends have never been closer than a kiss on the cheek. There can be an *air* of sexuality, a physical responsiveness without actualization similar to the intimacies between people of the same sex that often involve deep communication without physical engagement. Indeed, the fewer the sexual involvements, the more deeply each can be developed.

While monogamy may not be the biological design, it is a

much more emotionally practical one. Occasionally I have counseled patients toward infidelity, but I have always cautioned them never to let their mates know. Sharing one's secret, confessing in order to relieve guilt is one of the most selfish acts a person can commit. It is certainly not something you would ask a friend to understand. If one has the need for a separate sexual life, a "his" or "hers" rather than an "ours," then it must be kept that way. Respect for your partner necessitates it. Honesty here is only infantile selfishness at best and hostility at worst.

I once counseled a forty-five-year-old business executive to have an affair. He loved his beautiful wife of twenty years, and she returned his love. He had been unable to father children, and consequently they had adopted two boys and a girl, who were teen-agers and doing well. My patient was in the throes of a painful middle-age identity crisis. Programed by our society to fear aging, he questioned his sexual competence, his ability to sustain his business position against the onslaughts of younger men, and his worth as a person. All this questioning was taking its toll in both his business and personal life. He was in an agitated depression complicated by ulcerative colitis. He was also intelligent, tyrannical, narcissistic, and infantile.

After several months of deepening depression he asked me if an affair with a younger woman might help. We explored his feelings about how an affair might convince him that his aging was not the end of productivity and experience. In no way did he want to hurt his wife or lose the family he deeply loved, but he felt almost dead. His wife had not failed him, but he knew she could not help him, as she would prefer to lie to him rather than hurt him; nor could supportive or even analytic psychotherapy help—it would take too long. He became obsessed with the idea of proving himself with another; he had no guilt —only an intense desire not to make anyone he loved suffer.

He met a woman, had a brief encounter of less than three months and assured himself he was still a capable and attractive man. He quickly had realized the relationship could go nowhere and how much more he had shared and built with his wife; he went home to a better and stronger marriage. Ten years later they are still happily married.

To the existentialist, nothing exists until it enters your consciousness; therefore, the affair of a partner does not exist or has no relevance unless the other knows it.

A Second Passing Aside

Even though I love my husband greatly, it has never interfered with my noting, rejoicing, and often commenting on the physical beauty of another man or a woman. I rejoice in appreciating beauty in all its forms, but it always amazes me how astonished my young male staff are if I comment when someone attractive passes. There is no need for our role models, therapists, or parents to be asexual. It is much healthier to know our leaders as three-dimensional fellow human beings. It is reassuring that the Fords sleep in the same bed.

A woman friend and I once had a discussion about a male colleague. She asked me if I knew where he hides his penis; for no matter how tight his clothes are or whenever he wears a bathing suit, that pleasant bulge isn't visible. I thought for a second, and I realized she was right. Since I knew him better than she did and found the situation intriguing, I asked him the next time we met. He was astonished and asked me if women did indeed notice such things. I assured him that either consciously or unconsciously everything had to be right with the world, and made the analogy to his noticing the shape of a woman's breasts or behind. He laughingly responded, "Truly tit for tat."

He is a precise young man, fastidious to an extreme: he had always pushed his penis back in tight jockey shorts so that there would be no revealing outline to embarrass others. He was delighted to learn such precaution was not necessary—the Victorian bunting could be removed from the table legs.

A Domestic Story

Michael and I began our marriage in the Japanese equivalent of Niagara Falls—Atami. Japan's honeymoon village is a straightforward confrontation with one-half—the more important half?—of sexuality. There are huge statues of penises throughout the village. You cannot get away from the penis. In the temples there are nuns who place milk, nuts, and other gifts at the base of the penis statue which is the center of every altar. The central temple has a phallic representation seven or eight feet tall with the foreskin pulled back. Wooden Atami bears with huge genitalia are sold as souvenirs of the honeymoon visit. As a young bride I wasn't offended. I was titillated by my sophistication at being there, at a village dedicated to penis worship. It was Japan—romantic and different. We took baths together, as is the custom, and learned about our bodies in an atmosphere of acceptance and joy. It was a good way to start.

Bathing played a funny part in the days of our honeymoon in Atami. We had been married only a few weeks when Michael came into the bedroom and announced that he wanted to take a bath. I said, "Fine." He repeated, "I want to take a bath," and I said again, "Fine." After the third time I said, "What are you driving at?" He answered, "Well, aren't you going to draw it for me?" He had never drawn his own bath. His mother had always drawn the bath for him and for his father. He did turn on his own shower, but a bath, never. I told him to learn quickly and to draw one for me afterward. It's a laughing happening in our family now when he draws my bath and I his.

Michael is extremely competent, stubborn, very strong and not easily manipulated. He is definitely his own person. He had decided he was ready to find the woman to marry a few months before he met me. It was time; so he made a list of the positive things he wanted in a wife. I fit the bill, and the fact that I was engaged to someone else only stimulated his competitive nature. Michael is a man who is used to getting what he wants. He also makes his points in unique ways. I love him dearly.

Of Clam Juice and Lambchops

It was the last trimester of my first pregnancy. I am very tired, so I send Michael to the market with a list—juice, eggs, bacon, bread, jelly, cream, and coffee. Michael dutifully returns with everything including a nineteen-cent half-gallon of clam juice. It was the least expensive and best buy. He definitely lets me know he doesn't want to waste time at supermarkets; he has more important tasks to do.

A prominent woman writer within the sisterhood writes that women will never reach total equality and freedom, liberation will never be ours, until we and our husbands alternate the responsibility for calling home if there is a cook or for remembering ourselves to take the lambchops out of the freezer. Lambchops and clam juice are the bottom line.

For the past several years Michael and I have been fortunate in being able to afford help. The difference exists now only in the overseeing of the house. If the laundry is not done, Michael wants to know where his shirts are, but he never considers it his responsibility to see that they are done. And he doesn't appreciate the fact that if he fights with the laundress for one reason or another (she has lost a button), I will have to do the laundry if and when she walks out. He has absolutely no concept of catering the least bit to the needs of domestic help; I must because my career is so dependent upon them. We haven't a family to pitch in at a time of crisis—and our youngest is a baby of two.

It is impossible in our culture to be a successful career woman with a demanding husband and dependent children if you cannot find and keep good help. Ambrozene Bean, the governess-housekeeper, has been with us almost fourteen years, and Ramao Alves, the cook-butler, for over eight. They make it possible for me to be me. Domestic helpers are an integral part of our extended family structure, upon which a successful combination of career and home must depend. They are desperately needed and appreciated, taking pride in their work and loved by us all, particularly the children. Having no mother or sisters to help, I would not have been able to start Odyssey unless I had people to rely upon.

One of our recent marital fights concerned the butler. I am terribly programed and organized. I had just returned from Odyssey New Orleans to face a weekend of summer houseguests in Connecticut. I had everything arranged: instructions as to how the butler was to be transported from New York to Connecticut, lists as to his work assignments, cooking, laundry, cleaning, and so forth. Somehow while I was two thousand miles away, Michael got in the middle and gave Ramao the day off. As I stepped off the plane, they were both there to meet me smiling boyishly. I was dumbfounded.

When we arrived home, I asked Michael to join me upstairs —and then I let go. The inequality of our roles had gotten to me. I paced, I ranted, I raved, I screamed, I yelled, I threw things, I was uncontrollable. I was too tired after four twenty-hour days to come home to the laundry for a family of ten people in residence and twenty-three more expected for dinner the next day. What senior executive male faces this? My anger at the unfairness is still overwhelming. It is reported that the Chinese and Russian women have equality in the outside world but when they and their mates come home from working, it is still the women who do the housekeeping.

It never dawns on my husband that there is ever anything to be done. Somehow the house runs, takes care of itself. He is absolutely unaware that there are basic time-consuming tasks involved in running a household for a family of eight. It is never within his reality that he has to come home from a hard day at the office and make certain everything is right. I am going to do my best to ensure that Trissa and Sarah have it fairer. I know my daughters-in-law will—Judson and Lindsey are learning differently.

One time Mrs. Bean, Ramao, and I were all away, so Michael was in charge of the children. Lindsey, who was six, returned home first from school at three o'clock. No one was home. Michael was working at his office; he had forgotten. Lindsey sat on the steps of the house, patiently and securely waiting. Our neighbor saw him sitting there about four and asked him over to his house. Lindsey refused; he said he would rather wait, as he knew Daddy loved him and when Daddy realized what time it was, he would rush home and if he didn't find him, he'd panic. He would rather just wait and not upset Daddy. Eventually Michael came home and found him. It had happened exactly as Lindsey had anticipated.

But when things are going well, I can fly into New York from Chicago after being away for a week on business meetings. I can arrive at the airport at 7:00, be home by 7:30, bathe and dress for a formal dinner party at 9:00, and be less than ten minutes late to greet my ten guests. Ramao carries the evening off perfectly. Most of the time my life is little different from any other busy executive's, and I love being a guest at my own table and being surprised by the menu.

Our favorite form of entertaining is to have five couples in for a formal dinner and good conversation every Friday night when we are in town. One Friday, recently, Michael decided to give a party in spite of the fact that it was Ramao's vacation and I had another seven P.M. airport arrival. Michael has always contended that I make much ado about nothing, so he asked each of the male guests to undertake one course. The guest of honor was John Gummer, the vice-chairman of the Conservative party of England, a great conversationalist and preparer of Welsh salt ham hocks and cabbage. However, a slight problem arose: the closest butcher able to supply salted ham hocks was located outside of Philadelphia. Fortunately, John, as an English visitor on holiday, had four hours to make the round trip to Philadelphia to market for the meat. The wine was magnificent—one of the guests was a partner in Sherry-Lehmann—and another, who was 6′ 10″, turned out to possess a gem of a recipe for gazpacho.

Let me describe the evening as if we are all there now. Dressed in evening gowns, we sit by candlelight at the table for thirty minutes, eagerly awaiting the soup. However, it is served by our tuxedoed menfolk in a three-piece, covered cold-soup service, and each piece is brought in separately—the saucer, the bowl, and the cover—times twelve. Sans soup. No, that is an exaggeration; it is times six, as two pieces are carried at once; fortunately, man is born with two hands. Sadly, the dishes have an unnoticed, thick, gummy film of New York dust on them; but then, the goal is to serve the soup, not wash the dishes. Suddenly I become hysterical with laughter; ten covered soup bowls and two matching sugar bowls complete the setting. The gazpacho which arrives in the lobster steamer with a punch ladle is delicious, as are the ham hocks and each vegetable, which is somehow individualized as to its time of arrival at the dinner table. One of the women takes pity on the six men and helps clear and organize the washing up, which occurs before dessert. Four hours after grace, dessert arrives. The crêpes are thin and superb, as delicious as the jelly, which joins us after we've finished the crêpes. This experience strengthens Mike's claim that it is my problem when I get uptight and strive to coordinate meals so that dishes comprising the entrée arrive together, hot or cold as the case may be, on time, in clean proper dishes. However, he has never offered to stage a repeat performance.

It is time men are taught to take care of themselves. It took years for Michael to learn to put his dishes in the sink when he had come home late to a supper that had been left on the stove for him. He learned one Sunday, when Trissa was twelve. She had been studying biology and genetics in school, so she casually asked her father as she was loading the dishwasher after lunch, "Daddy, tell me where on the X chromosomes is the gene for moving dishes from the sink to the dishwasher—or is there an inhibitor on the Y?" That was the last time I ever came downstairs to find dishes in the sink. I wish all consciousness-raising were so easy.

Recently I was asked to join a new club in New York called the Atrium. I responded affirmatively, because it is the first club to my knowledge which invites career women to belong in their own right, even if they are married to prominent men; second, because I am still smarting from my Alta Club experience in Utah, front doors all the way; and third, because it's right next door to the First Women's Bank of New York and I serve on the board.

I enjoy the Atrium because it admits women in their own right. When you are the hostess, it is convenient to be able to sign a check and balance the accounts later rather than when your guests are present. Most men are uncomfortable when a woman pays, and I have been sufficiently programed to feel awkward reaching for the check even at a business luncheon which I request. I was so conditioned that it is only within the past year that I am comfortable, when I am with Jimmy or Fred, doing my share. Of course, this situation never arose with Michael. I earn more than Michael, but he pays all the bills, even when I have invited him to dinner—until the Atrium Club, where *I* am the member. I remember a happening.

The first week it opens, I take Michael to dinner. After several false starts, the maître d' and the waiters realize I am the member. The drinks are ordered, the menus arrive, and Michael is paralyzed. He can't order. I am the host; he is the guest; his menu has no prices; he is bewildered; he had never ordered from a menu without prices; he manages. Later, when I go to the powder room, he persuades the waiter to show him the other menu with all the details; he feels fine again and in control. So programed are we to the most exquisite detail. He still *leads*. I follow on the dance floor.

The Women's Bank is the first bank designed to meet the financial needs of women, both actual and advisory. Gynecological guarantees that we will not leave the job market because of pregnancy or child care will no longer be a prerequisite for mortgage loans, nor will our husband's permission. It is high time that women are considered people in their own right. Financial acceptability and power are important factors in being taken seriously. It is imperative that women receive equal pay for equal work. In our capitalistic system no man is paid according to the needs test. A man with seven children is not paid more for the same work than a bachelor. There is no sense or fairness to the rationale that women can be paid less because they have husbands to support them at home. Indeed, over one-third of the women who work are heads of their households, and often they are the sole support. It is an unfortunate reality that employers believe that women need and can adjust to lower pay scales. A college-graduate female earns on the average slightly less than a male with an eighth-grade education. I discussed the question of salary with all the women I interviewed. I was surprised how little most of them are earning in relation to the jobs undertaken and to men of comparable positions. I was struck by the weekly starting salaries of most: Glynn at twenty-five dollars, Baldridge at eighty dollars, Mink at one hundred dollars (not so bad), but Kelne at ten dollars. The situation of Jackie Nokes has already been shared.

I demand to be paid well on principle, as well as for the enjoyment it provides. I refuse to be taken for granted. I work hard. I believe I earn my pay the same as any male physician. He certainly commands adequate compensation. I refuse to be persuaded by the attitude "Well, you don't need it, anyway" —that is not the concern of the person requesting my services. The wealthy collect their dividends. Until women demand the respect inherent in equal pay for equal work, we will remain second-class citizens, never taken seriously.

Furthermore, if there is one thing that makes our political systems move, it is the power one holds, be it prestige, voting, or money. Women must not be ashamed to ask without guilt for adequate salaries. Too often women volunteers are taken for granted. We have to be serious about ourselves and our work. I don't mean to imply that I never do anything for free or never volunteer for worthwhile causes. I do so frequently —but of my own choice, not because it is expected. Indeed, it is about time there is a woman's bank.

A Story Where We Tickle Each Other

Any man and woman who love each other must have time for each other, away from responsibilities and demands. Michael and I have always cherished these private interpersonal moments. Sometimes these are sexual times because the best birth control in the world is the presence of four active children; there is almost no time to be alone, simply to tickle and to talk. Occasionally we spend a night at a hotel in New York, most often the St. Regis. We did so one delightful evening in 1966, July 27, to be exact, Michael's thirty-second birthday.

This is how it went. I have just begun the Odyssey. I am working night and day, as I am still a resident at Metropolitan Hospital. I seldom see my husband, and time together is rare, considering we have three children; the youngest, Lindsey, is not yet a year old. Michael informs me that the nicest birthday present he can imagine would be dinner together alone somewhere. I promise to arrange it. I'll make all the plans. However, I decide to play a game, and Michael's boss agrees to help me. At the time we are to meet I call Michael to apologize that once again my work detains me and I'll be delayed at least two hours. The hurt in Michael's voice is overpowering, almost divorce-begetting; after all, it is his birthday. Then as prearranged, his boss sends him out on a special case: Sir Hubert Humphry-Smith, a famous diplomat who a few minutes earlier has died in the arms of Countess von Trachtenberger-und-Taxis—during what the medical examiners politely refer to as "in flagrante delicto" (sexual intercourse). Actually, Michael first refuses to go, as it is almost eight P.M.; it is his birthday; he is waiting for his wife; and he is uncooperative, hurt, and pouting. Finally he is prevailed upon to go because of the potential international incident with offended ladies and cuckolded counts. His annoyance visible, he arrives at the St. Regis, where the manager is pacing back and forth, appearing most agitated and alarmed at the scandal brewing. Meanwhile, I am waiting in the suite, cocktails and hors d'oeuvres ready and a supposedly deaf and blind waiter on call to serve dinner. I am wearing a bright-colored caftan and a feathered mask. The doorbell rings; masked and caftaned I open the door, not realizing there is a long mirror behind me. I say, "I am ze countess." He looks at me and replies, "Don't you tell me that; I'd know your ass anywhere."

Then there is the year that on Christmas Eve I give him myself, stark naked, with a ribbon sitting on my pelvis, carrying a tag: "I'm your Christmas present."

Another time it is a Sunday afternoon and Michael is listening to Governor Rockefeller on television when the phone rings. The voice asks for "Judi," and Michael, startled by its familiar sound, inquires, "Who may I say is calling?" "Nelson, Governor Rockefeller," comes the reply. Michael comes upstairs to the bedroom, where I am reading, to inform me of the call and I begin to speak on the phone about drug issues. While I am talking, Michael proceeds to take off all his clothes. Then, standing stark naked, he challenges me to concentrate on Rocky. I giggle so much that I have to beg off the phone. I lie to the governor, telling him that the baby needs me and I'll call back shortly.

Maybe it wasn't a lie. I was desperately needed, and Michael's male desire to compete and win was satisfied. In quieter, less absorbing moments, I finished my conversation with the governor.

On Pain and Joy

For every painful incident there should be a minimum of ten joyful ones. You grow through pain, but you also grow through joy. Joy is essential for health and success. We do not place enough emphasis on joy; if you only punish yourself, you cannot grow. Much of modern-day literature focuses on tremendous pain; this is particularly true of feminist literature. It is better for women to stress developing themselves than to blame-assess and hate the male. It is more productive and viable to be positive. We teach a lesson at Odyssey: "The only person to blame is yourself; stop talking about X, Y, Z, and begin looking at how you can make it better, how you can carve out your own destiny. You have the power to change and to control only yourself. Rather than emasculate the male, find an affirmative identity for yourself: black is beautiful, Puerto Ricans pretty, Jews jolly, women wonderful, and so on." Positive attitudes go a longer way, as does emphasizing health rather than sickness.

Too often a woman enters into a relationship with a man because she fears loneliness; frequently she maintains an intolerable one for the same reason. The first step to personhood is to be able to be alone with yourself—that ability gives tremendous freedom and power.

While I place a great value on togetherness and enjoy time

with the children and Michael, I have a great need for time alone. Every woman is entitled to time to herself without interruption or guilt. Many women define themselves in terms of meeting the needs of others without setting limits on the demands of others. This is not healthy—or fair. For instance, when I am traveling on business, I take from four to seven P.M. to dress for dinner. I change for dinner in order to ensure those three hours to myself. Do I need three hours to dress? Certainly not. But this affords me the time to rest. I put my feet up, I share with close friends special delightful matters without problem-solving, I take a little nap, I talk to myself, I call home to hear happy children and reports, I organize the remaining day. I need only six hours of sleep a night because of this break. Sleep, while necessary, is a missed part of consciousness; I love my dreams and realize I work things through in that private world, but I'd rather give it a quarter of the twenty-four hours than a third. Sleep habits do differ from one person to another, and emotional factors play a significant role. Sleep patterns are often passed from parent to child; my father sleeps four or five times a day for about a half-hour and then four hours at night. This patterning allows for much more creative time.

Freedom has always been important to me; I never have worn a girdle because I cannot stand the constraint. In spite of my hang-ups—and I am a thoroughbred for hangups—I have continually striven to be myself. I do not cultivate conformity, but there are many things about me that do conform. If something fits, I don't reject it just because it conforms; I am more comfortable being happily married and having four children than I would be with changing partners, marital instability, and "his, hers, and ours" children. I would not relish waking up and not knowing the name of my bedmate; nor would I like to have to call my partner by a general appellation, such as honey or darling, in order to avoid saying the wrong name. Such oversights easily happen at intimate moments. Infidelity doesn't outrage me; it simply doesn't fit. I am faithful not on principle but because it works for me. My being and doing have to be harmonious—essence and existence. Existence fulfills essence, and essence is the refreshment of existence. If a woman is safe in her other relationships—self, children, career, and friends—she is better able to make demands and set limits on her relationship with her mate. That's the one most for enjoying; sex is a good thing; if it feels good, do more of it. Martyrdom and suffering are not my bag. Perhaps that is the message for this book: if it fits with your life style, if it's integrated with yourself, if it feels good, if the shoe fits, do it.

Despite popular conceptions of career women, none of those I interviewed believed in extramarital relationships personally for themselves. They all expressed it would compromise them as well as their careers. An adulterous relationship to me wouldn't feel good. It might feel good mechanically in my pelvis, but it wouldn't feel good in my soul. It must feel good everywhere: in my head, in my role as a woman-person —as a wife, as a mother, as a psychiatrist-lawyer role model. It's similar to the story I shared before. When I wake up in the morning, I say, "Judi-woman, Judi-wife, Judi-mother, Judi-physician, Judi-lawyer, get up and face the day." All of me wakes up, and all of me faces the world—not just one of me. I can't do any action that violates any one of my roles and still like myself. I can't do anything that would be marvelous for Judi-woman but would be terrible for Judi-wife, because I can't really separate Judi-woman from Judi-wife. Plurality is the richness of my essence. My existence is a bit of everything. While I am working, the baby often interrupts me to straighten her dress or give her something to eat. She knows she belongs everywhere in my world. I change a diaper, sign a contract for a quarter of a million dollars, or telephone for Michael's car pick-up. Each thing is taken in order; I don't separate them depending on my role. I have no problem making love in the middle of the day rather than in the middle of the night. Daytime we simply tell the children, "This is the time for Mommy and Daddy to be alone." They accept that Mommy and Daddy have special times together, and they look forward to finding their special person when the time is right. We don't flaunt sex, nor do we hide it. Our children accept its rightness as a good part of life.

Epilogue on Sex

In 1959, when I was pregnant with my first, Trissa, and Michael was an enthusiastic fourth-year medical student, he informed me that Dr. Sophie Kliegman, professor of obstetrics and gynecology at New York University, had asked for volunteer donors for artificial-insemination projects. He wanted my permission to help out some disappointed couple. Even though it would be impersonal, via a test tube, I was overwhelmed with jealousy. I needed to know only *I* was carrying his child, not hundreds (and I was emotionally positive it would be hundreds) of other women walking around with swollen bellies à la *my* Michael. Scientific-doctor-me couldn't prevail upon woman-me. Michael didn't volunteer.

Earlier in the same pregnancy, another assault on our marriage occurred. It happened like this.

It was at the hospital's Christmas party. While we were dancing, Michael received a call from one of the medical students —a young woman who asked him to join her in the lab, as she was having trouble interpreting several slides; she had a very sick patient. Michael excused himself, leaving me with one of his good friends. We chatted for over an hour until Michael returned, in apparent amazement and shock, to share the following tale: "As I enter the pathology lab, I am startled to realize Doris is stark naked. She calls, 'Come in, Michael, I want to make love.' I sense she is very confused and upset, so I sit down to talk to her to see if I can help. I ask, 'Doris, what's happening? Why are you doing this?' She rambles for a few minutes and finally sums it up by saying, 'Michael, I want you; I can't stand to see a happy marriage. Judi has everything; it's not fair. It's Christmas Eve, and I should have a Christmas present, too.'"

Michael explained to her that she needed to seek help, and that love in the lab yields no answers. Only my husband would have spent an hour alone in a laboratory with a naked woman doctor counseling her to obtain psychiatric help; I am glad no other professor decided to visit the lab that evening. Explanations would have been difficult to make and more difficult to believe.

Michael was visibly shaken by the experience. Fate is strange and coincidence amazing; about six months later, Doris became pregnant by still another doctor, a resident in Chicago. She had been previously married and had given the custody of her three children to her husband at the time of her divorce. She was a dropout wife and mother, trying to find herself in medical school. I wonder whether she ever found happiness as a person or as a doctor; I doubt it. Unfortunately, many young women are taking this road. But people find themselves best by standing still and evaluating themselves rather than running away. In evaluating oneself and designing life style changes in order to be more fulfilled, it is extremely important that one meet legitimate responsibilities. Life is an evolution —an odyssey, not a phoenix, the symbol of self-destruction and breaking all ties with the past in order to be reborn. I couldn't find myself or ever be at peace at Michael's or the children's expense.

But back to Doris and her pregnant dilemma. She was not married; her paramour had recently been divorced. Our good friend called me, asking me if I remembered Doris. With a mixture of laughter and harshness I replied, "Of course I do. What now?" He told me that he and other friends believed that if the three-day required waiting period that is law in New York between marriage license and ceremony were not waived (a requirement written ironically into law by my own Mother), the alleged father would disappear into the hospital corridors of Cook County in Chicago, never again to be seen by mother and child. He asked if it were possible for me to find a judge who would waive the period and marry them promptly. I promised to try. I hurried, was successful, and rejoiced in watching a full-bellied, fully clothed Doris walk down the aisle. I wonder what ever happened to her?

Actually, many, many times women pursue Michael. He's gentle. He's kind. He's giving. He's warm. And he's a very physical person. He is also tall and handsome. Michael doesn't have the inhibitions that many people have about putting his arm around you or patting children or picking them up. It doesn't dawn on him that he cannot touch you, that touching will be construed as sexual. I'm sure he feels that way because we have such a good relationship. He's not constantly uptight, not constantly looking. It is secure to have that feeling of safety. Ours is a relationship not of dependence, but we never feared giving up our independence. All good relationships are based on mutual interdependence.

It is from my relationship with Michael, my other half in the platonic sense, that I venture forth to my other relationships with the children, my career, and the sisterhood. In summary, the thing I share with Michael is good. I like me—I like him—I like us.

Bridges to Woman Faces Her Child

First Bridge

Yesterday I chanced upon the following article in the New York *Daily News:*

Slaps Wife-Beaters

London, September 28 UP—A House of Commons Committee called today for sweeping changes in the law to protect wives whose husbands beat them.

"Home is for many a very violent place," the Committee of eight men and five women reported, "yet the law provides barely any protection for maltreated wives." It said that police refuse to interfere in domestic quarrels, and social services too often stop at the front door.

The Committee said that it heard evidence from one wife who, in 16 years of marriage, had had all her teeth knocked out, her cheek pierced by a red hot poker, and several knife cuts that required stitches. In one case, she told the Committee, her husband doused her with gasoline and flicked burning matches at her.

The Committee's major recommendation was that local governments should provide temporary "refuge" homes for battered wives and that the national government should finance emergency accommodations.

Over the summer, I lectured at a major New England college and was consulted by a woman professor whose husband brutally assaults and beats her. She won't leave him because she believes divorce will ruin her children's lives. I don't understand her reasoning. At some point you must evaluate a marriage to a brutal man and walk away from it. This woman professor is destroying her children more by letting them see her helpless in this sadomasochistic relationship, without a sense of dignity, than she would by rearing them in a single-parent family. No woman should remain helpless in deference to the brutality of her mate, the physically stronger male. Nor should she endure other indignities in order to receive financial or emotional support. Many women don't leave their husbands even when those men commit incest with their own daughters, for fear of losing the monetary security. No one should be that much of a slave or afraid of self-reliance; but the job market must be open and fair to receive these women.

The English suggestion of temporary hostels doesn't solve the problem of why a woman stays in such a relationship. Only fear of loneliness and providing for oneself can be the rationalization, even if love is the cover.

Just because you made a bed doesn't mean you must forever lie in it. If a marriage is not based upon mutual growth and well-being, grounded in respect and trust, and productive of security and love, then one should evaluate it, and if improvement is not possible, it should be dissolved. Children are safer in an honest divorce than in a deceptive marriage.

Detachment doesn't get it, either. Children need parents who care about them but also about each other. A woman can't be just a visitor in her wifely or motherly relationships; nor can she go off to "find herself" and abandon all prior responsibilities.

If a marriage is no good, it should end in an atmosphere of dignity and respect. The children don't necessarily have to stay with the mother. Custody should depend upon the child's needs. Sometimes the father can play a more significant role in the child's development than the mother, particularly with teen-age sons.

Suppose, for the sake of illustration, I were to leave Michael or Michael me. Ideally, we would sit down quietly to decide with which parent each child would do best, the other having maximum visitation rights. It isn't a given that the children would do best with me or that automatically all four children would be better with him. Each child is an individual with a unique personality who would adjust to either Michael or me differently. It isn't a rejection or failure if one child would be better with me and another with him. When hard choices like this must be made, the best interests of the child should be the major consideration. If I love my children, then, as in the story of King Solomon and the two women, I would give them up rather than see them suffer. After all, Michael must be a good person or I wouldn't have married him. The idea of any one of my children loving and needing him more than me doesn't threaten me. Custody should be based on a logical, dispassionate, concerned analysis of the situation. But happily, divorce from Michael is only hypothetical and fortunately, not something I ever imagine facing.

It is vitally important that people permit themselves to understand that even within the close confines of a marriage, there is individual territory. You have to respect each other and avoid invading each other's space. Often I tell Michael I need more room. He doesn't personalize this as indicating hostility toward him; he isn't hurt—he realizes I need distance for my own self; it is part of my make-up, not a rejection of him. Often at a cocktail party a person will get too close while talking to me and I'll back away or if cornered, excuse myself. I can't stand someone's face right in mine. I need a certain amount of territory. This need for distance is not only physical but emotional. Too many demands smother me, and I feel trapped or suffocated. I up and leave, later to return refreshed. I do this without guilt or apology. After all, there is a "me" as well as a "they"—a fact too many women forget.

Monday evenings over dinner Michael and I share our calendars for the week. It never dawns on us that he or I can't go to this or that particular meeting. Many times husbands are tired when they return home from the office. However, their wives, having no one to relate to except the children all day, want to do something, anything, just to get out. There is no reason groups of women can't do things together, and the husbands, when they want, can stay home. Many American women tend to feel martyred. In many ways the women's movement has not helped matters; to blame the male for our predicament is not real. Both men and women have been conditioned to sexist stereotypes. No man is responsible for a woman's suffering; she is in charge of her own destiny and responsible for herself. Vengeance or hostility to the male or men in general is wasted effort. They, like ourselves, are victims. It is time to build, not destroy, to emphasize health, not disease. If a woman feels martyred, exploited, abused, she should analyze why she is masochistic and make the necessary changes. You can change yourself—never another. Be not afraid to look into yourself, to discard the parts you don't like, and to reinforce the good. Remember to build on the positive and not be defeated by the negative.

For instance, if your husband breaks your jaw, while it is being wired on the oral surgeon's table, you shouldn't ask, "Why did he break my jaw—what kind of man is he?" and "What did I do wrong?" but rather, "Why was I there for him to break the jaw?" and, "Why do I stay there so he can break my jaw next week?" And when you wake up from the anesthesia, get out. Love doesn't excuse or cure anything; it only obfuscates reality in a bitter relationship or sweetens an already good one. About 25 percent of all women face some kind of physical abuse, and double that verbal abuse. When a husband continually talks to a wife in front of the children as though she were a piece of shit, healthy children do not survive. Positive adults are reared only in homes of mutual respect and trust. Remember no one mate can fulfill the other's needs completely; therefore each of us must allow healthy friendships without jealousy beyond the marriage to the other.

This doesn't imply sexual infidelity but rather enjoyment of a play, a good meal, and interesting conversation.

Women should stop demanding that men always be strong. Men cry, just as we do, are afraid of failure, and have moments when they feel inadequate, frightened, depressed—all the emotions women feel. After all, we are only the other half of each other. Respect him as you would yourself, and he should do likewise. To denigrate one-half of yourself is to denigrate the other half, as well. You are both human; sometimes strong, sometimes weak; sometimes right, sometimes wrong; sometimes brave, sometimes fearful; sometimes winning, sometimes losing; sometimes positive, sometimes negative; but all times better because you face the world together.

Second Bridge

Early in our relationship Michael and I had the usual minor adjustment problems, and we sought an outside mediator who knew us both well. Indeed, it was Jimmy Murphy, the second in charge of Odyssey. One evening, after a particularly difficult session, Jimmy made an interpretation about our marriage that I have always remembered and been comforted by. Jimmy said that he observed the same dynamic operative with both Michael and me: no matter what our individual selfish needs, we both have a commitment to something outside ourselves, and that is safeguarding the marriage and protecting the children. The marriage has value above and beyond our momentary needs. This is indeed true. Both Michael and I are children of bitter divorces. When we married, we promised to be adults and resolve our differences so that our children would not experience what we did. This does not imply that we will stay together because of the marriage, regardless of how we feel, but rather that we try to work things through, each giving a little. We have an "our thing" commitment equal or greater than the sum of our individual commitments to each grow in "her thing" or "his thing."

Selfish, narcissistic behavior does not develop healthy children. The basis of good parenting is role modeling. Children need both mother and father to grow into healthy adults, and they need examples of stable relationships to follow. It is essential that there be mutual respect between husband and wife and between parents and children. Love is not the glue that holds a family together. Many of the most brutal relationships I have seen are defended on the ground that the participants stay together because they love each other. The boundaries of love are not rationally definable—they are intangible and personal; those of respect are clear and sharp and are best understood in terms of the Golden Rule; only included in the verb *do* must be the verb *say*. Out of relationships of respect develop deep feelings of trust. Trust is the emotional security that another person will do the best he or she knows how to do at any given time, in your best interest, without personal gain interfering. Good parents set limits for the child's sake even if they must suffer momentary rejection and loss of affection from the child. Unfortunately, more times than not, I have seen parents defend their lack of setting standards or making demands on the child by the rationalizations "I want Johnny and Jane to know I will always be there; that there is love behind them; that I'll never reject them; that no matter what they do, Mommy and Daddy are there; and that we love them no matter what." What this nonsense means in essence is: "I am terrified if I say no, even if it is to something as wrong as taking heroin, then my children won't love me any more, and I need their love more than their happiness or safety." This is the kind of love I see destroying children each and every day.

Children need less to love their parents than to respect and trust their life styles and decisions. Children need value systems and guidance—occasionally even rejection. Hitler's mommy at some point should have said, "My son's acts are so unconscionable that I cannot continue loving him but I must reject and walk away from him." It would have been a good day when Dracula's mommy disowned him.

Another prerequisite of good parenting is the ability to make decisions, set limits, and have expectations for your children. At Odyssey we believe "the loving hand is the firm hand." The results of the opposite are clearly articulated in the recent book by Midge Decter, *Liberal Parents, Radical Children*. The disruptive, self-destructive actions of the young of the sixties and seventies have many roots. Parents did not communicate with each other; men and women faced realities so separate and isolated that there never was a mutual commitment, a sharing of an "our thing." Parents prided themselves on being liberal, which was interpreted to mean allowing children to make their own decisions, regardless of their state of preparedness, giving them all the alternatives, and then saying "You decide," as if a two-year-old thrown into deep water could swim. As expected, many drowned. Dostoevsky wrote, "If there is no God, then all is permitted."

The most striking confrontation with the outcome of this permissive attitude of giving the child everything he or she wants because of the fear of rejection is seen in the photograph of Patty Hearst manning the machine gun while labeling her father a fascist pig. Randolph Hearst professes he still loves her, provides her with a team of lawyers and psychiatrists, and is willing to meet bail, no matter what the cost. All this, in spite of the fact that Patty continues to spew forth hatred. While she smiles in manacles, her mother stands by her side, comforting whenever possible but never photographed with a hair out of place. Better a spanking, less "understanding," and no concern for appearances!

Hearst stories saturated the press, asking the question "Why?" The answer is simple. Give someone everything, make no demands, never say "No" and mean it, have no reasonable daily concrete expectations, set no limits, communicate no value systems, and you will develop someone with an empty head and an even emptier soul waiting to be filled by whatever is first articulated by a charismatic leader, be it Charles Manson, Field Marshall Cinque, or one of the new all-absorbing religious cults.

It was the drug culture, the hippie movement, the rebel antiwar demonstrations, that captured the alienated youth of the sixties. In the seventies it is violence, destruction, murder, and crime, juxtaposed or occasionally combined with fanatical religious commitment. Often we read now of parents hiring questionable people to kidnap their children from religious communes.

Desperate, confused, and frightened parents are spending fifty dollars a session to attend Parent Effectiveness Training, appropriately abbreviated *PET,* which to me is the crux of the problem: our children are not "pets," possessions, toys, or duplications of ourselves. They are simply newer people whose development and upbringing are entrusted to us during their formative years in the most special and protective of fiduciary relationships. Each human being is first a mini-person (baby-child), then a midi-person (child-adolescent), and finally a maxi-person (adolescent-adult). Each time in life has its special privileges, responsibilities, and rights. Democracy in a family doesn't work; an eight-year-old should not have the same vote as Mother and Father—certainly, the parent's judgment is more mature and experienced than the child's. If it isn't, then that in itself is a major problem. There are some eight-year-olds who not only decide with their six- and ten-year-old siblings where the family takes their summer vacation but also are exposed to the various religious philosophies of the world. They are expected to choose a religion for themselves. Only confusion results. I emphatically repeat: children need guidance and a backboard of values against which, as emerging adults, they can find themselves. By the age of twenty, thirty, forty, fifty, or sixty an adult can define a personal religious orientation. In the early years, a foundation for each of us to build upon must be laid down, and it must be firm and secure.

Parent Effectiveness Training should not be cute, as the acronym suggests; nor is it possible to accomplish in three or four easy sessions. A good first step would be to change the word *parent* to *person.* Effective, happy people who know and like themselves and their life partners make good parents. The quality of the primary relationship, that of the breeding couple, completely influences and colors the secondary one of parent-child. Some couples are happy with each other but are so absorbed in their own narcissistic pleasures or work that they have little time for the children. These youngsters are shipped to boarding school or left with servants and have little if any real contact with their parents. These jet-set parents have not come to grips with the special responsibility of parenthood, and are therefore unresolved. Having children is a sacred trust that must be equally shared by husband and wife. Children need two parents, and boys in particular, in order to grow up into normal, healthy, adequate males, need fathers as role models. No woman, no matter how self-actualized she is, can teach her sons how to be men, husbands, and fathers.

I remember a particularly touching moment when Trissa at age eleven called me while I was on a lecture tour with her father to tell me that she had begun menstruating. At first she didn't want me to tell her father, saying she would rather do it when we arrived home. However, upon reflection, she said, "I know, Mommy, you'll never be able to keep a secret from Daddy, not the way the two of you share everything, but when you tell him, give him a message from me: Tell him I won't get pregnant before I am married. I know that daddies are very necessary, no, *indispensable.*"

Michael and I laughed and cried at the same time over that simple but so special, charming message. There was no denial that premarital sex can occur, nor hesitancy to mention such a possibility to us, even at age eleven. There was a shocking openness—but even at Trissa's age, there was a clear conceptualization of the needs of children, a sense of appropriate limitations on one's behavior, and an acceptance of the responsibility not to hurt another. There was also a deep expression of love for us parents, male and female.

Perhaps some will criticize the fact that our children so openly discuss sexuality with Michael and me—but it is impossible not to and still remain honest in today's environment, which is so saturated with explicit sexual references and replete with sexual innuendos. Such discussions are necessary if parents are to be effective guides. It is impossible to rear our children to read, ask questions, to be curious and knowledgeable, and not to have them aware. We must be ready to answer their questions appropriately. We discuss issues such as sex, drugs, rebellions, and so forth, within the context of values, always emphasizing whether any one act will help or hurt the development of the "who am I?" of the child involved or of others intimately connected. We clarify for the children that whatever they do or whatever relationship they enter into is an integral part of their being and will shape their future lives. We admit of no dissociative experiences, and we expect them to face the consequences of their actions. Actions are always evaluated within the context of the identity crisis: "Who am I?" "Where am I going?" "What am I going to become?" Only actions which move the individual in an affirmative direction, in a happy course, are encouraged. Our young are demanding a value system to live by. It is freeing to have one.

Our four have been given responsibility within the family setting from the time they could toddle. Our two-year-old already knows that she either puts her clothes in the laundry or folds them for the next day before she goes to bed. Rules and structure reinforce security and well-being. It is important to have a place and be counted on. Children need a role to play within the family other than that of spoiled possessions for whom mother does all and father provides everything.

It has repeatedly struck me as ironic that people need a license to fish, to hunt, to own a gun, to practice many professions (law, medicine, barbering, massaging, to name a few), to operate most businesses, to marry, but nothing is required except operable mechanisms to fornicate, beget, and conceive, and thereby become a parent, entrusted with the care of another human being, a helpless infant who cannot fend or speak for him or herself. This most difficult of human undertakings is the one for which we are the least educated or trained. Training in human relatedness and values should begin as early as the first grade; remedial courses and therapy are too late. Classes should continue and become more and more sophisticated until graduation from high school. Human relatedness is as important as reading, 'riting, and 'rithmetic. We should begin to think in terms of a basic four *R's*, not three. I am not suggesting government licenses or intervention around the right to have a child. We have enough government control of our lives; but I do advocate good preparatory educational courses in child rearing. We all need guidance and help in the difficult, confused world of today.

The importance of considering our children, *our nation's greatest resource,* cannot be overemphasized. We are all becoming more aware that millions of children live and suffer under conditions that cannot help but lead to alienation and isolation and eventually to violence and mayhem. Odyssey has a motto which clearly states our belief: "Today's abused, tomorrow's addicted."

In the late 1960s I wrote a paper for the American Academy of Forensic Sciences, the theme of which was that the then occurring drug-addiction epidemic represented only the tip of the iceberg of youth's alienation. Furthermore, the frustration and desperation which the young feel because they have no meaningful control over their own destiny must be compared to the rage of trapped animals who first turn against themselves but as the social disruption continues, turn on one another. Any behavioral scientist well versed in the dynamics of social breakdown knows that relatively intact animals will first take their frustrations out on themselves in suicidal equivalents—head-banging for rats, drug addiction for humans. Then, as there is less and less socialization of the baby rats by the mother rat, they turn on one another. For our species, when we have less and less to believe in, such as government, church, and family, the rage finally turns homicidal, with rape, assault, and murder the convenient channels for ventilation. The strong overpower the weak, and terror reigns supreme. This is explicitly demonstrated in the excellent anthropological study of the Iks entitled *The Mountain People,* by Colin Turnbull.

This book describes a small tribal African people starved for food, who dwell in unbelievable cruelty toward one another. Each person stands only for self, and no relationships develop between people. The constant guiding refrain is that there is only enough for oneself. The strong rule; children are cast out in the jungle to fend for themselves when they are three years old, and the aged (between thirty-five and forty) are left to die.

Men and women mate and mate and mate constantly and promiscuously, either through rape when there is enough food to provide sufficient energy, or prostitution in exchange for food that the stronger male can provide. If the girl has reached puberty and has had enough nutrition to ovulate, a child may be conceived. Conception is dreaded and is seen only in terms of another mouth to feed. Sarcastic humor and pranks at the pain of another replace folklore and tradition from the absent grandparents, who would, if they were permitted to live, be the storytellers of the tribe. No one alive today within the tribe remembers love or God.

There is almost nothing described by Turnbull that I cannot relate to my everyday work. This saddens and frightens me. Only one story goes beyond; it is about a young mother who goes to forage for food. Even though she has seen the tracks of a leopard, she leaves her three-month-old baby by the side of the water hole; because she knows that after the leopard feasts on her baby, he will sleep and be easier to capture by the men of the tribe for their dinner. So it comes to pass, and the men eat first, leaving only bits and pieces for the women. Turnbull with scientific dispassion notes the tragic irony that the young mother obtained only the entrails, the stomach of which contained the partially digested arm of her baby.

This, I haven't seen—but there are no lions or leopards on the streets of our cities or the roads of our countryside, and that is probably the major determining factor. I have treated children pregnant at nine who were prostituted at three by their mother (fellatio until five or six, until the genitals become sufficiently large to permit penetration). Forty-four percent of Odyssey's female patients have been involved in incestuous relationships, 25 percent of which were with the mother's knowledge and consent, 75 percent of which began before the child was twelve, and 45 percent before nine. Perhaps this is why of the nation's 1 million runaways—1 million throwaways —the largest single group is fifteen-year-old girls. Children need safety, security, and proper love to grow normally. The increased incidence of crimes by juveniles, particularly against old persons, was clearly predictable and preventable if our leaders had cared—but our leaders or elected officials only concern themselves with what the electorate demands, and we have been strangely silent about "Concerns of Children."

A shibboleth of "the American way of life" is that the family is sacrosanct, good or bad, and it is considered good unless someone takes the initiative to prove otherwise. Therefore, usually no one takes a look to see whether or not children are safe within the family. The reality is that many children—4 million approximately—are in danger of their lives and go to bed at night calling their enemy Mommy and/or Daddy. The unfortunate ones survive to kill or maim others. Unless you and I realize that a child reared in danger will grow up an angry and hostile adult capable of pulling the trigger on a Kennedy or a Ford or on you or me or our children, such will happen —such happens. Americans must realize that for better or worse we are one another's keepers. We cannot rear our children in isolation. The child to the left or the child to the right can sell drugs and influence your child in the middle. The teen-ager brutalized as a child can mug your grandmother. The gangs, addicts, and other malcontents on the streets of New York can wreak such havoc that eventually the hard-working people flee, bringing the city to financial ruin and leading to nation-wide repercussions. There is no place to hide. Trissa, Judson, Lindsey, and Sarah must share this earth and defend themselves if necessary from you and you and you, whoever you are, who are angry, hurt, hungry, wanting.

Recently I was asked by the White House to prepare a memorandum for James Cannon, chairman of the Domestic Council, on my idea for a cabinet post for the Concerns of Children (see Appendix A). Certainly, children, our nation's future, are as important as Defense, for whom are we defending? as Justice, for whom are we judging? as Labor, for whom are we laboring? as Health Education, and Welfare, for whom are we ——, and so on. The delivery of services to children is fragmented and sketchy at best, poorly coordinated, with more money often going to the maintenance of the bureaucracy than to the delivery of care. The needs of our children are lost in the mammoth structure of HEW. It is too big and too inefficient. Separating out Concerns of Children will make HEW more manageable and will provide more direct accountability in children's programs. Juvenile justice, health care for children, education, and nutrition for children belong together, not scattered across the Washington power scene. Good programing would not cost more, as money desperately needed is currently being wasted. A better job could be done for less than present costs. The nation must have an ombudsperson for its children so that the children at America's bicentennial birthday party will be laughing, not suffering.

The idea for such a cabinet post was well received initially —and then silence. These issues are part of a book about women because I believe the priorities for women are different from those for men; ours include the rights and needs of children. Women are by nature interdependent, symbiotic, with their young. When I am working, my ear is always cocked for the sound of Sarah's cry, a cry that I can distinguish from 100 other children's. Her distinctive cry is not an ever present concern to Michael. The parasitic—no, symbiotic (I received so much emotional sustenance during pregnancy) relationship creates the difference. My four children were within me, physically part of me, an experience that can never be understood or intuited by the male. These are differences too great to be denied by even the most militant of antisexists. In many ways womanlife is separate, though it is equal, frequently special. The priorities of men have too long shaped the policies and direction of this nation. Unless the concerns of women are articulated and heard, there will be no earth left for men to play their one-upmanship, competitive games, nor any men or women left to play.

A cabinet post for the Concerns of Children is but the first step—a declaration of a resetting of national priorities for our second two hundred years. Let us together begin to demand this of our elected officials—we vote; we have the power; we must demand. I am not sure that what is good for General Motors or Exxon is necessarily good for the nation—nor am I sure that what is good for party politics or our cities or our farms is, either, or labor or management, but I am sure and I can categorically, simplistically state that what is good for our children is good for our nation. Together let us demand the nation's birthday celebration be for *laughing,* not dying children.

Last Bridge

In July 1963 Michael and I argued over circumcision. Our older son had just arrived. All I wanted to do was discuss the pros and cons of the circumcision. However, not a word could be said to my rational, scientific, academic, agnostic Michael, without rage resulting; Michael personalized; he could not discuss it. He adamantly stated that his son had to look like him. I queried, "But your daughters can never look like you in that sense. Furthermore, there is medical evidence that circumcision is an uneasy early trauma, at best a concession to tribal rites." Tribal Michael bested me because he felt so earnestly. Later I matched him, because when Sarah arrived, I told him that I had decided to have her ears pierced in the newborn nursery before she left the hospital. Mine are pierced, and so are Trissa's, but ours were done as teen-agers. When I informed Michael that Sarah had to look like me and Teri, he objected with grave concern, stating it would be too traumatic. He felt it was unnecessary and barbaric. I asked him to defend the concept that ear-piercing was more difficult than penis-hemming.

We reached diplomatic accord; we had circumcised our sons, and we would pierce our daughter's ears.

Woman Faces Her Child

hallelujah,
HALLELUJAH,
HALLELUJAH
                a child is born.

A First Story

At the particular moment I was pushing out a baby, I didn't give a damn about anyone. I have read *Our Bodies, Ourselves,* the excellent book from the Boston Collective, and I am convinced that women need to help other women; we must understand our own bodies. I have had eight pregnancies and except for one baby, I felt mercilessly at the hands of someone, a male, and a system that didn't care or understand me as a person. The relationship with the male obstetrician-gynecologist contains no possibility of identification. More often than not, he has an overriding hostility to the female or a feeling that she is a functioning reproduction machine in the service of the baby. The epitome of this concept is to question the conclusion that a therapeutic abortion to save the life of the mother is permissible. The mother has history, life, and relationships. Often there are many who depend upon and need her; she is a person known and loved; the unborn child has yet to begin. To sacrifice her for her child is unconscionable and is only possible within a formulation that values the birth of a child more than the worth of the mother. Do many fathers with families to provide for consider dying themselves in order to save an as yet unborn child, who has no identity nor actual meaning? I doubt it. I grant that life in and of itself has symbolic worth and that a woman's greatest moment of glory is to push the baby out, but it is not her only glory or value. Only a culture which conceives of women solely as childbearing vehicles and not persons could establish such rules.

I remember my second date with Michael. It followed by twenty-four hours our first in the morgue. He was still a struggling medical student, with little money, so he took me to see a delivery. It was an exciting free date. He was furious when the staff told him to wait outside; they had recognized him as a medical student. However, they accepted me in the delivery room, assuming incorrectly that I was a nurse.

I remember it, as if I were standing there right now.

While Michael paces the hall with the expectant father, I stand at the right arm of the patient who is a nineteen-year-old, slim, frail Puerto Rican girl, weighing no more than ninety pounds, and in labor. She has been moaning in the agony of almost twenty-four hours of labor with little if any progress. X-rays have not revealed any gross pelvic bone pathology, and the baby appears in good position. She has been put up on the table, into the stirrups and arm restraints, draped and sterilized, for the resident doctor to begin his examination. Though it may be through lenses distorted by emotions, I visualize him now as a cross between Hermann Göring and Charles Manson, looking more like the former and acting like the latter. The patient speaks no English, and none of us knows Spanish. Indeed, it is veterinary medicine, with the woman the dumb animal, for not only can't we communicate with her but she is unable to understand enough to help us on her behalf. She struggles and wrestles to be free of the restraints that hold her arms and legs fast to the table and screams at the top of her lungs. The ambiance is that of the medieval torture chambers of the Marquis de Sade. Indeed, women are bearing in chains; I intuitively know it doesn't have to be that way.

The time is the late fifties, and I have sneaked into a delivery room because birth processes have been hidden to us. We haven't had sex-education movies or seen anything in these dark ages. There is only mystery; our mothers have taught us that suddenly you have these terrible pains, you are rushed to the hospital and doctor, only to be knocked out and when you awake, there is a baby. Imagine me, a naive law student in the delivery room at Bellevue Hospital. The operating-room lights are glaring, and the nurses are running around. The patient is pushing, bearing down, and screaming, screaming, screaming. And Göring is pressing on her abdomen, and she's screaming, "Mamma Mía" and the baby can't come out. And she is thrashing around, and she's breaking out of her chains. And her whole body is shaking. I shall never forget it. You can't imagine it. It was everything my Mother had always warned me about. And she is screaming and yelling, and the resident finally identifies the problem: she has a double vagina; she has been born with a septum in the vagina, dividing it into two parts, one a dead end and the other leading to her uterus which contains the baby; but the baby can't make the turn—the baby can't get out; and she's yelling, and she's screaming and she can't talk with anyone in the room, so that there is no one who can really help her. They don't want to give her too much anesthesia, first, because of possible complications and second, because there isn't much anesthesia at Bellevue for charity patients in labor. We continue to hold her down. By now, she is almost psychotic from the pain. All of us who remember the second stage, the head coming, can imagine the pain if the head can't get out. And Göring becomes the butcher, fat and heavy. He's sitting there on his stool between her chained legs, and he says, "Give me the scissors," and he macerates her vagina—literally, cuts it to bits, cuts out the septum, throws pieces of tissue on the floor, and finally having dredged out passage "a child is born," and I am literally lying across her body to keep her down, and the room is laughing. They're laughing about the fact that if her husband has any sense or his prick, eyes, he would have always used the side with the dead end; then she would never have been pregnant. They joke that he should have steered his penis always to the left and what a shame it is that now this natural contraceptive is no more. More jokes pass back and forth about her finding a man with a forked penis—no, better yet, forked tongue. Humor in the delivery room is not uncommon, nor is the attitude, "Well, she had her fun; now she pays." I have always wondered, does the male not have "fun"? "The Hallelujah Chorus" isn't her reality. She is little more than an object which belongs to her husband and a handy one, at that, particularly with that dead-ended-barren-vagina to choose between.

I have attended many births since that initial experience, where women scream in anger and fright. They know too little about the natural processes of their bodies and the joy of giving life. Too frequently, they have no communication with their husbands; after five or six children these women often want tubal ligations, but their husbands will not consent because *machismo* states that the more children a man has, the more man he is, regardless of whether or not he adequately provides. Abortion on demand is a recent practice, and there are still states that demand a husband's consent for sterilization. Only in the past five years have women been permitted to care for themselves and to control their own bodies. Prior to this new attitude, women were reproductive machines and childbirth was enmeshed in the concept of sin and punishment, not glory and creation.

During my first delivery I accepted the fact that my legs had to be tied down in the stirrups, but I insisted that no one was going to tie my hands. I didn't want the feeling of being trapped. After Trissa I wasn't bound at all. Michael was always with me, and each time we had to argue with the delivery-room personnel, ending usually with my threatening, irrationally of course, to get up and leave if they attempted to tie me up, down, or around. Being a lawyer, I had previously written a letter to each obstetrician when retaining him, stating that I refused to be tied and would only engage him if he respected my wishes that as long as I was conscious and cooperative and not endangering the sterile field, I would be free to bear in joy and not in traditional humiliation. I suppose my adding that any other action on his or the hospital's part would be construed as assault and battery and thereby legally actionable had something to do with my wishes being respected. It is a shame that one must resort to such tactics to have sane medical practices toward cooperative, sensitive women. 1963 saw Jud's relatively uneventful arrival.

My best delivery was Lindsey, who arrived twenty-seven minutes after the first pain, in the labor-room bed in an unsterile field, happily without my being shaved or purged. He is none the worse for it, and only the delivery of the placenta had the nonsense of the pomp and circumstance of the operating room. Michael and the doctor, who was a kind, real human being, had been busily watching the election returns and missed most of my action. I had voted, marketed, and instructed the governess before I drove to pick up Michael to take him to the hospital. He was in the morgue and had to shower before walking me to the admitting room. It was this shower lag time that almost produced the first morgue baby.

After Lindsey's birth and before I had been bathed by the nurse in the recovery room, I prevailed upon Michael's guilt for having been watching TV to surreptitiously get me a cheeseburger with double grilled onions and a chocolate milkshake. The nurse found me approximately twenty minutes postdelivery, sitting in the recovery room in Buddhist fashion, munching away and unwilling as usual to stop my eating even to bathe. After all my deliveries I walked immediately upon returning to my own room. A difficult but informed, happy, healthy patient is my style.

Much has changed in obstetrical procedures in the fourteen years between the birth of Trissa and Sarah. I remember the shock among the nurses when Michael took movies of Trissa's birth (which he now delights in playing backward) and the laughter when he said as she emerged, "Judi, it's a girl. I guess we'll have to start a boy," and I tried to close my legs in spite of the stirrups, and I said, groggy as I was, "Not now Michael, later; I'm simply not in the mood."

Michael recently shared with me how symbolic it is to him that a baby is born head first; for there is a second or two when the father sees his child as a person before he knows whether it is a boy or girl. Michael says that is a very special moment.

Sarah's birth *was* very special. She weighed 10½ pounds, and the doctor needed all my help and cooperation to push her out. I barely had anesthesia, and not even a stitch was needed. Since we knew she was a healthy girl, Michael had little anxiety and could concentrate totally on the photography. By 1974, in contrast to 1959, obstetrics had undergone a revolution. The doors were open, largely due to the growing awareness and demands of the sisterhood. No longer do we bear against gravity. Now the delivery table rotates into a chairlike position, and women are able once again to squat as they did for centuries. That a birth chair provides a much better position than lying on one's back is apparent to anyone who has ever tried to have a bowel movement in a bedpan, lying flat in bed. We all instinctively want to be in sitting position. Romantic illusions aside, the same muscles are involved in birthing as in defecating. Indeed, it strikes me as bizarrely appropriate that if there is not enough time to prep the mother before delivery, that is, give her an enema, the baby is born face down in shit—a fitting symbol for beginning life's journey. It really does begin with all our body fluids and processes letting go.

With Trissa, I wanted to squat, but the nurse forbade me sternly, saying, "And where do you think the doctor would be with you squatting." In reality, as I said earlier, I didn't give a damn for his convenience. By Sarah's time I pseudosquatted, and Trissa comforted me. She was with me through almost the whole experience and the only trauma was to Michael. For as he left the delivery room, he was greeted by a colleague with the question, "Have you just become a grandfather?" Michael said "No, a father," and his friend responded, "New wife, huh, old boy?" And Michael said, "Same wife, no mistake, just love of each other and children."

Trissa has been programed differently from the way I was. I remember my Mother and aunts and their stories. Trissa has experienced that childbirth is a joy, not a punishment. She has no concept that labor is to be feared; it's necessary, hard but good work that has to be done in order to have a child. There is some discomfort, even pain like severe menstrual cramps, but you're not going to be devastated by the experience. She looks forward to it.

hallelujah
HALLELUJAH
HALLELUJAH.

An Aside

My experience and that of the Puerto Rican woman are total opposites. Mine is woman understanding and in control of herself; hers a blind, noncommunicative, hostile, painful one. I found out after her experience that many lower mammals have double vaginas, and indeed one male animal, the opossum, has a forked penis to accommodate the situation.

Later I learned a bit more comparative anatomy—for instance, that the male whale's penis, when erect, is over six feet long. For some unconscious reason, that special fact intrudes on me at the most inopportune times. Whenever there is a particularly obnoxious male chauvinist doing his thing, the thought always flashes through my head, "What would you say if I made you aware at this very moment that you are no bigger than a whale's "hard-on"? Of course, I never do it, but it is frequently the thought behind my Mona Lisa smirk.

In psychiatry one of the techniques used to gain insight in a nonthreatening manner is to ask patients what animal would they like to be if they were to be born again. I have heard everything from the usual lions, cheetahs, and so on, to jellyfish. One's choice is very revealing. If I had to do it over, if I couldn't choose to be a white Anglo-Saxon Protestant male, I would probably like to be a great big elephant. Though I love being a woman, it certainly is easier the way the world is put together to be born a Rockefeller. There are fewer hassles and more opportunities to build. However, other than that, the elephant will do.

I have wanted to be an elephant, obviously because of the strength; but, what I like most about the elephant is the elephant's social organization. Michael frequently teases me about luxuriating in pregnancy, being doubly precious and all; and it is true that during each pregnancy, when I feel one with this new life, I am tremendously fulfilled and never feel alone. Pregnancy has a special emotional quality and a unique beauty. A society that admires and prizes Twiggy is a society that has lost the softness and the reassurance of curves. It's a masculine, sharply-defined society. When you can't tell whether people are men or women, there's a basic confusion.

Elephants are pregnant for twenty-two months, and in fantasy I have been jealous of their long specialness. Elephants don't labor and deliver alone. They need the help of two other female elephants, two "auntie" elephants (that's what I call them). The auntie elephants apply force with their trunks to the mommy elephant's abdomen, pushing the baby out. Knowing about this meeting of her need produces a terribly warm feeling in me. Elephant sisterhood is a good thing—females aiding females. This is the message of the sisterhood, and the elephants have done it already. Women share a unique experience; and we need each other.

Recently I had the opportunity to play auntie elephant. The director of Odyssey Louisiana is a young woman named Maggie Pike. Her first delivery was complicated by the fact that the baby was a breech. During one stage of labor the baby's body compressed both sciatic nerves, so that Maggie's legs went into painful contractions for almost thirty minutes. She remembered the pain vividly, so vividly that she seriously questioned whether or not she wanted to go through labor again and bear a second child. She and her husband, Barry, are warm, loving people who have taught Mike and me a great deal about the positive direction our young people are taking. Barry came to work for us about two years after Maggie, so he is perfectly comfortable being assistant director under her directorship; after all, she earned it. I can't imagine being Michael's boss, but that is our programed hang-up.

Maggie and Barry shared with me their concerns about having another child, and I volunteered my services. I promised to teach Maggie to hypnotize herself for suppression of pain and also to teach Barry how to reinforce the suggestions. She conceived within the month and we began hypnosis training last March. In May the test arrived.

I am in New York, Maggie in New Orleans. Barry calls because Maggie's anxiety level is so high that neither she nor he can put her under; he asks me to do it over the phone. I promptly do, and she is out like a light; but in the excitement Barry has forgotten to inform me that Maggie is still at home; he questions: how is he going to get her to the hospital?

I demand he put her back on the phone; I order her to take Barry's hand and follow him. Without waking, she does as commanded; she goes right to the hospital, and several hours later, still under, she delivers a second perfect baby girl, Amy, without pain or unpleasant memory. Amy is a welcome replica of their first daughter, Jennifer, an ideal imp. Every time I look at Amy I am overwhelmed by Auntie-Elephant feelings.

Another Animal Association

For many years I have admired the paramecium with his/her/its tenacity of purpose and direction. The paramecium became a symbol or role model for me early in life, probably in high-school biology.

The paramecia are tiny organisms of the level of sophistication of the amoeba. When you observe one under the microscope, you note that whenever the paramecium meets an obstacle, it will butt against it, then retreat and try from another angle until it gets around the hurdle. It never gives up when thwarted but always tries a different path. In other words, if it hits an object at a 45-degree angle and can't get around it, it then tries 47, then 50, until it succeeds. I've patterned myself after the primitive paramecium; it never bothers me to back up and try another way. I am goal-oriented, not problem-fixated. Problems are to be solved, not surrendered to. When something must be accomplished, then that is where I head, always making sure, however, that the attainment of ends does not corrupt the integrity of the means. My strategy in business is like that. I seldom stand and fight on a point for its own sake. I'd rather walk away, looking thoroughly defeated, only to return tomorrow, than waste energy on trying to defeat my opponent. My ego rests more on accomplishing the task than vanquishing the enemy. I believe many women operate this way.

The amoeba is also a favored symbol of mine. I used to watch him/her/it, fascinated, for hours. The paramecium is a bit ahead of the amoeba; it has cell walls, is clearly defined, and has a shape. The paramecium is only one cell, but a highly organized one, and it appears to have a real sense of direction. Many times I have observed the drama of a great, enormous glob, called the amoeba, amorphous and larger, enveloping the paramecium and digesting it, so that all becomes amoeba.

For hours and hours I have watched one digestion after another until all was formless and moving. It was frightening, to say the least. An attribute that makes the amoeba so attractive is the fact that it is absolutely immortal. The amoeba never dies; it simply splits into identical daughters when it gets too large from ingesting paramecia and other passers-by. It has no parenting questions or generation gap, for parent and child are one and the same, so that theoretically, the first amoeba is still out there somewhere, easing itself along. It can be crushed or killed, but then its identical twin is still creeping along. There is no death for the amoeba.

I had a fascinating conversation one night; a long, long conversation with a man I felt extremely comfortable with, Duke Ellington, whose real name was Edward Kennedy. He was vice-president of the Odyssey board and one of the world's great conversationalists, a Leonardo creative genius. During that evening he discussed a movie for which he was writing the theme song. The plot line concerned an old white man who had a brain transplant from a young black man, and the identity confusion that resulted. Ellington was making fun and puns on the song from *My Fair Lady* which begins, "The rain in Spain stays mainly in the plain"; something like "the brain is not the same," when suddenly he became pensive and quiet. He took my hand. He asked me in an almost childlike way, "Wouldn't it be marvelous if some great doctor could take this brain of mine, which is so gifted, so creative, and has so much more to give, and transplant it into a young, healthy body that is owned by a defective brain?" That night he was very much into himself, maudlin with thinking about dying before all the music in his head was put onto paper. He felt possessed; the music had to be written, and he knew there never would be enough time. He wasn't ready to die until every note that was in his head was shared. Sadly, there was no way, and he died shortly thereafter. He died May 24, 1974. Funny, I remember it very clearly. He was seventy-seven.

He loved Odyssey because he had watched so many talented musicians destroyed by drugs. He never understood why people needed them, and he always became angry when a musician claimed that drugs made him play or write music better. Duke saw through that excuse. At two or three in the morning he would sneak into Odyssey to bring unexpected joy to the residents. They'd all tumble out of bed to have a surprise Ellington concert till daybreak. Ellington feared being alone in the dark so he slept in the day.

Ellington would have admired the amoeba. He had the thirst for immortality, the tremendous drive to accomplish everything he wanted and dreamed. It is ironic that one of the most undeveloped of life forms has conquered the major affront to man—death.

An Awakening

Recently Trissa told me that there have been several times that she has been depressed and unhappy without my becoming aware. I was mortified but not because of her sadness. I expect my children to have ups and downs and to experience the full range of human emotions, just as I do. I have no need to deny them laughter and joy, sadness and tears. I spare them not death nor grief, I protect them not from the knowledge of the human condition, nor do I fool them that I am omnipotent and will always be there to guard them from harm—but I do pride myself on being there to comfort them when they need me, and now I had just learned that I had been oblivious to her pain. I pride myself on being a loving, good, warm, touchy-feely, kind parent, and I had missed the whole thing. I was devastated, but she informed me that she had wanted it that way; she had wanted privacy in her feelings; she didn't want an all-knowing-caring-analyzing-psychiatrist Mommy; she had wanted a human Mommy who missed something important, and she had carried it off. She was delighted even though, she told me, she was depressed and there was nothing I could do about it; it was simply the raging hormones of teen age. So all I did was hold her; I cried, I felt, and I nibbled on her ear. I often nibble on my children's ears. Affection and eating are interchangeable to me, so I sort of nibbled. I had no answers, and all I said to her was, "Teri, I'm here." Then I went to tell Michael that she was unhappy. Our oldest baby was undefinably sad. The next day, Michael had some work to do in Albany, so he decided to take her along as his aide. He spoke to her on the way about nothing and everything, and when she came back, she said she guessed that anytime she felt that way, Mommy and Daddy would be there to share it with her. That's all a parent can do.

On the Need for Privacy

The last anecdote illustrates Trissa's need for privacy. Too often parents forget that their children are people in their own right and need as early as the "negative twos" to differentiate from their parents, to be their own selves.

Ask yourself: how would I feel if every day I had to tell my husband whether or not I had defecated or if every day he told me whether or not he had. It would be highly peculiar. It doesn't mean that defecation is dirty; only that it is a personal matter. I remember one mother of a twenty-eight-year-old drug-addict son who was concerned most because heroin was so constipating! Yet many parents invade their children's world with these kinds of questions long after there is any need. To read a child's mail or diary is wrong even if a parent suspects wrongdoing, such as using drugs or having negative sexual relationships. I would confront the child and ask—but never spy. I am a parent, not a policewoman. Mutual respect mandates that I don't spy and that they don't lie.

I never enter my children's rooms without knocking because I don't expect them to enter mine without knocking. I close my door at night, and the children do the same. Michael at first found this uncomfortable; he questioned, "Suppose the children need us, how will we hear them?" I responded, "They'll come down the stairs and knock." This morning, two-year-old Sarah knocked before coming in to say "Good morning." Attitudes begin to develop simultaneously with words. Each child's room is as much his or her sanctuary as mine is to me. We each deserve our own territory.

Don't ever try to be your child's friend; he or she needs a parent more. There are plenty of others to be friends but only one mother or father to guide. The parent must be a fair, just, authority figure; the extent of the control changes as the child moves through the states of being a mini-, midi-, maxi-adult. When I am talking, sharing, enjoying theater or another happening, swimming or boating, my children are always aware that I am their mother. There is no one I like or enjoy more than my older daughter, but we create things together, like each other, share mutual respect, as mother and daughter. We glory in that special relationship, and it is unique among all her relationships. She expects her mother to do things with her, to walk with her, to share with her; we have a mother-child relationship. It is a deep interpersonal relationship.

I never relate to my husband except as my husband. That, too, is a very special relationship with a very special person, a very precious sharing which colors everything we do together

—even to simply reading a book. What we share best and with no one else is our children, half of each of us, intrinsically joined together four times. During the time I was writing my book with my daughter, at night I would lie in bed next to Michael and recite the day's activities, and he would say to me, "Aren't the children delicious?" and I would rejoin, "Aren't the children delicious?" We must say that to each other many times a week. There are no other human beings with half my genes and half his genes in four little bodies. What other person could feel about Teri, Jud, Lindsey, and Sarah the way Michael and I do? I cannot imagine how we could ever hate each other enough to hurt the children. Children need parents who are able to make decisions, not necessarily right ones, but decisions nevertheless. It is better to be wrong and decisive (you can admit your mistake later and apologize) than to be wishy-washy and noncommittal. Children need to know who you are and what you stand for. You must make decisions at the time when you must make decisions. And that is that. The mandate of the parent is to make the best possible judgment based upon the available data at the time of decision-making. So much of what is wrong with this country, with all decision-making, is people saying, "Tomorrow I'll decide. I'll know a little more then." We all know tomorrow, by definition, never comes, and we must realize that decisions are made as much by omission as by commission. Frequently there are disastrous consequences of doing nothing. Good parents, like good leaders, are rare today. People are not trained for decision-making. We are not trained to take responsibility for the human condition, which is imperfection. No one knows everything at any given moment, but you do the best you know how on Monday morning at ten o'clock because a decision has to be made, and if you learn something new at four o'clock, you hope you can rectify any mistake made earlier. But if you can't, you shouldn't whip yourself.

The most destructive thing parents do to their children is not give them direction. However, it is imperative to permit the greatest possible latitude in the children's own self-actualization. The more self-actualized the parent, the greater flexibility for the child; the less actualized, the narrower and more rigid are the acceptable choices. A good parent provides the child with a wide range of normal alternatives but indicates clearly to the child what is beyond the pale of normal; self-destructive behavior should never be condoned or accepted. I see myself as extremely rigid, but my children and friends consider me quite flexible and able to tolerate wide variations in behavior without being threatened. But when I say "No," I mean "No." I just don't say it too often.

It is critical that parents realize where they begin and end versus the child. The journey toward individualization, or weaning, begins at two. Symbiosis is necessary until the negative twos. After that if symbiosis continues without modification, it cripples the child. The negative twos are the first of several landmark identity crises that the human experiences throughout life. We experience a series of identity crises at different stages of our maturational development. We all remember the adolescent one, the time when we made the break from our parents necessary to starting our own home and family. The healthy adolescent must be permitted to stand up to the parents and correct them when they are wrong. There are other identity crises, such as the one at middle age which was clearly shown in the Art Carney television show. This is the time when each of us evaluates what we have done and wish to do with the remaining half of our life. This often coincides with menopause or the climacteric, and is accompanied by wide mood swings and hormonal imbalances. Frequently, it is at this point that people attempt to begin again with new mates and careers.

Unfortunately, the adolescent identity crisis of the child occurs simultaneously with the middle-age one of the parent. Therefore, each clashes with the other at a time when each is struggling. The adolescent questions the values of the parents at the same time the parent is reevaluating and must, for his or her own sake, cling to the past and vehemently defend it. It is too threatening to question whether or not one has wasted the first half of one's life. It is even more difficult not to resent challenges from the young who still glory in the ability to do it all differently. Little wonder the old often grow to hate their successors.

Trissa had a gentle rebellion recently. Michael and I desperately wanted to wake the baby. We wanted to show her off to some late-arriving guests, but Trissa absolutely forbade us to do so. She stood there telling us in no uncertain terms, as if we were the grandparents, to stop the selfish nonsense and selfish acting out at the baby's expense. We didn't wake the baby. She had to defy us, mild and right as it was, so that she could gradually leave the values of the family and develop her own, meet a peer, marry him, and have her own family. It's done in small steps, and if you understand the steps, you can enjoy your children's adolescence even more than their babyhood. Adolescents being afraid to leave home but biologically driven to do so, cling to one another and desperately conform. They need absolute ideals as anchors in the chaotic search for individualization. Moderation and compromise are virtual unknowns. The insanity of adolescence is an imperative; it cannot be touched—it should be quietly tamponaded. Children have to crawl, to toddle, before they are able to walk, to run, to skip. Children do the same things emotionally that they do physically.

One of the sadnesses which today's children face is that romance, courting, flirtation, and sexual expectancy are fashions of yesteryear. Today sexual intercourse takes place almost simultaneously with the introduction. Many young people like my daughter have postponed dating, except in large groups or packs as Michael and I call them, in order to avoid having to grow up too soon. It is easier in the city, with its many activities, than in the country. In our day, merely a generation ago, there were definite limits and yeses and noes, which young men respected without personalizing and feeling rejection. There was real inexperience and myth at college.

I remember a bright and popular girl at Bryn Mawr who drank nail polish remover one night when she returned home from a date because she had been soul kissed, and she knew —knew for certain—that she was pregnant. Gone are those funny, silly experiences. At college I was shocked when I realized that there were girls in my class, whom I even liked, who were no longer virgins. Trissa realizes this in high school and has to make a conscious decision that such behavior is not for her.

Too many so-called liberated parents who feel they missed something in their teens encourage their children toward early sexuality. Parents must not try to find answers through the lives of their children. Recently Mike and I went to a party given by an aging hippie psychiatrist and his very "with-it," swinging, liberated interior-designer wife. Shortly before, he had written several articles extolling bisexuality, group sex, and the like—stating the more one experienced, the more one experienced—another of those profound psychiatric statements. Before joining the group, Michael and I had made a bet with each other as to how long we would be at the party before someone asked us if we were bisexual. Mike said five minutes and I ten, or vice-versa, but whatever it was, we both lost. It only took two minutes for our host to state loud and clear, "Everyone, these are my most conservative, straight friends, Judi and Mike. Have you seen my article on bisexuality? What do you think about swinging that way?" I had prepared! I turned to him and said, "In my case, Sidney, I'm pansexual, rather, in love with my Teflon frying pan, with which one never gets stuck."

Everyone laughed, and the embarrassing moment passed. *Pan* means "all," as in *panphobia, panobsession,* and *pantheism.* Pansexuality is the obsession of experiencing everything so that you don't experience anything. Ergo, the whole hippie movement: you love the whole world so you don't have to love anybody. It's the diffusion of the intensity of feeling; consequently, you can live without commitment. Western culture discourages feeling, gentleness, and caring and encourages competition, aggressiveness, and performance, even between lovers.

We have to stop the Western world, get off, and take a look. It is absurd, all this doing and no being between man and woman, parent and child. We have to stop it—we really do.

A Poem

Since I had a mother
whose many interests
kept her excited and occupied,

Since I had a mother
who interacted with so many people
that she had a real feeling for the world,

Since I had a mother
who always was strong
through any period of suffering,

Since I had a mother
who was a complete person
I always had a model
to look up to
and that made it easier
for me to develop into
an independent woman.

> From *I Want to Laugh
> I Want to Cry
> Poems on Women's Feelings*
> by Susan Polks Schutz

I hope this is how Trissa and Sarah feel. It is how I felt as a daughter.

A Bridge to Woman Faces Her Career

During the period when I am writing this book Bryn Mawr, the college from which I graduated, asks me to join with several distinguished alumnae who have chosen medicine as their life's work to speak to the women seniors who are pre-med. Out of a class of approximately two hundred, forty-five have applied to medical school in spite of the fact that tuition has risen to $12,500 per year in some schools. Many of the girls are scholarship students, often indentured from undergraduate days, whose aspirations must now overcome not only the additional eight to ten years of graduate training but also an expense of $50,000 to $75,000. It seems incredible to me, and I am warmed by their enthusiasm and commitment. What a far cry it is from the days of Elizabeth Blackwell, M.D., or Mary Walker, M.D., on whose behalf I wrote the letter on the following page.

Medical schools are now admitting a 30-percent female enrollment, and by 1980 they anticipate 40 percent. I mused as to whether the girls' experiences would ever parallel mine. While I didn't have to sit behind screens during anatomy in

Odyssey House New York, New Jersey, New Hampshire, Utah, Michigan, Louisiana, Nevada, New Mexico

Executive Offices 210 E. 18 St., N.Y., N.Y. 10003 (212) 260-3300
Executive Director Judianne Densen-Gerber, J.D., M.D.

June 1st, 1975

Ms. Anne Walker
2449 39th Place N.W.
Georgetown, D.C. 20077

Dear Ms. Walker,

It is with the greatest pleasure and reverence that I forward this letter to you highly commending your Great-Aunt, Mary Edwards Walker, M.D. 1855 Syracuse Eclectic School, to the American public. That Dr. Walker be rightfully acknowledged now for her outstanding contribution to the role of American Women is doubly important.

First, at this time of our struggle to have the Equal Rights Amendment passed, the Anti-ERA forces constantly state that if ERA becomes law, women will have to serve alongside men in the Armed Forces. Dr. Walker is a role model to us all, having been the first woman to serve as an Army Doctor in United States History. Participating in the Civil War as a woman physician, Mary Edwards Walker proved that American women care as passionately as their men about the freedoms of this country and are willing to fight to preserve them. She is a dramatic example that bravery and patriotism know no sexual distinctions.

Second, on the eve of this nation's bicentennial, Mary Edwards Walker is to be honored as the first woman to receive the Congressional Medal of Honor which was awarded and affixed on January 26, 1866 by President Andrew Jackson. Too few have followed in her footsteps.

The position of women in American Medicine has too slowly improved since the days of the Blackwells and the Walkers. Though all medical schools are now open to us and we no longer have to sit in a physical purdah hidden behind the curtains and screens designed to protect us and our male colleagues from the embarrassment of mutually facing the anatomy of men and women, we still sit in intellectual purdah hidden by the rationalization that there are female specialties for us to be relegated to, such as pediatrics, psychiatry or obstetrics (albeit to the benefit of our female patients) with little or no opportunity in surgery, orthopedics, etc. and almost none in Chairmanships of Departments in Medical Schools and Academia. And even more distressing, we sit in emotional purdah hidden in guilt because we displace a male when one of us occupies a seat in school; it is generally accepted that a woman will not use her medicine during her child nurturing years and if she does, then the confrontation of deviancy in redefining the mothering role is ever present.

We, who must live within the confines of social deviance, salute a great woman, an inspiration to us all - Mary Edwards Walker, M.D. 1855. United States Army Physician 1861-65. Congressional Medal of Honor Winner 1866 - She dared to be different - She dared to be herself - She dared to be a full functioning person.

Sincerely yours,

Judianne Densen-Gerber, JDMD

Judianne Densen-Gerber, J.D., M.D., F.C.L.M.

JDG/ss

order not to embarrass the men, as did the early women matriculating in medicine, I remember the open hostility of several of my classmates. In anatomy there were four students assigned to dissection of a cadaver. Happily, my partner, who later was to marry a woman doctor, was very supportive of women in medicine; however, the other two boy students were furious that I had taken a man's place. The first day of dissection, they drew a Maginot Line vertically down the body from head to foot. Bernie, my partner, and I were not permitted to cross that line to see the anatomy on the other side. Fortunately, we had the left side of the body, so we copped the heart, the spleen, and the stomach, but to this day the liver remains an unknown to me.

However, as was the custom, when dissection day for the testicles and penis arrived, strangely, every group which had a female student working with them waited for her to begin. Around the room were all those male bodies undergoing minute cutting by women. The rationalization for this custom was reputed to be to see if the females were "men enough" to handle it, but I have always had the opinion that it was based more upon castration reticence than on a concern for developing a withstanding toughness in the ladies.

As an intern in surgery, I received support for this opinion in a unique way. The chief resident in surgery insisted that I personally do a rectal on every male patient on his service. He was a Greek and enjoyed putting me and them in this position. Though rectals were not my favorite ritual in the comprehensive physical, I didn't avoid them. However, for many male patients, my finger in their anus caused much embarrassment and unnecessary anxiety. Usually one of the male residents covered this part of the examination for me as he did the "cough, stress, press on the scrotum" test for hernia. I didn't feel any guilt that I was missing an indispensable part of my training and hence might not be an adequate doctor, since I had already decided to commit myself to the opposite end of the patient.

But orders were orders, and day in and day out for three months, the ritual of the rectal was my reality—and then one day I had a patient whose penis once upon a time had fallen off. It afforded me an opportunity not to be missed. That whole night I stayed in the hospital library researching all the possible causes. The next day for one hour I held the entire surgical rounds captive. Attendings, residents, and interns were at attention, hands carefully crossed in front of their groins, while I dispassionately discoursed on all the possible differential diagnoses causing absence of the penis and the lack of remedial treatment, such as Leriche syndrome, leprosy, carcinoma of the penis, trauma, including (but not limited to) biting, and kuru, to name a few, finishing of course with congenital absence and hereditary chromosomal abnormalities, such as XX. Within twenty-four hours, swiftly and inexplicably, I was transferred to the female surgical service.

This pattern of tongue-in-cheek revenge or awareness exercises for my male chauvinist contemporaries had begun that day when I was busy tearing about the genitals of my cadaver. All eyes were upon me when I called out a question to the anatomy professor, Herr Pick—a German with a heavy accent, austere manners, double-lens glasses, and sarcastic, witty humor. "Herr Pick," said I, "I am most distressed. Almost an hour has passed since I began dissecting these presenting parts (the penis and testes), and still I cannot find the brain. I had assumed it would be a large organ, but I have missed it and cannot even locate a ganglion. Will you kindly assist me?"

Herr Pick in his most solemn voice inquired, "And why, Fräulein Densen-Gerber, think you the brain is found *there?*"

"Why, Herr Pick," said the most ingenue of me's, "is that not what enables my two associates to be so much more intelligent and therefore more entitled to be here than I?"

Stunned silence and then laughter followed, and the Maginot Line crumbled.

Why is it that when men cannot handle a situation with women present, it is assumed that it is the women who must be removed? For instance, if coed biology classes might embarrass the men, women are excluded; if men can't concentrate in synagogue or mosque or church, hide the women; if men are distracted in their work by sexual thoughts on seeing women, then the answer is, no women can participate. Always the frame of convenience is the need of the male, not who is at fault. This is one of the most frequently quoted excuses for keeping women out of politics: that women make the men uncomfortable, as the men cannot take their coats off, put their feet up, drink like fish, swear like troopers, and . . . ?

During the administration of Golda Meir, when there was a wave of rape in Israel, several members of the government approached Prime Minister Meir with a solution—a curfew for all women to be off the streets by eight o'clock. This would obviously drastically reduce the rape rate. Mrs. Meir quickly agreed, changing only one word throughout the proposal. Since men were to blame, she substituted *male* for *female*. To no one's surprise, the legislation was never effected. It is all attitude.

It was good to return to Bryn Mawr. Many of the most formative experiences in my life occurred there. There, unlike high school, I learned not only academic discipline but that the proper emphasis for me was upon organic chemistry rather than tea-pouring. I learned to relate to young men in a positive, mature way; gone were the days of the high school headmistress lecturing to us students that when we were possessed with "the strange tingling between your legs, go climb a tree, straddle the thickest branch and let your legs hang down" or her other favorite lecture, the text of which centered on "always retire at night clean of mind and body, for that night might be the night that the Lord chooses you his handmaiden for the Second Coming." It was years later that I was freed from the absurdity of this latter construct and the always waiting.

Since its founding, Bryn Mawr has emphasized the worth of women, educating them with the same enthusiasm as educators of men do. It is correctly assumed that women have the same potential. It was this commitment that led me to study there and never to regret that decision. The Quaker humanist values also have had a profound effect on me, for which I am forever grateful. Thus, I was flattered by the invitation to address the students, encouraged by the warm reception given to my remarks, which were selections from these pages, and honored when I was asked to serve as a consultant to design an innovative program for a new graduate master's degree in law and social sciences to be awarded by the college.

As a freshman in medical school, I had responded to the challenge of Professor Jack Geiger at Tulane who stated, "Problems will never be solved as long as physicians treat only the rat bites and not the conditions that allow rats." It is this kind of physician I have become; from the patient material I see, I extrapolate, using the modern technological tools of mass media and communication to bring to public awareness problems that have remained hidden. I believe once the American people know, we are sufficiently free and strong in this democratic society to push our leaders to action.

Woman Faces Her Career

I see myself as treating health and mental-health issues, not ones we make up in laboratories but real ones that my patients suffer from and show me daily—drug abuse, juvenile crime, prison conditions, child abuse and neglect, denigration of women, blacks, Hispanic peoples, all Third World peoples; learning disabilities, abandonment of the retarded and mentally ill, welfare dependency, urban blight, family disintegration, apathy, cynicism, indifference, self-centeredness, and last of all, garbage. We are symbolically drowning in our waste. In his books *African Genesis* and *The Territorial Imperative* Robert Ardrey points out a fascinating fact: cave animals take care to preserve the territory in which they live; they soil outside the cave; tree animals drop their wastes wherever they are. Man is a tree animal, and he believes he can simply move on to the next tree. Unfortunately, due to current pressures, we are running out of trees and had better begin to conserve what we have. It is the development of the tools to enable us to live constructively close to one another under crowded conditions that occupies most of my professional time.

The most important task facing American medicine and government today is to provide a healthy soil upon which American children can thrive, so that they can become happy, constructive, full-functioning adults and heads of positive family units. Earlier in this book I shared with you the memorandum I had submitted last May to the White House for the establishment of a cabinet post for the Concerns of Children. Recently I addressed a congressional breakfast in Washington. I had invited the members to meet the eighty children of the Odyssey Choir. I wanted them to share some of their stories with their representatives, to make them realize that today in America no one prominent and powerful is speaking for children who are not as yet old enough to be able to speak for themselves.

Children suffer a dual impediment in obtaining their rights: first, they are too young and immature to formulate and articulate their own needs, as other groups can, and second, they are without the vote. Imagine for a moment how much power a

The children of the Odyssey choir, many of whom were abused, neglected, and addicted, singing in the Halls of Congress. *(Photo by Susan Pappas)*

mute disenfranchised group has, particularly one which in the past was always considered the property of another—and there you have the situation confronting children. The following is the statement that I prepared for the Congress and the President; if it moves you, write to them and to me. Your concern and help are needed.

I stood at the podium in the vast room which seemed even larger because so few congresspeople had cared enough to come to meet their children. By the light of huge crystal chandeliers, midst the quiet noise of plastic knives and forks against paper breakfast plates, I tried to tell the most powerful in the nation why they should help children. I began:

> Across America there are children crying out from hunger, from fear, from neglect, from abuse. Do we hear them? Will we heed them?
>
> We call upon the White House to establish a cabinet position for the Concerns of American Children—to recognize our children as our greatest natural resource and our nation's first priority. A national ombudsperson is needed to examine the social institutions most affecting our children and to represent their interests in our highest councils.
>
> The system of prenatal, perinatal, and postnatal care and nutrition provided for those who cannot pay is inadequate. Delivery of health care to children in general is badly designed and frequently ineffective.
>
> Educational training for day-care centers is nonexistent, or poor at best, depending upon the state.
>
> American law, for all intents and purposes, except in cases of infanticide, equates the child with the property of his or her parents. There is a harsh, nearly total indifference to the soon-to-be-born. Our piecemeal system of juvenile justice often punishes the child for the abuses or omissions of his or her guardians.
>
> Protection is sadly lacking for battered children who fear for life and limb at the hands of the enemy, whom they call "Mommy" and "Daddy". The Director of The National Center for Child Abuse and Neglect, Mr. Douglas Besherov, states that 1 million children suffer danger this year and 200,000 die annually from the *disease* of child abuse and neglect—in other words from our indifference (yours and

mine). More children will die from this cause than any other this year.

The Department for the Concerns of Children would coordinate and direct a two-year survey of all existing resources, including social, legal, educational institutions, as well as juvenile-justice and child-protection agencies on all levels of government. The study will evaluate existing legislation, the nature and quality of the services and providers, and inventory where we are now and what must be done.

The department would also design and develop model systems and programs based on the evaluation to make the changes that must be made. It will initiate and implement programs which will right the wrongs that are destroying our most important natural resource—our children.

Here is a brief sampling of the histories of a few of Odyssey residents, many of whom stand before you now as part of the Choir. These cases are typical rather than extraordinary; there are hundreds of others and hundreds of thousands throughout the nation. We will only solve the problems if we open our eyes and care, not if we turn away and deny. Listen how American children are growing up and why Odyssey believes "Today's abused are Tomorrow's addicted."

JANE

Jane is a white, Catholic, fifteen-year-old girl from New Hampshire. She is currently a resident of the Odyssey Adolescent Program in Hampton, New Hampshire.

Jane claims she can remember her father trying to drown her in the water of the toilet bowl when she was a year old. Her father also beat her, and her mother eventually divorced him over such incidents, when Jane was three. At age seven Jane was sent to live with her maternal grandmother and grandfather; she refers to this period as her only happy childhood experience. Following her grandmother's death, when Jane was nine, she was sent back to live with her mother, who became extremely physically abusive toward her.

By age twelve, she became a ward of the state and was placed in a series of foster homes. (Jane indicates she went to the state and told officials she didn't want to live with her mother.) Between the ages of twelve and fourteen she had two terminated pregnancies, one the product of forced intercourse with one of her foster fathers. She told her caseworker about being raped by her foster father, but the caseworker refused to believe her. Also, during this period she was raped by her brother, who is two years older than she.

Unable to cope with the stress, she made two childlike suicidal gestures, once breaking a mirror over her head and scratching her wrist with a piece of glass, another time by running in front of a car (the car stopped).

At fourteen Jane tried once again to live at home, but the situation quickly deteriorated and Jane's mother committed Jane and her two brothers to the Youth Detention Center. From there Jane went to a short term (ninety days) residential center. She liked it there but had to leave at the end of three months, and after another brief stay at home, returned to the detention center.

Jane has indicated that she has been depressed since the age of nine, when her grandmother died. She maintains that this grandmother was the only person who did not beat her and the only person who cared for her. It is also to be noted that Jane has been an alcoholic since age nine.

Jane's primary need, understandably enough, is for a safe, secure environment where she will not be abused or rejected. Odyssey has assured her that she can stay with us as long as she wants and that she will be safe here. She is being counseled in a special group designed for child-abuse victims and is protected from contact with her mother in the early stages of treatment.

Jane delights in singing in the Odyssey Choir.

Lucy

Lucy is a twenty-six-year-old, black, Protestant middle-class female from a Michigan family of eight children. Her parents were divorced when she was thirteen.

Although in her mother's custody, Lucy was repeatedly rejected by her mother. After her mother's boyfriend attempted to molest her, when she was seventeen, she turned to drugs. Her mother did not protest these actions and married the man, anyway.

Lucy has had two children from her prostitution activities; one has been placed with an aunt and one with Lucy's mother.

At one time when Lucy tried to stop using drugs, her addicted boyfriend broke her jaw, stabbed her, and fractured several of her ribs.

Later, when Lucy was twenty-five, her stepfather raped her in the presence of her mother. In the course of the rape, the stepfather ripped her vagina with an icepick, necessitating a hysterectomy. Lucy screamed to her mother for help, but the mother's reply was, "Don't ask me for help, you black bitch."

Lucy was hospitalized in a mental institution and is now a resident in Odyssey House. Prior to coming to us, Lucy attempted suicide several times. She is now for the first time experiencing the feeling that someone cares, and she has found something to believe in, someone to trust.

Lucy's mother has continued to haunt her, however, by writing letters stating that Lucy's child is dead and implying that the child has been killed.

Lucy's greatest need is not to be left alone.

JILL

Jill is a white, twenty-three-year-old, upper-middle-class Jewish female from a large city in Pennsylvania.

Jill's parents were separated when she was eight, and she went to live with her mother. Her mother introduced Jill to marijuana at age nine and began subjecting her to Lesbian activities at age eleven.

On Jill's thirteenth birthday, as a bas-mitzvah present, her mother decided to have her deflowered by the mother's boyfriend and as an additional gift, introduced her to LSD. From that time on, her mother and any boyfriend of either of them, engaged in group sexual activity. Jill always felt rejected and inadequate, believing the men preferred her more experienced mother, who was only sixteen years her senior.

At age sixteen, when she returned from school one day, Jill found her mother hanging by the neck, a suicide. In shock, Jill was hospitalized for a month. Upon release she began shooting heroin. At twenty-two she became pregnant and addicted to methadone. She was severely injured in an automobile accident and was hospitalized for six weeks, paralyzed from the neck down.

Jill's greatest desire is to be a good mother to her daughter.

TOM

Tom is a white, nineteen-year-old, Methodist, lower-middle-class male from Texas.

When Tom was one year old, his father committed suicide and Tom spent the next four years drifting from hotel to hotel with his alcoholic prostitute mother.

At age three Tom suffered a ruptured appendix. Because she was entertaining a trick, his mother responded to his screams of pain by yelling at him to shut up. She slapped him to silence him. She took him to the hospital twelve hours later. Tom's mother rarely wore any clothes in the house and repeatedly prostituted herself in front of him.

At age five Tom set fire to a hotel room—his mother's place of employment. She was subsequently found to be unfit, and he was placed in foster care for two and a half years, until he was finally adopted.

Tom began using alcohol and sniffing glue at age eight and turned to heroin, cocaine, amphetamines, barbiturates, and hallucinogens at age sixteen.

Tom's fantasy goal in life is to become a hermit and live in a cave where he can be alone and will never again have to be with people who can hurt him.

BETTY

Betty is a black, twenty-three-year-old, middle-class, Protestant female from New York. Betty was raised by her great-grandmother until she was six years old, when she was transferred to her maternal grandparents for two years. She then lived with her parents until age nineteen.

Betty first experienced sexual activity at six years of age with a cousin. At age eight or nine she was fondled by her mother's boyfriend. The mother prostituted herself and Betty, without her husband's (Betty's father's) knowledge.

When Betty was nine, the mother burned the child's vagina with a marijuana cigarette after Betty resisted joining in sexual activities with the mother's boyfriend. From the age of ten until she was nineteen, Betty suffered numerous and repeated beatings by her father.

When she was nineteen, Betty's father became enraged when he caught her with her boyfriend's arm around her while they were sitting on their living-room couch. The father beat her about the head and face until both eyes were swollen shut. This beating caused temporary blindness and a hospitalization for three months, and has left residual severe headaches.

Betty married at nineteen. Within a few months after the

marriage Betty, who was already pregnant, found out that her husband had gotten another woman pregnant as well. At this time Betty was hospitalized, having become mute for one month.

At age twenty-three Betty was raped by her brother-in-law. While she was pregnant, her mother tried to give her an abortion with a coat hanger. The baby was born premature, weighing three pounds, but survived.

She and her two sons are now in the Odyssey Parents' Program. Her greatest hope is for someone to love her.

John

John is a white, twenty-three-year-old Morman male from Utah.

John, at age three, was abandoned by his natural mother. His father, a serviceman, remarried.

At age seven, John was suspended from the second grade because he pulled down a little-girl classmate's panties. His stepmother punished him by chaining him every day, all day, to a pipe in the basement. From eight A.M. until six o'clock at night, when he was permitted upstairs to eat, he was not fed; nor was he able to use bathroom facilities. If he couldn't control himself, he was horrendously whipped. Currently he suffers from many problems concerning elimination and sexuality.

Almost at the end of the year's "sentence," at age eight, John was brought upstairs one evening early and chained to the refrigerator. While he was chained, his six-year-old brother came home from school. The brother made a demand on his stepmother that so infuriated her, she beat him to death with a baseball bat. This took place in front of John, who was tied up in the kitchen. He struggled but was unable to free himself to help his younger brother. His father was present in the house during the beating. The next day John was placed in foster care; his parents were arrested, placed in jail and subsequently convicted of murder.

Eleven foster homes later and having received foster care which can be described as minimal at best and in reality as destructive (including but not limited to sodomy with one foster father), John escaped to the world of alcohol.

He came to us in fear because he did not know how to be a father to his two daughters.

John's greatest striving is to understand how he can stop being so evil a person, one whom God sees fit to constantly punish.

JOANIE

Joanie, a black Catholic female, was born in 1958 in a major city in Pennsylvania. Her mother was an eighteen-year-old, drug-addict prostitute; her real father was unknown, and her substitute father, the mother's paramour at the time, was a twenty-two-year-old unemployed alcoholic.

At five months of age Joanie was abandoned by her mother. The paramour took Joanie to Michigan, where they lived with his mother. This woman—sixty-six years old, living alone and cared for by neighbors, deaf and blind from birth, and having recently had both legs amputated—was the sole adult caring for baby Joanie until she reached six years of age.

After her "grandmother" left to die in a nursing home, Joanie lived with her alcoholic foster father, who put her to work doing farm chores, severely beat her, and starved her as he ate the food provided for her by the neighbors. At age ten Joanie became a ward of the court after complaints by classmates about her severe body odor prompted an investigation of the home. She had never had a bath. She was placed in the county children's home, and all parental rights were terminated.

Over the course of the next five years Joanie was placed in numerous institutions and foster homes. In no place was a treatment plan even developed, let alone followed up. The responses to Joanie's outbreaks of misbehavior were typically corporal punishment or discharge from one institution and transfer to another.

On several occasions Joanie was subjected to sexual activities (heterosexual and homosexual) by guards, supervisors, or foster parents. At age fourteen Joanie became pregnant while in custody, by an attendant at the state juvenile home. Finding herself pregnant, Joanie requested permission to marry a nineteen-year-old known heroin addict pimp–drug dealer. Her request was granted by her social worker. She was married by a judge. She then supported both their drug habits by prostitution almost until the onset of labor.

Her first baby was born in April 1973. In June 1973

Joanie requested an annulment because of her husband's frequent beatings of her and the child. She took the baby to the Receiving Home for temporary custody. An examination of the two-and-a-half-month-old baby revealed that she had been beaten and scratched, but no report was filed with the legal authorities.

In spite of the obvious physical evidence of child abuse, when Joanie moved alone into a separate apartment, the helpless infant was released to her on June 29, 1973. Within twenty-four hours, the baby was brought to the hospital and pronounced dead on arrival. Evidence indicated that Joanie and her husband had spent the night together and that either or both were responsible for the beating to death of this child; no one else had been present. However, the prosecution of Joanie on charges of homicide were dismissed for insufficient proof.

In January of 1975, when sixteen-year-old Joanie was six months pregnant with her second child, she was placed by court order in the Odyssey Parents' Program, a program for pregnant addicts and new mothers and babies. Her husband—not the father of either child—was returned to prison for the criminally insane, for violation of parole.

However, Joanie's first chance for successful treatment—and perhaps her last—was cut short in May 1975. With the help of her civil-rights attorney paid for with federal funds Joanie took her three-week-old baby from the Odyssey facility and returned to the streets of her Michigan city. She has since returned to drug abuse and prostitution. After abandoning her baby, she finally consented to placing the child for adoption. Hopefully, he is at least safe.

All she expects out of life is to destroy herself.

JACK

Jack is a white, nineteen-year-old male from a Jewish and Protestant Virginia family.

Jack's father, a Jew converted to Christianity and a Protestant minister, has served six months in prison and six months in a psychiatric halfway house for molesting a child, a member of his church choral group. From age nine Jack was forced to perform fellatio on his father and to participate in group-sex activities (with his siblings and their friends), which were directed by his father.

Jack ran away from home at age sixteen and began using speed, THC, mescaline, and LSD.

Jack spends many hours hitting a punching bag he named *Dad* and screaming "Kill."

LINDA

Linda is a white, twenty-eight-year-old, Mormon, lower-class female from Utah. She was adopted by her aunt and uncle at birth.

She was raped by her uncle, whom she calls *Dad*, when she was five years old and continued having sexual intercourse with him for five years.

At age nine, Linda began using Thorazine. She started using speed and pills at seventeen and cocaine, heroin, and morphine at twenty-one.

She has three children, all in foster homes. The oldest child is twelve years old.

Her excessively promiscuous life of prostitution and repeated contacts with unclean men has resulted in cancer of the cervix and a total hysterectomy.

Linda presents herself to the world as she feels; she has permanently tattooed a tear under her left eye.

If you believe that America should have laughing, not dying, children at its birthday party, help us in our campaign to establish a *cabinet post for the concerns of children*.

Perhaps it is strange to include such an appeal—or plea—here, but this is my reality, my career, my doing. Case histories, stories such as these, are part of and color all my present experiences. My very being faces this challenge: One cannot be the camp physician at Auschwitz and go home to Christmas dinner unaffected.

The concerns of children must be a first priority as women find themselves. Ours is a special relationship to them. We must safeguard our young, not abandon them. I firmly believe that what changes I have been able to initiate and develop have been due solely to the great number of people who believed with me and pulled alongside. Change occurs because we are many, not few. Do write.

Another disturbing trend is developing due to population

pressures. For centuries woman has been prized most by her society not for her beauty but for the number of healthy children she rears to adulthood. Woman gleaned her greatest self-respect from her reproductive capacity. Man, the hunter, provides; woman, the bearer, mothers. Today esteem is being derived from zero population growth and bearing the two permissible children as close together as possible. Theoretically, this allows the woman more freedom for herself and her man, but in reality she has little upon which to base a sense of self and even less to occupy her time. Modern technology, the ease of homemaking, and small families make time the major factor with which to cope. Modern woman is bored—leisure-laden, superfluous, overeducated, and underutilized! No wonder both she and her children inevitably get into trouble. In families not as disrupted as those I described above, the mother tries to overmother her young because she has no other meaningful outside involvements. The children feel stifled and smothered until eventually they rebel, leaving their mothers even more alone and unchallenged and their fathers angry and hostile at the hurt inflicted. This is best summed up by a joke that appeared in *The New Yorker* years ago. A Helen-Hokinson-type woman emerges from a gorgeous mile-long Rolls Royce, followed by the chauffeur lifting her son out in a wheelchair. The doorman says, "Madam, oh what a shame! What happened to him that he can't walk?" She replies, "Walk? Of course he can walk. Thank God he doesn't have to."

If we continue to do for our children, they won't be physically able to walk in our shoes; their muscles (particularly those involved in adult responsibility) will have atrophied.

A Male Speaks

Once a year I treat myself to a week at the Greenhouse, the marvelous health spa in Texas, combining work with yet another attempt to diet. My weight consciousness is not based upon an obsession with glamour but rather an embarrassing defeat in will power that must medically be turned around; my health as a pre-diabetic demands that I behave.

At the Greenhouse the staff makes me feel womanly and physically good. I enjoy being cloistered for an entire week in a world of women without any men to distract me. It's fun, like the dormitory pajama parties we shared as teen-age girls. Many friendships are made and amazing intimacies are exchanged. Women like one another, and there is little competition. More than one woman remarked upon a special ring of mine that I always wear. Several years ago, Trissa had bought me the ERA aluminum bracelet, the one sold by the League of Women Voters. The bracelet is designed to be worn by all women until the amendment is ratified by the requisite number of states; it is similar to the POW bracelets worn during the Vietnam conflict. Joining her, I proudly wore my piece of tin everywhere. However, Michael noted that it didn't match my evening clothes or life style.

One night Michael surprised me with a ring from Bergdorf Goodman, which he had had specially designed. It was gold, with the initials ERA in diamonds. The card said, "Beware: gold and diamond chains are as real and hard to escape as iron ones. Wear this to confront and remind your sisters who have made it (or us)." Symbols always!

The women at the Greenhouse hunger for activity, for meaning in life, for something to do. They are intelligent and sufficiently wealthy to be able to undertake anything and everything, and yet, pills, alcohol, affairs, and boredom are the reality of more than one or two. Each time I visit, I puzzle on why this happens; yet, I hesitate to ask. The women often ask me for advice—how to be, how to become, how to overcome the emptiness, the loneliness, that even great wealth doesn't fill.

On the Wednesday of this past stay one of my Odyssey colleagues, Martin Hassner, who happened to be in Texas at the same time, paid a visit. We discussed the whys, the hows, of men and women, and I told him what I had been writing. He asked if I would like him to write down his thoughts as a male contemporary who had observed many couples. His birthday is a day after mine, so I replied, "The thoughts of a fellow Scorpio are always welcome. Send them quickly and I'll include them."

He sent them, and here they are. He sums up how some males feel trapped in the crazy stereotyped model that now faces so many. There are echoes of many clichés of our Madison Avenue type of programming. It is mandatory that we prevent this from continuing to happen.

Thoughts on Women and Careers
MARTIN HASSNER

The emphasis is on the wrong syllable. The problem is not women and "how to handle a career" . . . but rather why are we (men) allowing our women to waste away on tennis courts, in department stores shopping, at long lunches, mired in self-pity, and unable to get untracked and out into the world again.

Start with children and the end of romance. Take one energetic, reasonably well educated, career-girl type who really wants to "meet someone" and "work for a while" (of course, that seems respectable . . . I mean, why not?). And then "start a family." She meets "someone," and because she is all the things she is and all the rest, they are married. And also she does work for a while. He is "up and coming" and she works because she really doesn't want to stop just yet. They furnish a house together and work together. They share hurried breakfasts before rushing off, taking subways or buses or whatever, kissing good-bye, and starting the day. It is exciting, exhilarating, more fun than anything has ever been. They continue to share the day when it is over. They "date," eating out, going to movies. They rush home to homework for him and some semblance of playing house for her. The day stimulates their nights in bed, and bed feeds the following day—and off again. Time rushes furiously, and if he is full of his own successes, she is also enticing to all those married men who surround her with knowing looks and sly invitations. Because she is more exciting, and she knows it. Because she is now one of them, no longer to be feared because of what she might do at the end of an affair. She's safe. Married. She knows what it's all about. And her husband listens to her tales—and it stimulates him. She is desired by other men, she is exciting, full of life. And she goes home *with him* to bed. There is an equality. They are genuinely sharing. Time, success, "adventures." It's two of them against the world.

And then, after a while, she tires. She really never works at that "career." She has attained her goal. Now after months of zooming around, she wants to stop. Fix up a new and bigger apartment. Share her pleasure with girlfriends. Get off the rat race and slow down, like a nice married lady should. And her husband? Well, how could he deny her this? He doesn't need her money. It's been nice . . . but he's making money now, and it will be nice to have her playing house for him. It shows how he has matured, how respectable he is. And so he says, "Sure, stop."

And she does. Blissfully. And gets pregnant. And despite the occasional nausea, she continues to be blissful. Floating. Time stops. The rush is over. It's been replaced by this warm, lovely calm. And so it starts. First one, then several more. She assumes the responsibility for the children. She works at it. It is difficult. She reads about child development. She plunges into how they learn and develop and grow. She uses her heart and her mind. And she's good at it. And her husband tries, too, but not very hard. He's working and concentrating and succeeding. They're earning more than they ever imagined they could. He has a little power and a lot of worry . . . he's involved "out there," and he trusts her decisions at home. What house to buy, how to furnish, who their friends are, how they entertain, how she raises the kids, what she thinks of their schooling. They buy her a house in the suburbs because the school system is "good." At least, she thinks so, and she's been reading about all of that and she knows what the kids need and he's delighted that she's "taken over" this aspect of their lives. But he doesn't ever say that and really never quite reaches that thought consciously. It's just that she's there to do all of this and he doesn't have to worry about it.

He still tells her of his business conquests. She pays attention, often has opinions, but he doesn't listen to them after a while. How would she remember how it is in the office? It's been years since she's ever gotten into the big city for more than a few hours every couple of months. And yet somehow they continue to share . . . but the fabric, the texture of that sharing, shrinks to threads. He doesn't even know that he's stopped listening. If there are serious problems with the kids, he does concentrate but otherwise shuts it all off. He's doing his job; she's doing hers.

And that's the beginning of the end of the romance which was so easily changed by the children and by their presence in the house. Romance—that sweet time when their sex life was fed as much by the lives they were leading together as by the easy accessibility of two willing bodies—that romance is gone forever. The children, familiarity, separateness, and finally, his need to again be stimulated, to show off, to be involved, so that the pressure of business is not all—at last that romance is gone. Not love—romance.

And what of her? The children are all in school. Suddenly for the first time, she is no longer a slave to time. Suddenly she can control it . . . more so now than during her pregnancy. Then time had meaning . . . days moved into weeks and months, and the expectation of growing life inside her was so different, so consuming in itself.

What can she do? How much tennis? How much shopping? She could go back to work. But what of a résumé? What can she *really* do? What is she trained for? Who will be interested in her?

And the children do need her at home. And all the carpooling. And P.T.A. And she should be home when they come home. And he needs her. And who would do the shopping? And on and on. And she says, "Well, maybe next year." And the rotting of her mind, of her being, begins.

It's difficult to remember when she stopped reading. Her current events seem to come from television. But she never really cared about governments—local or foreign. She and her friends always have so much to talk about. For hours and hours. But what does she say to him? And does he care any more? He gets a lot of things outside the home . . . and maybe he doesn't care any more.

She could go to work, lead her own life. It says so in *Ms*. In *Cosmo*. In *Redbook*. In best sellers. It would be better for everyone. But it means getting into the city. Commuting. There'd be no time, no time . . . she doesn't even ask for what and how important the "what" will be . . .

And he permits it. He sees now how limited she is . . . especially in comparison to his new girlfriend. His wife's not into what's happening. She never says anything that interests him any more. What does she know? She's not even . . . she can't even . . . does she understand where he is now? What he wants?

What he wants and what he's been looking for and experimenting with is *romance*. Stimulation. Sex is really not the point. That is so available . . . but it is not the point. She doesn't interest him any more . . . but he loves her and it's okay. Her working would be a pain. So much trouble, so many arrangements with the kids. Who will watch them? Cook dinner? Too much trouble. Forget it. Why don't you take some courses at the community college? Learn to play bridge? Go back and relearn to play the piano? If she's back working, that will mean they'll travel together, go home together. He won't really have those extra hours with Ms. X for a drink . . . to talk . . . to . . .

And so she can't quite make the effort, can't quite get over the fear of rejection. The need to compete with all those women who've been in the job market . . . in the world, working and earning and competing. She can't quite give herself back to time; think about getting up at 6:00 or 6:30 A.M.; think about all of those arrangements. After all, she doesn't *have to work*. What difference will it make?

When a woman realizes that she is no longer what she was . . . or can be because her life has gone soft, the rhythm gone out of it—

When a woman realizes that having a career or simply working will put her back on the plane that she has left—

When a woman realizes that she is more when she is working, producing, being involved . . . more important to those around her, more interesting—

When she realizes that her mind is her most precious possession and that she must reclaim it by once again disciplining time, by making the physical effort that must be made—

When she realizes these things, she will make the effort to get back into the world, and romance will be reborn.

Life cannot be vicarious and be vital. Second-hand living through other people, a husband or children, is as addictive as any drug habit. The techniques for breaking that vicarious life habit are similar to those for the kicking of any addiction. An understanding of self, specific goals, self-assurance, positive self-image . . . on and on . . .

The status of women can be lifted when the self-image is lifted and the understanding of life's priorities are set once again.

The problem to be solved is not how a career woman handles her house, children, and husband. If she is a career woman *SHE HANDLES THEM QUITE NATURALLY. IT'S PART OF THE DEFINITION.* Harder perhaps, yes, much more difficult . . . but nonetheless true. The problem then concerns the millions of women who waste into a living death because they can't kick the habit of living through other lives.

The divorce rate, adultery, drinking. It's all part of the overall problem of lives gone soft. Of people—productive, once successful people—left behind. If there ever was a need for consciousness-raising . . . we have one.

We must prevent this waste of womanlife. We need a *withstanding toughness*. This doesn't mean to imply selfishness or lack of sympathy. Withstanding toughness is the ability to make good decisions, to handle competing priorities fairly, to use time efficiently, and to conduct one's life according to internal value systems, regardless of the pressures faced. Withstanding toughness is imposed on self not on others. One must begin to be oneself even if it means aloneness. There is a difference between aloneness and loneliness. Loneliness is a painful feeling of not having anyone with whom to share. Many people are lonely even in a crowd, and many marriages are little more than legalized bonds between two separate, no-longer-communicating, widely-experientially-separated persons. Status doesn't necessarily yield togetherness.

Aloneness is a human reality. It is the realization that much of life's sadness, pain, joy, is faced and felt alone within one's private being. Withstanding toughness makes it all possible.

A Bridge to Woman Faces Her Sisterhood

There is so much I want to say. Women are full-functioning people and to define ourselves and be defined as derivative of husbands or children is as much a crime against them as it is against ourselves. Yet the answers are within only our control. Women must change, seek, act and . . .

I have had to overcome the strong desire to tear up this whole manuscript and begin again to write the book I had first contemplated. I wanted to filter out all the negativity I had experienced and select inspirational stories to encourage young women—no, all women—to stretch out, move forward, and *be*. I wanted to tell only the good for fear that being totally honest would frighten the timid, weary the brave, and defeat us all.

I wanted to write about Bernice Lavin, dynamic vice-president of Alberto-Culver, who side by side with her husband, has built a gigantic corporation while overcoming the physical handicap of a leg left lame by polio; or to write about Dorothy Speller, M.D., black woman physician, whose father struggled against poverty, educating his children until one son was the plaintiff in the landmark Supreme Court case that integrated the United States Armed Services in the 1940s, and until another became general counsel for the NAACP. Dorothy herself is one of the most successful physicians in the country. She flies her own airplane, has an art collection, and two of her children (a daughter and son) have finished medical school and received fellowships in psychiatry at Harvard. Another daughter was brain-damaged at birth, and both Dorothy and her husband, when he was secretary of health of Pennsylvania, saw that special work programs were developed by state government to enable the educable retarded to support themselves.

I had to resist the temptation to begin again and write the propaganda so desperately needed. Books like *Total Woman*, by Marabel Morgan, irritate my core being and turn me completely off, as do all statements, works, feelings of, by, or for women that express in any way that we are less than helpmates, companions, sharers, friends, and equals to our men. I wondered if the kind of honesty that shows it all is a good thing, and as usual, self-doubt set in—and I was paralyzed. I just couldn't write. Deadlines drew closer. Panic progressed.

I went to the opening of the First Women's Bank in New York. Since Lucy Jarvis had proposed me to be a board member, I looked for her. I wanted to ask her, "How goes it?" She wasn't there, but her charming son Peter was instead. He shared with Michael and me that his mother was fine, busy as ever producing TV documentaries, and being sought after by all who are in the know. Lucy is a truly remarkable woman, with everything she touches turning to success. Certainly, all of you should share her story, and that of Lenore Hershey, who recently attained that coveted pinnacle in the world of women's magazines, managing editor of *The Ladies' Home Journal*. This took work, dedication, competence, and commitment; Lenore has them all. After thirty-nine years on the bench, Judge Justine Wise Polier has retired to devote herself to the Children's Defense Fund. She is one of the few ombudspersons for children the nation has. She becomes more beautiful with each passing year; she leads us all in the positive use of retirement hours which are full-functioning and in the service of others. She triumphs over the aging process which cripples so many other women who have based their beauty on the exterior, rather than on completeness within. And I cannot forget Jeanette Picard, who defied space forty years before she defied men, to finally be ordained in 1974. She, too, has the special glow of achievement. Patsy Mink has announced her candidacy for the United States Senate, which with its total absence of women members, painfully confronts the nation as to the true position of the female within the policy-making echelon of this country. I wish her well in this, her statement for women, even though politically we are far apart. Women are found on all sides of the political spectrum—and correctly so; we differ in our beliefs, the same way men do, but we must stand together on women's issues and we must speak with one voice for our children. I intuit the pain of a mother, regardless of her background, who must rock her baby to sleep at night because he or she cries from hunger; but I am even more horrified at the mother who has become so alienated from even her own child that she subverts the food money for her baby to buy drugs to shoot into her or her old man's arm.

The point must be made as strongly as possible again and again: *women make it.* We can successfully combine being people with marriage, children, and a full career—*success is ours,* though the road is hard and the system designed against us. What has happened to me in the last few years since I started walking this trip to awareness of womanlife is that I have lost my illusions that life is fair. I have realized that appreciating the injustice does not cause me to cop out, nor do I become overwhelmed with such hostility that I stop growing, experiencing, succeeding—legitimate fears to which too many women succumb.

I have become tolerant and at ease with myself. I am no longer embarrassed when a woman is foolish or empty. I know plenty of men who are; and a woman has a right to be herself. I no longer feel every woman is a reflection of me, but rather that we can move together, each in our own way, for the betterment of us all. Men are not our enemies; as we read in

Hassner's letter, they are as trapped by this foolishness as we are.

This book is probably filled with inconsistencies and compromises, even muddled philosophy. That is important and should not be changed. Consistency is not the *sine qua non* of truth or of being or of worth; I know that one day I feel one way, and then there are days I feel another. This book is an outcry of the feelings that I have—and they are valid for me and perhaps, I hope, for others. The freedom to think, experience and feel as you will, undefended and floating, is an invaluable step toward being, becoming, self.

And so, I finally decided to leave it as it is and trust it will be a *cinema verité* of womanlife. Many thoughts, many journeys. For me the experiences with the prostitutes provide a Fellini backdrop to the world of womanlife.

Early in my first analysis with a woman therapist I remember being amazed to learn how much people could differ without one being right and the other wrong. We are limited by our own experiences, always walking in our own shadows. As is natural with me, I became aware out of an experience with food.

Lindsey had just been born, and it was my thirty-first birthday. Michael surprised me with a birthday party at Pavillon; he challenged Henri Soulé to outdo himself. No simple task. Michael and Soulé had become fast friends years before over a duck improperly carved and a Musigny slightly turned. When Soulé was to die years later during lunch at Côte Basque, the staff pleaded with the office of the chief medical examiner to let Michael sign the death certificate. They knew Soulé, who was a master of details, a true perfectionist, would have wanted it that way.

I was in the midst of telling my woman analyst about this perfect party, with the special asparagus soufflé au gratin and the marvelous cake with crème de menthe icing and so on, until it became free-associated with sexuality, simply because a great many things in my head translate into sexual satisfactions—especially Soulé's salmon mousse in two sauces, lobster and champagne. I explained enthusiastically that the mousse was absolutely orgastic—it was the total gustatory experience, the salmon mousse, with its own flavor, combined with the two sauces, and the texture ... And then she interjected, "Judi, I'm having a hard time following you. Let me share a story from my own life. When I was a beginning resident doctor, I had tuna-fish-salad sandwiches every day because I never even thought of eating anything else. I was actually afraid to taste anything else, too insecure to try to order something unknown. And then one day the food counter at the drug store sent me chicken salad by mistake. I was almost devastated, but again, I was too unsure to send it back or make a complaint. So I ate it, and I liked the chicken salad. From then on I was able to rotate between the tuna and the chicken salad." As she told me this story, I remember suddenly having cold chills on the couch and feeling, "There's no way she'll ever understand me." There was no way I could cross from my experience to hers. But still we were both expressions of womanlife.

She doesn't get her feet, as well as her mouth, into every single food experience there is. My couch, my way, is sensual, endlessly sensual. I see things in sensual terms or perhaps *earthy* is a better word. Sensuality and sexuality are not the same. An example is how I feel about furs. Tactile. One night I returned home from a dance with a borrowed, full-length, gorgeous mink coat. It isn't the mink I remember, but the coming home, taking off my clothes, turning the coat inside out, and having Michael photograph me in it. Michael claims my idea of a perfect gift for him is a mink jock strap turned inside out and that one of the reasons he loves me so is because I taught him to feel that way. Having been trained, before he married me, to be a "Portnoy," Michael subconsciously frequently got guilt feelings about skin pleasure.

A classmate of mine married into one of America's richest families, and I'll never forget my shock and surprise at her cotton trousseau: cotton tank shirts, cotton panties, and on and on. Every time I could afford to, I bought silk and lace. I inquired, "Why do you save money this way?" She responded honestly, "No one knows what I wear. No one sees what's underneath." But I thought, "I'd know it; I know what I wear. It is next to my skin."

People are obviously different. But that doesn't mean that one is right and the other wrong; there are problems when we don't communicate or learn to respect one another's ways. I trust I have shown the many different kinds of women I've walked beside—from the whores of Las Vegas to the women at the top—all intimate reflections of womanlife. Sisterhood has to speak for all women. And women are vastly different. Some of us wear cotton underwear, and some of us wear silk.

At Odyssey the chronic depressive patients receive a special "awareness" to help them grow. An awareness is a repetitive exercise which hammers home a message that a person must learn in order to get well. Each depressed person receives a pan of white beach sand; before morning and evening meeting he or she must heat it in the oven. Then, in front of the entire community at meeting time, the patient has to remove his or her shoes and stockings, stand in the sand and cry out three times, "Someday I am going to enjoy walking barefoot in the sand." Many people have to be freed to enjoy pleasure, to feel good, to love and be loved. They—we—have to cry out until we actually want to live.

Two Proverbs (No, better yet, Two Inspirational Sayings) for the Sisterhood

The first is carried on a calling card—or should I say business card?—to be used in moments when faced with male chauvinistic conduct. It reads:

> Sir, you have just insulted a woman. This card has been chemically treated. Your penis will fall off in three days.

The second is best engraved on a plaque in offices wherever women work. I found it first at Nellie's Place, a hostel for distraught, lost abused women in Toronto. June Frayne, who sits on their Board of Directors, had referred me there to see the outstanding work they do. They see over 4,000 women a year. The saying goes as follows:

> Whatever women do, they must do it twice as well to be thought half as good. Luckily it's not difficult.

You know, I think I'd like to change the title of this book once again—to *Walk In My Shoes and Leap Over the Wall.*

A Manifesto for the Sisterhood

One of the most articulate, charismatic women in the early anti-slavery and women's rights movement was a black freewoman, Sojourner Truth. She had spent half of her life within slavery. She is one of my role models; from her gut-level intelligence came words more eloquent than the Boston Harvard prose of the aristocratic abolitionists.

On one occasion she became incensed at the rhetoric which was pouring forth on all sides about the special, delicate nature of women which mandated extraordinary care and concern on the part of the male. Indeed, we still hear echoes of this today in the stop-ERA movement, whose adherents often claim that they do not denigrate or consider women inferior but on the contrary hold them in such high esteem—on pedestals—that they wish only to ensure that the special protections traditionally afforded women are preserved. Too high a price is paid for these "considerations." The same goals could be accomplished by non-sexist legislation. For instance, ERA might eliminate alimony for women as a matter of course, but in no way does it prevent child-care allowances and additional support to the parent regardless of whether that parent is male or female. Often there are situations where the woman should pay alimony. A great number of women are earning more money than their husbands, thereby substantially changing the family's lifestyle; frequently, the husband contributes time and energy to helping his wife advance. Certainly mine has, as has Patsy Mink's husband, who has relocated several times when she has won elections and changed jobs. If divorce comes later, husbands who have contributed to a better lifestyle are entitled to the same compensation as wives. This has always been true in community-property states.

One of the most difficult problems faced by two-career families is that of a geographic relocation offering advancement opportunity for one of the couple. This has been solved in various ways within different marriages—traditionally one or another, usually the wife, follows, but lately more and more couples have been living separately in two cities and commuting to share time together. For many this new life style appears to be working well, but how it will affect children is not yet known.

But back to Sojourner Truth and her anger in the 1840s. She rose to her feet to disclaim the frailty of woman as follows:

> Well, chilern, whar dar is so much racket dar must be something out o'kilter. I tink dat 'twixt de niggers of de Souf and de women at de Norf all a talking about rights, de white men will be in a fix pretty soon. But what's all dis here talkin' 'bout? Dat man ober dar say dat women needs to be helped into carriages, and lifted ober ditches, and to have de best place every whar. Nobody ever help into carriages, or ober mud puddles, or gives me any best places . . . and ar'n't I a woman? Look at me! Look at my arm! . . . I have plowed, and planted, and gathered into barns, and no man could head me—and ar'n't I a woman? I could work as much as a man (when I could get it) and bear de last as well—and ar'n't I a woman? I have borne five children and I seen 'em mos' all sold off into slavery, and when I credit out with a mother's grief, none but Jesus heard—and ar'n't I a woman?
>
> Sojourner Truth
1st Women's Rights Convention

Amen, Sojourner Truth

In a treatise from the Proceedings of the American Philosophical Society Volume 117 No. 2 April 1973 entitled "Education and Sex: The Medical Case Against Higher Education for Women—England 1870–1900 author Joan N. Burstyn quotes a leading doctor of the day:

Those grievous maladies which torture a woman's earthly existence, called leucorrhoea, amenorrhoea, dysmenorrhoea, chronic and acute ovaritis, prolapsus uteri, hysteria, neuralgia, and the like, are indirectly affected by food, clothing, and exercise; they are directly and largely affected by the causes that will be presently pointed out, and which arise from a neglect of the peculiarities of a woman's organization. The regimen of our schools fosters this neglect. The regimen of a college arranged for boys, if imposed on girls, would foster it still more.

The need for women to rest while menstruating did not cease once menstruation had become established. The period of menstruation was always one of heightened danger to the nervous system: menstruation resembles pregnancy in giving rise to an exalted central nervous erethism, and ovulation is a primary exciting cause of epileptic, womitive, and hysterical convulsion. While women's nerve-centers were always in a state of greater instability than men's, it was during menstruation that overwork was most dangerous: There are few (physicians) who have not seen bright careers of mental work and usefulness cut short, never to be resumed, after a few days of hard mental strain during a menstrual period. It cannot, therefore, be too strongly insisted on that, with the young and the delicate, at any rate, and to some extent with all women, the period of menstruation should be a period of comparative repose, mental and bodily, but especially mental.

This nonsense was not dispensed with until 1926 when Britain's Air Ministry needed women. Then the official stand changed:

> Any doctor who has really studied the subject knows that menstruation is a perfectly physiological and not a pathological process, though many medical men are biased, largely because they judge by the patients they see, instead of by normal people . . .
>
> The menstrual period has been brought up as an objection to every profession which women have wished to enter. It has never yet been found to be a practical objection, and remains merely a theoretical one.

Ms. Burstyn concludes by writing:

> According to Anderson, women could undertake higher education without endangering their reproductive capacity.
>
> That the views of Anderson, and those doctors who thought as she did, prevailed was due also to a shift in attitude, by the turn of the century, among the middle classes in Britain. Their ideal of protected womanhood, so vehemently defended by Maudsley, Thorburn, and Withers Moore, had never been extended to women of the lower classes, who worked as domestics and factory hands. When a growing number of middle-class women found it necessary to join their lower-class sisters in earning a living, the ideal had to be changed so that unmarried women, at least, could enter occupations that did not demean their families. In the end, not even the power of medical argument could stem the tide of human ambition and economic necessity.

Amen, Ms. Burstyn.

Woman Faces Her Sisterhood

Human ambition and economic necessity wrought more changes than simply an acceptance of menstruation as a natural physiological phenomenon; they ushered in a era in which not only did women have the vote but they were elected to office. Many began to serve in state houses across the nation. These women formed the Organization of Women Legislators, acroynm OWL.

It was at an OWL annual convention in 1972 in Salt Lake City that I met Representative Chris Miller, a dynamic woman who represents the Fort Worth area. It is she who carries the first proverb on a handy business card. Once again I had been asked to give the keynote dinner speech to the assembled women. I had every intention of being light and witty, but all that faded when I learned that Arizona had sent a contingent of stop-ERA women legislators to block the affirmation of a resolution by OWL endorsing the passage of the ERA.

I could not believe that women who served in government could become so confused as to the real issues that they would be willing to accept second citizenry. Indeed, once one was through all the rhetoric, it was easy to realize that everyone in favor of the family, traditional values, and maintenance of the home had to support equal dignity and position for both mother and father. NOW was sponsoring an enlightening advertising awareness campaign. The ad showed a picture of a beautiful baby girl. The caption began: "This healthy, normal baby has a handicap. She was born female." It went on to describe the adverse economic conditions she will face the rest of her life. It ended by saying: "Think about your own daughter—she's handicapped too."

Certainly those who claim the loudest to believe in the American way of life must work the hardest to see that all have the opportunity to participate.

I was pained by the actions of the old women of OWL which ironically enough shares the same acronym as the Old Women's Liberation Movement, a very strong feminist group. No single group of women suffer more than the aged, if and when a woman's primary value is based on her sexual and reproductive appeal. Old women live longer and have less relevance than almost any other group in our nation. But here were old women, chosen to lead others who were more concerned with defending their life style choices than securing fairness and justice for other women, many of whom had great responsibilities of single-parent child care and long lives ahead. To maintain the status quo at their expense was unconscionable. I threw away my prior speech, I began *this* book, I put on my shoes and leapt over the wall.

I would like to share with you that first speech of my new awareness, born out of anger and inability to continue to rationalize. I would like to share it in toto, even though it repeats some anecdotes already written on prior pages. It summarizes many thoughts and because I like symmetry, it pleases me to end as I began.

A Recalled Speech

I'm delighted to be here in Salt Lake tonight but I must admit, slightly uptight. This is the most difficult subject of all for me to write or speak on: the identity crisis we, as women, face today in the United States. We are confronted with finding a new role for ourselves, as well as redefining that part of our old role which we will keep. Actually, I am delighted at the opportunity because I have signed a contract with Saturday Review Press to write a book on female identity. As I research the topic, I am finding it almost impossible to begin. The conflicts make it too painful.

However, tonight it begins. As I speak to you, the beginning of my first chapter is being taped.

The toastmistress introduced me as recently having had a baby. Overdue by about two weeks, Sarah was born on Friday the thirteenth, weighing ten and a half pounds; she already had a mind of her own. The doctors had tried to induce the birth three times before her actual arrival date; she resisted successfully the "pit" drips. It was as if she were saying from "the get," "Mommy, I intend to meet the world on my terms." My second daughter is actually fourteen years younger than my first, and she faces a different reality as a woman than her sister, myself, her grandmother, or the great-grandmother for whom she is named and who chained herself to the White House in order to secure the vote. Since my mother successfully practiced corporation law for years, I represent a third generation of emancipated females. My other grandmother was a real-estate broker. Sarah has running in her veins two bloodlines of women who have functioned in many diverse roles.

In the thirty-five minutes allotted to me—and it will be thirty-five minutes because I believe in structure and discipline—I will share with you a few thoughts which I have jotted down. I want to talk to you as one woman to another, as women of accomplishments engaged in the challenge of finding self. I cannot believe what I have found here: intelligent women opposed to the Equal Rights Amendment. Not all of you, of course, but too many of you—one would be too many. You, women legislators who enact the laws of this country, must stand firm and lead us in the conviction that we who represent one-half of humanity are equal to the other half. Equality does not mean sameness. We can be physically different and respect those differences without being discriminated for or against economically, civilly, religiously, legally, socially, or even emotionally.

The issue of the draft doesn't bother me; I am willing to fight along with my husband to preserve this country, and I would grieve for my daughters, the same as my sons, if one died in action. As to coed bathrooms, there is one in my home and I am not destroyed, but I agree with most people that there is a logical, nondiscriminatory reason for providing separate but equal public bathrooms. However, if the lack of rest rooms for women is given as the justification for why women can't attend law school or join the bar association (as it was in my Mother's days), then I'd integrate the rest rooms; it is the lesser of two evils. I feel the same way when such nonsense stands in the way of a woman receiving equal pay for equal work.

Ladies, women, sisters, when you get down to the nitty-gritty and all is said and done and the rhetoric finished—*we are equal.* There is no other way to look at it.

Since I usually teach through vignettes which make a point, I'd like to do so now, sharing with you several personal experiences and the thoughts they evoke in me as a female person trying to find my own personhood.

Perhaps the most important crisis in my own search for self occurred when I was in Washington in 1971. Why it took that long for me to begin the questioning stems probably from the fact that I am a third-generation liberated female and therefore was most protected from acculturating destructive stereotypes. It never had dawned on me that women could not go to law school; my Mother had. Or that women could not go to medical school; my pediatrician had. Or that women couldn't be or do whatever they wished to be or do; my early experiences had been with women doing whatever they wished to do.

They were fortunate, having come to America generations before and having succeeded. Adequate wealth made possible a different set of circumstances; my Grandmother had raised her children through governesses, as her Mother had before her; hence, it wasn't considered wrong or incorrect for a woman to leave the care of her children to others. Actually, that was the way things were always done generation after generation. Women were expected to do civic work, church work, and so forth. Criticism and guilt for doing activities outside of the home were not part of their reality.

In 1971 I had been invited to Washington at the request of the Republican Party. Then as now, I considered myself a conservative Republican, since I believe the minimum government is the best government. People should be allowed to grow and develop with the fewest controls, but government must provide a milieu of opportunity, challenge, encouragement, and justice for all Americans, regardless of their packaging.

The Republican Congressional Task Force wanted me to discuss the crisis created by drug addiction in Vietnam. We believed—and still believe—there were twenty-five to seventy-five thousand young men addicted in Southeast Asia. We feared these young men would come home to every town and hamlet in the United States addicted and having formed a network of supply which would infect the entire country. Odyssey had a plan to prevent this from happening. We wanted those in power to listen and act. They didn't, and the plague came to pass. But this is not my topic tonight.

While I was lecturing to the Republican task force, I became quite emotional. I talked as the American wife and mother I was. It was the same kind of reaction which had caused John Lindsay to characterize me as hysterical a year before when I confronted him on the epidemic of adolescent addiction facing New York City's children. I don't resent the word *hysterical,* since the uterus is definitely part of my destiny (the Greek word *hyster* means "womb").

I did my thing in my emotional way. I cried out my demand that my children be able to go to a drug-free school. American-mother me expected these congressional fathers to do something to ensure my children's safety. I just knew action would be forthcoming, and I was pleased with myself as I went to lunch with one of the members of Congress. As we walked into the Senate dining room he turned to me and asked, "Judi, when you were speaking, did Congressman X have his fly zipped?" And I responded, "I beg your pardon?" And he repeated, "Did he have his fly zipped?" I retorted, "Really, Louis, I was not in the mood to notice, one way or another, but why do you ask?" He clarified: "Well, if Congressman X had his fly zipped, that would be the first time he has ever spoken to a woman with it zipped."

One might be expected to have a sense of humor about this, but not I; I'm known for my quick and abrasive retort. And I turned and said, "I hope you'll run somebody against him in the Republican primaries because I don't want the likes of him voting on the SST, since obviously all the blood in his body is displaced downward into his genitals, leaving an insufficient amount to sustain good brain function."

My day was ruined. I had learned once again that when a woman becomes adequate in the vertical, many men must strive to place her once again on the horizontal. [I vowed that day I would never publicly be ⊢ but always I.] Though the SST quip was satisfying to me, it didn't answer the question. I was angry but troubled. I met with several of my staff to consider whether even though I served as adviser to fifty-one members of the United States Congress concerning drug addiction and the problems of the socially disadvantaged, it would be better heard if the problem of "the Vietnam menace" were articulated by male members of my staff rather than myself.

I asked my staff, male and female, the pointed question: "Would the men in Congress listen better if my words were spoken in bass or baritone?" The answer came back gently but firmly: *a unanimous "Yes."* And then I had to make a choice between my right as a woman to articulate my opinions based on my expertise or getting the job done, which could be accomplished more effectively by my writing the speeches for one of my male assistants to deliver. I am sorry to report that

I acted as women have done for centuries, as Abigail Adams did. I elected to defer my needs to the service of others. I stepped aside and let a man speak my words.

Another silly, small incident brought home the foolishness of today's attitudes toward women, particularly when we attempt to do consciousness-raising. I had received a letter from the Columbia Law School Alumni Association signed by a distinguished alumnus, Colonel Melvin Krulewich. It began, "Dear Brother-in-Law." I laughed and thought as I looked at my pregnant belly, "How truly inappropriate." Since I knew Colonel Krulewich, as he had been in the same law office with my mother, I wrote back a letter stating that I would be happy to donate to the Columbia Law School Alumni Association when they included me in the salutation. I suggested that "Dear Brothers- and Sisters-in-Law" would be nicer, but as it now stood, I was excluded and therefore I interpreted that I was not expected to send money. (I am continually amazed, hurt, and angered at how difficult it is for so many—men and women—to call me Doctor.)

Krulewich never answered. However, two years later, while chatting with my Mother and in response to her question, he told her that the letter had been mysteriously lost but miraculously found. Just the past week it had appeared on his desk. But he still didn't answer the issue raised—he did an even more interesting thing; he suggested, "Bea, do something about your radical daughter. Explain to her that we at Columbia didn't mean anything. She should be mature enough to learn to behave as a grown-up woman. At Columbia we are used to saying 'brothers-in-law,' and we will continue to say 'brothers-in-law.' It is her problem that she doesn't realize it is the generic which includes your sex." Whereupon my Mother called me up on the telephone to say, "Judi, please stop making waves! Will you please behave?" And I replied, "Mother, when will you please accept the fact that I am almost forty? If you had stood firm, I could behave. I'll stand firm so that your granddaughters never are left out."

Yet another awareness for me occurred just last week, when I did the staffing patterns of our new facility in New Orleans. The head of nursing from New Hampshire will become the director, and her husband will be her assistant. Initially, I had automatically listed them as co-directors, even though she has been on staff two years and he is new. However, she confronted me, saying, "Judi, I have had two years' experience with Odyssey, which should count more than his higher degree or his maleness. Why am I not in charge? Haven't I earned the top position?" I replied, "But Maggie, you'll destroy your marriage. No husband can work for his wife." She asked, "Why not?" To which I replied, "Women's liberation is different from 'wives' liberation.' There is no possible way that I could be my husband's boss." Maggie responded, "Barry will understand; he knows that I deserve the position." This younger generation is so much further along than mine. It is beautiful to experience.

It's extremely important to realize the differences in generations and in awareness due to present-day consciousness-raising. An outgrowth of the whole liberation movement—the *human* liberation movement—is that we are beginning to ask the right questions, questions which previously we thought we had answers to. And so I feel good when looking at my newest daughter, who since five days old has worn beautiful diamond earrings given by her godmother (ears pierced in the newborn nursery after tremendous objection from my husband, who thought it was too traumatic but who acceded to my argument that it was no more so than the early operation on our baby boys that he insisted upon).

In the hospital I had the newborn's horoscope read, but my husband would not listen because it predicted great success for this younger daughter, partially based upon her very positive manipulation of her male associates later in life. My husband retorted, "Never; she belongs to Daddy."

We, women of one generation, must realize we talk a different language from the younger women of today or tomorrow. And yet we must sit down to listen to them—for we make the rules they have to follow or rebel against. It is they who must do most of the identity-crises solving. We can make it easier or harder for them by what we do today. We must try to identify with them, not with our own past conditioning and foolishness. We have a sacred trust to make it better for them as women. Our movies, our ads, our general education—our everything—militates against a young woman's approaching resolution of her adolescent identity crisis with a concept that the world is open to her.

Recently in New Hampshire, while driving with the family, my older son said, "When I grow older, I don't know if my wife will be able to work." I responded, "Why, Jud?" "Because, Mommy, there will be nobody to take care of the children." He was perceptive and right. The whole area of privately afforded child care, which my generation and those before knew, will not be the reality for the next group of young women. And unless adequate day-care centers or alternate family life styles are provided, many young women will have to stay home. My son continued, "I wonder how many babies my wife and I will have. She has as much right to be a mommy as I have to be a daddy, so I guess I'll work Monday, Wednesday, and Friday, and she'll work Tuesday, Thursday, and Saturday. On Sunday we'll rest and make babies." I suppose that will be an answer for some, but in professions such as law, medicine, government, and so forth, such alternation does not seem too practical a solution. It would be better to develop an adequate system of alternative child care which doesn't tie one parent to the home. Certainly, other countries, such as China, Russia, and Israel, have been able to do so. However, my younger son, who has a more conformist, less innovative solution-seeking personality chimed in, "You know, Jud, your wife may be as intelligent as you are, and when you're the doctor and she's the nurse, you can't really succeed working part time."

I report this with great pain. My husband and I are both physicians, and yet my eight-year-old, who experiences us both every day, has been so conditioned by society that already, regardless of what he sees in his own home, he assumes that the man will be the doctor and the woman will be the nurse. Not that I consider it is less to be a nurse than a doctor, but both options should be open to both sexes. Indeed, recently more men are becoming nurses and women doctors. We must present a world to our children that allows them to find whatever is their own level, based upon what they themselves are and not on the sexual difference.

My Mother's generation had a different way of coping. Her attitudes are probably similar to many of yours in this room, as you are nearer in age. In the 1920s and '30s the concept was, "Don't make waves, be supercompetent, accept that you must get better grades than the men in order to be admitted into male-dominated and -controlled professional schools, play by their standards, compete from their ballpark; remain feminine, dress and look good to please them sexually; be ready for them." I have seen this again and again and again, and now I am fighting mad. I am tired of women who are much more qualified than their male peers constantly apologizing and saying, "Well, naturally, as a career woman, I am more comfortable with men. I find the concerns of women frivolous. I can't talk about diapers and other things like that."

Yet I know from my own life that while I may be very competent, diapers and things like that are equally important to me and I do not reject womanlife, with its special concepts and values. This can best be summed up by a remark that Simone de Beauvoir made when she was forty. She reported that for the first forty years of her life, she actually blossomed in the constant compliments of her father when he said she thinks like a man, but now she realizes how sexist that is and she is proud to be and think like the woman she is.

My generation has a slightly different attitude. At least we say, "Be yourselves. Find your being, but remember, under no circumstance, compete with the man. Don't be castrating. Above all, be feminine. Never let the men know that you are bright." We were taught when you left the classroom, take off your glasses, bat your eyelashes, and play the game because "boys never make passes at lasses who wear glasses." It was upon this basis that for many years I opposed coeducation, feeling that if there were males in the classroom, girls would hide or even suppress their capabilities. Sadly, in many of the schools recently turned coed the girls are finding male domination overwhelming and their priorities not heard. Books like *The Feminine Mystique*, by Betty Friedan, came out of this game in the forties and fifties, a game of sexual omnipresence. These were days in which women were rightfully extremely angry at the lies they had bought. And so many of these women are the leaders of the women's movement today. Their anger arose from the hypocrisy of being educated on one hand and having to play the unfair game on the other. They were trained to meet challenges and succeed and yet were forbidden to do so.

It was after World War II—which had allowed and needed women to find themselves in order to work for the war effort, in addition to maintaining the role of wives and mothers—that things became even worse. We were told when the men returned home, that it was our lot to return to the background. Women were told it was wrong to compete in general and most unladylike to compete in particular with the male, who needed to have a job first, as he was supposed to be the breadwinner. Though it is true that men are the traditional breadwinners, a third of the women of this nation rear their children without a man; what of them? That is what ERA is about; guaranteeing that if a woman does the same job, she will be paid the same salary. The passage of the ERA will hold families together, not destroy them, as alleged by ERA's opponents. Anything but the passage of ERA is antifamily and antichildren, no matter what the rhetoric of the short-sighted claims. When you go to vote in your state house, remember the many, many single-parent families throughout the United States in which the woman is the sole breadwinner. Nonratification condemns her children to a lesser life style. It is a national disgrace that the woman with the college education earns the same amount as the man with an eighth-grade education.

ERA with its guarantee of economic parity is the first step toward the finding of our self-esteem and our rightful place in this nation. We must value ourselves. My generation and my Mother's still accepted life on male terms. We were valued according to whether or not a man chose us. Being attractive to men, being chosen by them, determined our status. It was *Miss* or *Mrs.* It took years for *Ms.* to arrive to match *Mr.* Recently I overheard a mother instructing her daughter that she must remain a virgin because her hymen is the most valuable asset she can bring her husband. Such nonsense makes our world. She is the most valuable gift, not a small remnant of vestigial tissue. The pros and cons of virginity are issues to be discussed in terms of the young woman's needs and feelings, not of potential property value to a man. It was, is, and will always be her body to do with as she feels best. Young women of my older daughter's generation are questioning the clothes they wear (unisex dress), the use or the lack of make-up, going Dutch on dates, living together before marriage, and so forth. Before we can condemn them and before we say it is wrong, we must take a look at what they are trying to say and accomplish. Those of us who are psychiatrically trained sorrow that the uncertainty of questioning and a world without rules are so painful, but we also rejoice that so much growth is occurring. Now it is a less safe world but in general, a more real one. I believe the world of young women will right itself and be back on course again—a more direct course to knowing self. Trissa's pain will make a better world for Sarah and Sarah's for my granddaughters.

The handful of women who are emerging today as pseudomen are loudest and most vociferous, obscuring—with their bra-burnings, lesbianism, hostility toward the male, and other noises—the real work that is being done. And yet they are probably essential to get women like you and me moving. We must not be scared away or confused. They are symbols of what is so wrong, and we must right it. Pseudomen reflect a world still being articulated in male terms. What I demand is a world which permits my daughters the freedom to grow and develop as they wish and as they are capable of doing. I have four children, divided equally into hes and shes. I would give my life to ensure that they walk side by side.

If the only way to get a piece of the action is to act as the male, then movements such as Lesbian Nation, the New Regiment of Women, serve a purpose. Somehow, some way, they will force the locked doors open. But I seriously doubt that many women desire to be Lesbians. I'll defend their right to be but do not wish this life style for myself or my daughters. For some it is the only way to express the fact that they are constantly being left out or to react to the brutalization of their mothers by their fathers and an uncaring society. Many are asking questions that we "normals" are afraid to ask. If they hurt anyone, it is only themselves. We must build a world where men will be permitted to be men and women will be permitted to be women, and we will be full humans together, walking two by two, as in the time of Noah. Nowhere in the story of the ark does it mention that the female animal walked two steps behind the male. We went two by two, and that is what the women's movement is all about—and the goal of the sisterhood. It shall come to pass!

There are many right ways and expressions of female being. The sisterhood is designed to bring us together to work for the concerns of women, their innate right to partake in the goodness of this country. The country, with its myriad of problems, needs the creativity and participation of all its citizens. It can't afford to exclude anyone from the problem-solving. When the sisterhood succeeds with the basic minimum, the passage of ERA, then I will be assured that my daughters have the beginning of equality with their brothers. I had it easier than they will because there were fewer women struggling to be self-actualized. We were such tokens, so rare, that we did not threaten the workings of the established order. Today the avalanche of women clamoring for opportunity is a different matter.

Recently an attorney colleague of mine who is very familiar with the Asian countries remarked to me that in countries like India where there is a marked class system, women have a much better time because the ruling-class male accepts the fact that a Brahman woman is higher than an Untouchable man. Conversely, in a society where there is no rigid class structure, there are no upper-class women to be given "the freedom to develop" and to do whatever they want, to show beyond a doubt that women have the same capabilities.

Furthermore, every culture needs an underdog to feel superior to, and in our democratic society women have suffered from meeting that need, as well. As our society has fewer and fewer Third World citizens, such as the blacks, Chicanos,

Puerto Ricans, to discriminate against, only women will be left. Therefore, we must assert ourselves now to ensure that our children receive their rights and are protected. As our young women ask relevant questions and find answers, we mustn't be confused by answers such as lesbianism, drugs, revolution, or communism. These constitute attempts to ventilate and to enter society in a full-functioning way.

What will ERA mean to your children and your grandchildren? What will your daughter or your granddaughter feel if you do not proclaim loud and clear that she is equal? You may not have needed such affirmation when you were fifty or even when you were sixty, but young women of today, facing a more difficult, confused world, need this affirmation of their equality, and we must give it to them. This is the only truly conservative way of doing things. Conservatism to me means that each person is allowed the freedom and tools to find and to take care of her or himself. And I think that is the true conservative message.

Your actions in the near future must open up the world to young women to the extent that they will not have to sacrifice the joys of a wife, the joys of being a mother and a total human being, in the severity of the struggle for personhood. When women are trapped, they take out their frustrations on their young. We must examine American child rearing and family structure. Women today are living through their children. And when you live through your children, you make unreasonable demands upon them; they cannot find themselves. If we are to fulfill our unique biological destiny, which is motherhood, we must answer these questions. Each passing day brings new tales of child abuse, neglect, and the destruction of the family and American values. We can't be good mothers unless we are good people; we cannot be good people if we are frustrated and unfulfilled.

We must consider the female identity crisis in the light of five issues: woman in relation to herself, woman in relation to her mate, woman in relation to her child, woman in relation to her career, and finally, woman in relation to the sisterhood, to other women.

These are womenly responsibilities, and these are especially your responsibilities, since the majority of you are women who have learned how to negotiate the system. As women legislators, you have the direct mandate from your electorate—women, children, men—to find ways to ensure freedom and opportunity for us all. You have no other option.

I thank you.

On Guiding Young Women

Several times since entering Exeter Trissa has shared with me her shock at the attitudes of many of her classmates. Both boy and girl colleagues boast of talking disrespectfully to their parents, defiance even to the point of occasionally hitting their elders. Trissa stands up to this faction, telling her unhappy peers that she respects and listens to her parents. She would not dream of ignoring and not evaluating what we say because she knows from experience that what we normally say has a solid base. She trusts and believes in us. We serve as her role models. All teen-agers need a backboard of value systems against which to differentiate and individuate themselves. The worst thing a parent can do is deny a child a person to evaluate, to react to, and to move forward with and from. Without capable, strong, decisive parents to imitate, children become angry, hostile, and devastated. Kent State is the final symbol of the war between young and old, in which everyone loses.

In too many instances, because adolescent girls do not respect the roles their mothers play in relation to their fathers, they do not want to pattern themselves after these mothers. Young women are lost without boundaries or structure; women are groping to find new definitions of self, both within and without marriage and family. Many compensate by forming a total career alliance to the exclusion of all else. They disrespect their mother's lot. Traditionally, the housewife's job is not compensated. Such work is not deemed worthy of recognition in our monetarily oriented society. Therefore, the housewife is denied the trappings of prestige and the tools to control her own destiny. She cannot cause change. In our society "money talks." To deny women that power or to place them in the position of not having the security of knowing where their next meal is coming from makes women as powerless and as much slaves to men as their children are.

I was horrified by the cover story in a recent New York *Times* Sunday magazine section, called "The Total Woman Greets Her King."

The cover shows the man dressed in red blazer, blue pants, white shoes, and a red, blue, and white open-necked shirt; he is the bicentennial personified, and she is in a black leotard, without undergarments, with matching sombrero and knee-high boots. As if the final touches of thigh-high red garter and black stockings are not enough, this all-American picture is completed by her silver-studded gun holster, replete with gun. It is not necessary to ask me as a psychiatrist why women are shooting at President Ford or concretely expressing penis envy; simply look at the tasteless nonsense being sold and bought by the American public. Eighty-four women, the *Times* article reports, paid fifteen dollars apiece in Muncie, Indiana, to learn how to get their husbands to say, "Praise the Lord" when they returned home from work to find them naked except for black mesh stockings, boots, and the trusty kitchen apron. Better to spend money on assertiveness-training. To spend money learning how to go from pussy to panther in six easy lessons is better than this demeaning nonsense.

Certainly, it is apparent from the stories of Michael and me that fun between us is fun between us. I have no objections to sexuality and a multitude of expectations, but I would never insult him or even more myself and you, the reader, by advancing the idea that once a woman reaches orgasm, she will be materially rewarded by her husband's buying her a piano or a fur coat or new refrigerator-freezer. The whores in the first part of the book give me a more honest feeling than this outrageous propaganda, with its insults. The final affront is that it is all packaged in Biblical terms and supposed Christian virtues.

The *Times* article continues, contrasting Total Woman's concepts with the sisterhood:

> More relevant to their own lives [ordinary women's] is a movement that might free them within the confines of the fact that they are married. That is their security, and they will hold on to it. Faced with a choice between certain safety and a deadly uncertain chance for ecstasy they will choose safety. The fact of their marriages will not change, and neither will their husbands change. So they do what women do best—they adapt—they give in.

Hogwash and bullshit. Each of us has one life to live, and I opt for ecstasy. I don't adapt to Michael; we accommodate each other as full-functioning halves of a greater whole. I look him in the eyes as an equal—long before I look him in the crotch.

No woman should believe the way she wins is through a man. We win each for ourself and for one another. For a woman to read that it is correct to surrender her life, serve and worship her husband, and to follow him even when he is wrong is almost as insulting as the portrayal of each man, each husband, as an easy trick and each woman as a hooker. Sex, material gain, and personhood are more interwoven in Muncie, Indiana, than in the whorehouse of Nevada. In Nevada the girls remain separate and uninvolved with their business activities. They don't confuse sex and money with love and marriage. In the Total-Woman ambiance, women pay to learn that a man's most important sex organ is his eyes. I must have missed that lesson in anatomy; it must have been on "their side," the other side of the cadaver. I have always believed that a healthy man's most important sex organs are the same as a woman's, his head and his heart. One of the most pleasing and sexiest sights to me is an eighty-year-old couple, crippled with age, helping each other down the street. Years of profoundly touching each other's being are more relevant than Frederick's of Hollywood. Perfume and lace, facing after-shave cologne and silk pajamas, will never be enough without good conversation, wit, and involvement.

When I write of woman facing her career, I do not necessarily mean a full-time, paying job. A career is an outer goal-directed activity, separate from the immediate concerns of the family. Volunteer charity or church work, working for political campaigns or the betterment of the community, serving on the school board, are all activities which permit the woman to develop herself in relation to functions not derived from her husband and children. Woman must be able to define herself by herself. Obviously, paid career involvement lends a world or frame of reference uniquely its own.

Marabel Morgan, the opportunist behind this Total Woman nonsense, teaches her "four *a*'s" for women to lead a successful life. They are: accept, admire, adapt, adjust.

If you want how-tos from me, here is a categorical one: Throw her four *a*'s out and replace them with mine. They are: *aspire, assert, achieve, accomplish.*

A Bridge to the Epilogue: Dialogue with My Editor

ME: I don't know how to be meaningful and understood by the woman in Wichita, Kansas. Only she could tell me, and unfortunately, she is not here. I wish she were. Someday I hope to chat with her, face to face. We have so much to talk about. All that I can share with the woman in Wichita, Grand Rapids, San Diego, Waterville, or Miami Beach is a process, a style—telling how I feel, see, know, my world and the world of womanlife to be.

EDITOR: But we must make the book comprehensible and acceptable to many women.

ME: I accept that, but I need to know what you have in mind. I must have some direction.

EDITOR: I think most women believe that a successful woman is a ball-crusher. Either a ball-crusher or a kind of Mary Poppins. It seems impossible to be a woman who leads two lives.

ME: Not impossible—rewarding and good. A complete life is composed of more than one part or role. I've never been compared to Mary Poppins, though I delight in her. She has the right mix of fantasy and reality. I frequently hum in my head the song "A Spoonful of Sugar Helps the Medicine Go Down"; to me that signifies love and warmth of motherhood, combined with the professionalism of doctorhood. I have been compared many times to Auntie Mame because I experience each place and every situation I am involved in to its fullest. I hate to waste a second of living. Intensity is the key to my personality but intensity in joy, as well as sorrow, in fun, as well as work. It is good to feel, care, love, and even lose occasionally.

EDITOR: It shouldn't be a book relevant only to the New York woman, the feminist, or the housewife, or any set. It must describe us all.

ME: I agree. The values that I articulate should fit well with many groupings. The book will do that because I walk many paths, but I always put old-fashioned common sense before learning and theory. If my professionalism leads me away from my womanly intuition, I correct my training. In medical school we were taught that if the laboratory results don't confirm our own observation of the patient's state, we must check the laboratory again. We never accept the laboratory over and against our own experience. So it is with life. Formal training must only enhance, not supplant, basic good sense. My Grandmother understood womanlife better than Sigmund Freud. He expounded the theory of penis envy and the need for women to mature to reach vaginal orgasm, but my Grandmother had the right emphasis. She wisely taught me that if your husband wanted an evening out, let him go, for all human beings need some freedom. However, she counseled to be sure to feed him his favorite dishes before his departure, especially if one of them is made with garlic and/or onions. Practicality, reality, fun, and joy.

EDITOR: Carry on.

Epilogue

And finally it is the end. I pause to think through what I have experienced during this period of writing—where I wanted to walk, where I found myself, where I have led you, and where we shall go together.

Naturally, there is no way we could have seen it all together. Anecdotes are mere sketches of past happenings, scene memories of experiences; furthermore, each reader must add part of his or her self to complete and integrate the fragments of existence presented—some have been hyperbole, many muted. Birth touches death; laughter, tears; and anger, contentment. Many pieces make the whole, and still more remain. In these pages I have focused on only one issue, that of womanlife and the realization of its value and worth as a full-functioning, complementary part of humanity.

To have had this respite and time of evaluation has been like a miracle to forty-year-old me. At this, the midpoint in my life, writing afforded me the official time to contemplate where I shall walk in the remaining half. For that, I am deeply grateful.

Long ago, in 1867, to be exact, Sojourner Truth said it in a way that even today, over 100 years later, has relevance for us all:

> There is a great stir about colored men getting their rights, but not a word about the colored women; and if colored men get their rights, and not colored women theirs, you see the colored men will be masters over the women, and it will be just as bad as it was before. So I am keeping the thing going while things are stirring; because if we wait till it is still, it will take a great while to get it going again . . . I am above eighty years old . . . I have been forty years a slave and forty years free, and would be here forty years more to have equal rights for all.

There are no new truths, only greater and harder struggles to attain old innate rights. I echo Sojourner Truth's sentiments, I have lived forty years semiaware and now welcome the next forty of challenge. To be part of the continuity of the journey to fulfillment of women everywhere and every time is exhilarating.

It is as if, like all women, I am positioned in front of two doors—a "lady or tiger" situation (my favorite short story). Behind one door, the one of the lady, is the journey of constantly keeping up images, of pretense, of superficiality, of competition, of playing by the rules, of doing the expected, for which the reward is to look like Raquel Welch and be walking into the sunset, holding hands with a man who combines the best of Billy Graham, Robert Redford, and the current president of General Motors. Behind the other door, that of the tiger, is the odyssey of womanlife, of finding just yourself, shivering and naked but honest and willing to grow and learn. There stands a person secure because of a deep understanding that living is a process, confusing and paradoxical at times but moving—going someplace. There are no answers except being part of that *life style of goal-directed process,* for which the reward is a self in harmony and peace with herself and with others.

So be it for me.

Finis

Appendix A

Submitted To

James M. Cannon,
Assistant to the President for Domestic Affairs
Executive Director of the Domestic Council

April 23, 1975

Introduction

This memorandum is intended to serve as a brief, preliminary sketch of an office of a Special Counsel to the President, preliminary to the creation of a Cabinet post, to be created either by Executive Order or by legislation. The Director of this Office will be reportable directly to the President and to a Special Joint Committee of the Congress. The mandate of the Office will be to identify the significant problems of American children and the availability of resources and services to meet their needs. Once sufficient data are collected and assembled, the Office will design and recommend policy and implementation of programs to effectively and efficiently coordinate and administer the resources and services on the federal, state, and local level.

Proposed Activities

1. Coordinate and direct a two-year survey of all existing resources and services, including but not limited to health, social-service, legal, educational, juvenile-justice, and child-protection legislation, programs, and systems on the federal, state, and local levels. This would include an evaluation and analysis of the legislation or implementing orders, the nature of services, the qualifications of service providers, eligibility requirements of recipients, quality of services, and impact on the designated problem areas, as well as the coordination with similar programs or services from other sources, governmental or private.

2. Design and develop model systems and programs based upon findings of the research survey for implementation on national, regional, state, or local level to provide comprehensive services to children. Emphasis should be placed upon local or state responsibility, with coordination and supplementation from regional or federal resources where appropriate.

3. Hold public hearings periodically in each state with federal, state, and local officials, service administrators and providers, community leaders, and private citizens to receive maximum input on needed changes and to help monitor the progress of and public response to legislative and/or programmatic developments. Transcripts and findings would be submitted to the President and to the Special Joint Committee of Congress.

4. Conduct a public-education and awareness campaign to create a general understanding of the significance of children as the leading national resource, and the numerous problems threatening the health, safety, and development of children, individually and collectively. The campaign would present the

public and its officials with facts and statistics which would facilitate and promote greater effectiveness and efficiency of the various components of the present system. Support will be sought for establishing the concerns of children as a priority of public services.

5. Organize and utilize an advisory board of citizens, private foundations, religious leaders, professional groups, and service providers to meet regularly with the Director and to make recommendations on programs and policy matters.

6. Quarterly report to the Special Joint Committee by the Director on the activities, findings, recommendations, and problems of the Office. The Committee will be requested to take particular notice of any major issues raised which are of appropriate concern to the legislative sector.

7. Examples of coordination of resources and effort:

a. Law-enforcement monies and mental-health monies should be coordinated in services and programs to provide a comprehensive, effective effort at a reduced net cost to taxpayers.

b. Develop mechanisms for dissemination of information to the public of existing programs such as the WIC program.

c. Investigation of the problems of runaway children and abandoned children, and the coordination of resources allocated to their care and protection.

d. Promulgation of guidelines for educational materials and courses on parenting for use in public-school curricula.

e. Promote the development and use of materials and courses in public schools with which to acquaint children with American values and traditions and to update American-history courses to reflect the participation of women and racial and ethnic minorities in the shaping of the development of the United States' position of world prominence.

f. Promote educational and recreational activities designed to foster constructive and positive competition among children.

Estimated First-Year Budget Requirements . . . . $20 Million

Appendix B

(Selected excerpts from my first taped notes for this book, August 1972)
It is my personal belief that the capitalistic system allows for the greatest ability to mold one's own destiny but, unfortunately, that is primarily limited to white middle-class males. The white middle-class males have to realize that their future is interdependent upon permitting the same freedom and self-actualization to all people. And what is really being seen now is a struggle for this type of freedom and free society, probably the freest society ever known on earth, to heal itself before it is wounded from both within and without.

Certainly orgasm is relevant. It is as relevant as any other biological function but should certainly not be the center of attention. The entire debate upon clitoral or vaginal orgasm is ridiculous. It will take care of itself. When women are able to feel they are in control of their own destinies, that they are people, they will experiment and find themselves without fear.

To focus on this is again to continue in a new way the whole concept of sexuality as the center and all-being of life. We have only moved the concept of a woman primarily being meaningful through her uterus to her being sensitive in her clitoris. If I had a choice of which part of me was more important, I would prefer the uterus. At least it is larger and capable of greater expansion than the tiny, rudimentary residual phallic symbol.

This tiny little button ("Look, I've got one too. Mine is just hidden!") called the clitoris is certainly no penis. It has many nerves, it brings great pleasure, but certainly should not preoccupy us in our search for identity. Indeed, I personally believe that when the brain is fully developed and actualized it will bring its clitoral representation along with it. Again, at this time it can be noted that in all surveys women who have succeeded in careers and are fulfilled in the area of being able to cope with and manipulate and use the environment in a positive sense seem to be more orgastic and less troubled by concerns of this kind.

The right to have orgasm is extremely important but not as important as the right to earn a decent living. Because I would prefer—I would tend to think—that once I am earning a decent living with self-respect, my orgasms will follow. Under no circumstances do decent living and self-respect follow the ability to have decent orgasms. Again, I think this centering on orgasms is doing it in the male's terms. It is the male who is extremely concerned with this release of nervous tension in this way and again his sexual drives and presence of an erection inhibit his doing anything else. We fortunately or unfortunately do not have that. In other words, a man with an erect penis would have trouble sitting at his desk. We don't have any such anatomical problems. And erections do not occur or tumescence does not occur in exactly the same way with the female at odd times of the day. Particularly when we are signing Bills of Congress.

An orgasm is an orgasm is an orgasm and by any other name it is still an orgasm. Whether it takes place in the clitoris or the vagina is esoterically important but not important to the person who is supposedly going to have "the three minutes of unconsciousness." Though I've always considered myself totally free and actualized sexually, as well as in other ways, some of the other things that I am supposed to have experienced are way beyond my awareness. I have never been unconscious for three minutes at a time (which I will definitely confront my husband with this evening) but I also have never climaxed fifty times in succession. If this is what I have been working for I had better stop doing this book at this moment as I will have no time for anything else. It's all a bunch of shit. And again, I suppose that if one experiences fifty times three minutes of unconsciousness one would have approximately two and one-half hours every day that one was occupied in the unconscious experience of orgasm.

The chapter on pregnancy in the book *Our Bodies, Ourselves* is absolutely excellent as is the chapter on childbirth and postpartum. It really talks about pregnancy from the woman who has experienced it, rather than pregnancy from the male point of view. It clearly parallels the feelings that I have that no man can possibly understand and that perhaps part of the reason we have so much difficulty is the presence of male obstetricians and gynecologists who are technicians or specialists but cannot feel empathy is because it is beyond their existential set of the entire feeling of pregnancy. During my third pregnancy, which produced the abnormal child, my feeling was a sense of being trapped in the waiting room of the obstetrician. Knowing something was wrong, he and my husband, both physicians, saying that I was hysterical (all women get this way at pregnancy), refusing to listen to me, my having polyhidramnios, my feeling moribund, my knowing something was wrong, my being part of an assembly line. The interesting thing about it is that I came to that room not only as a woman, but as an attorney, as a highly intelligent person, and as a physician. And as a physician I was reporting in medical terminology the difficulties I was experiencing; but because it was pregnancy and because it was connected with my being a woman they could not hear me as a physician. They just heard me as a "hysterical woman at that time and you know we don't listen to her." The anger, the alienation, the feelings of resentment, both to that particular obstetrician and equally to my husband still linger now eleven years later because at that time no one listened to me as a person. Not being listened to is perhaps the most frightening experience any human being can have—to know that you are in difficulty and to have deaf ears turned to you. Many women blame the fact that they are not listened to on their lack of intellectual training; they don't understand that it is primarily the problem of the rejecting, hostile, insensitive male who refuses to realize that he could listen even if he cannot understand, and do things in the terms of a female who is having a different experience. The basic root of the problem is the lack of communication between the sexes. There is, of course, absolutely no understanding that I can see in any male—and I doubt that there *can* be any understanding in any male—for the process of reproduction and delivery. There is no way for a woman to understand this unless she has *had* a baby. I can remember before I had the experience and after. There is no possible way of bridging that particular unique life experience of the symbiotic relationship —and it is symbiotic and not parasitic—of the foetus and the mother and the knowing that relentlessly, whether you like it or not, you will go through that period of labor in which you will be torn asunder literally to produce a new human being.

That you cannot stop. You cannot stop the discomfort, you cannot stop the relentless growth—the child really takes you over for a period of time and will only be born through great pain. The process has begun and once it has begun it is inevitable. You have no control over that destiny once you have set it into motion, and the first pregnancy, since it is unknown, is a complete takeover. If you do it a second and third time, at least you know what you're getting into. There is no way that a woman can understand before she is pregnant what this experience will be. It does not mean that the experience is not worth it or is not rewarding or is not the most gratifying experience known, but it does mean that for a period of nine months one is caught up in what might be called, in some senses, a pseudo-death. It is inevitable, consequences flow from it, it cannot be stopped unless you intervene with an abortion which is another horrendous feedback. It just goes on and on and takes you over.

All this should be expanded as well as questioning the different women who are successful as to their feelings in a non-poetic sense but in a consciousness-raising sense toward their pregnancies.

It is my belief that children benefit and are less paranoid when they grow up with multiple adult role models and the acceptance that they can go to any adult without fear. Part of the problem of our particular child-raising technique is the binding of a child so that it is even unable to go to its own father. Decreased is the ability to love and touch others and the feeling of warmth; increased is the fear of threat that our present American child-raising techniques are productive of paranoid behavior patterns, cynicism, distrust, isolation, coldness, an absence of litter love, and a lack of community feeling. Our present child-raising techniques in the nuclear family tend to make the individual unable to make meaningful bonds, both superficial and deep with other human beings, to feel secure. In fact, our child-raising techniques are now asocial and hence we are having more sociopathy and nonproductive team work.

We have got to get rid of the primary relationship exclusivity between mother and child. In fact, the primary relationship of mother and child should almost never exist; at best it should always be a relationship between mother, father, and child, and preferably mother, father, child, and other sibs, in a kind of feeling that there is a mutuality. A dependency on one other individual in and of itself must fail. No other human being can take that kind of parasitic leeching. In addition, no other human being can meet the test, nor does any other healthy human being want someone else constantly at them. And indeed it makes the male irrelevant. It has to end because it is not good. It is not that we are now adjusting to a compromise because women want their identity and therefore the child must suffer. But indeed the present myth of the one-to-one at-home woman, something which never existed before, has to stop; it's just no good. It raises defective children and it has to stop; even if women were totally satisfied with it, it doesn't meet the needs of a child. It cannot produce healthy young, and that is what we are seeing with our drug addiction and other attendant disruptions. It does not—this system, or this method—produce healthy young. It would be as if an elephant mother attempted to bring her child up alone. She cannot do it without the rest of the herd. She would not be able to raise that child in a healthy relationship. Nor would a monkey. A monkey all alone with her young would not be able to raise it in a way that it could meet, mate, and reproduce.

End of Tape I
August 27, 1972

Curtain Call

Special thanks to

The women who helped make this possible:
    Grandma Sarah, who gave me love and courage
    My Mother, who gave me strength and direction
    The twelve successful women whom I interviewed and enjoyed
    The twelve prostitutes and the madam, who shared and taught
    Freedom Gavin, who organized the project
    Susan Pappas, who followed it through
    Sara Sander, who typed and typed it all
    Ellen Harrington and Susan Shutz, who contributed their poems

And the men:
    My Husband Michael, who was always there
    James P. Murphy, who first read it

Frederick Cohen, who first corrected it and
Martin Hassner, who brought his words to it

And last
A Special Dedication to Children everywhere

and especially mine:

Trissa,
Judson,
Lindsey, and
Sarah

for whom it is written, so that they may know a world of men and women together, equal and complementary.

Judianne Densen-Gerber, J.D., M.D., F.C.L.M.